HOW TO SET AND ACHIEVE YOUR FINANCIAL GOALS

OTHER ONE HOUR GUIDES

HOW TO SET AND ACHIEVE YOUR FINANCIAL GOALS

Bailard, Biehl & Kaiser, Inc.

Dow Jones-Irwin
Homewood, Illinois 60430

This publication is designed to provide accurate and authoritative information in regard to the subject matter covered. It is sold with the understanding that neither the author nor the publisher is engaged in rendering legal, accounting, or other professional service. If legal advice or other expert assistance is required, the services of a competent professional person should be sought.

From a Declaration of Principles jointly adopted by a Committee of the American Bar Association and a Committee of Publishers.

Project editor: Margaret Haywood
Production manager: Ann Cassady
Cover design: Image House
Cover illustration: David Lesh
Compositor: Eastern Graphics
Typeface: 11/13 Souvenir
Printer: Arcata Graphics/Kingsport

Library of Congress Cataloging-in-Publication Data

How to set and achieve your financial goals.

Includes index.
1. Finance, Personal. I. Bailard, Biehl & Kaiser.
HG179.H67 1989   332.024   88–33535
ISBN 1-55623-147-4

Printed in the United States of America

1 2 3 4 5 6 7 8 9 0 K 6 5 4 3 2 1 0 9

PREFACE

Our current times have been called the "Information Age." Never before in history has so much information been available to the average person. The widespread use of personal computers makes it possible for millions of people to access massive databases offering comprehensive facts about the financial world.

Unfortunately, this unprecedented maze of information does not guarantee better financial decision making. Professionals and amateurs alike can be overwhelmed with details if they do not have a logical framework for dealing with it all. In most cases all it guarantees is further confusion.

Our goal with this book, and others in the *One Hour Guide* series, is to provide you with an understandable, easy-to-use method for organizing and managing your financial affairs. We show you what information you really need and how to interpret it in light of your individual situation.

Advertisements for financial services tend to give the impression that the solution to all your financial concerns is finding the "right" investment. Typically that "right" investment is whatever the advertiser happens to be selling, whether it is insurance, stocks, bonds, real estate, or some other investment vehicle. But we have found over the years that what is right for one person is not necessarily correct for another. It is that "personalized" touch that differentiates the financial plan you will put together in this book from the canned, off-the-shelf variety that is widely hawked.

This book will help you achieve the kind of personal satisfaction that comes only from mastering an important aspect of your life: your financial affairs. You will learn a number of different ways to increase your personal wealth. You will learn about risk and how to control it to suit your personality.

The information in this book and others in the series has been developed during our years of experience as financial advisors. We have helped hundreds of clients achieve their goals using the methods we describe in these pages. These goals have been as varied as the people themselves. They range from achieving financial independence to traveling the world to paying for higher education to providing for a family's financial security in retirement years to name only a few.

Our popular seminars on personal money management have helped thousands of people from small business owners to corporate managers to recent college graduates to retirees become true *money managers*. They learned the importance of moving beyond being mere money makers and money spenders in order to achieve their life's goals.

Our college textbook, *Personal Money Management* (published by Science Research Associates and now in its fifth edition) is the leading text in its field. Hundreds of thousands of university and continuing education students have learned the fundamentals of personal finance through the book. Our own entrepreneurial experience, from our days together at Stanford Graduate School of Business to the top management of our own diversified corporation, has convinced us *personally* of the wisdom of these techniques. *We offer no advice nor suggest any course of action that we have not applied successfully ourselves.*

For many years this hard-won expertise was available only to wealthy investors and institutional accounts who can afford our specialized services and who appreciate the value of objective financial advice. Clients like these demand not only successful track records but also a deeper understanding of the role of money in achieving career and life goals. It was from our desire to make such counsel available to more people that this book and series were born.

Of course any publication owes its success to many people behind the scenes. In addition to the generous cooperation of our clients, without whose feedback and support this series would not have been possible, we especially wish to thank Jerrold D. Dickson for his ideas and presentation of the BB&K approach to setting and getting your financial goals; Jeri Hayes for her personal high standards in editing this work; and Brenda Locke for her organizational abilities in seeing this project through to completion.

To these and many others who helped us create, prepare, and deliver this book, we express our sincerest gratitude. With them, we take great pride and pleasure in welcoming you to our growing family of clients.

Thomas E. Bailard
David L. Biehl
Ronald W. Kaiser

CONTENTS

CHAPTER 1

INTRODUCTION: DEMYSTIFYING MONEY

ATTAINING FINANCIAL FITNESS

To their chagrin, many people have learned that achieving professional success does not guarantee equal success in managing their financial affairs. Many of us take for granted the notion that merely earning additional money will mean an easier, more fulfilling life. Unfortunately, it is not that easy.

The financial matters of many otherwise successful people seem to be governed by a kind of Parkinson's Law: "Living expenses expand even faster than the income meant to cover them!" But it doesn't have to be that way. The purpose of this book is to show you how to organize your financial affairs to achieve the "good life."

Over the last ten years there has been an increased awareness of the importance of good health and physical fitness in attaining the good life. At BB&K, we believe that *financial fitness* is an equally important ingredient.

Financial fitness is more than numbers in your bankbook or the profits and losses from your investments. It is a positive feeling about money and its role in your life. It means that you are at peace with your current situation and confident about the future.

You don't need a six-figure income or a massive Wall Street investment portfolio to achieve this goal. You do need to take the time and make the effort to carefully analyze where you are and what you want. How is it possible for *you* to secure financial fitness?

First, you must develop a money manager's mentality. As we alluded to above, there is a distinct difference between being a money maker and being a money manager. Money managers know that money is a tool for achieving goals and nothing more. For them, money is a positive force rather than a source of insecurity.

Second, you must learn the methods of effective financial planning. Financial planning and personal money management are skills that can move you beyond the harried paycheck-to-paycheck existence to a more productive, more satisfying lifestyle.

1

And finally, you must learn to be *yourself*. Whatever your career and life circumstances or personal values and beliefs, there is a state of financial well-being that is right for you. We all have different desires, goals, abilities, and values. What works for one person may not be appropriate for another.

Who Will Benefit from This Book?

This book is not meant for everyone. It will most benefit those people who:

1. have a strong sense of responsibility for themselves and the members of their household.
2. want to deal with life's realities in a positive, productive way.
3. want more control over their personal and financial destinies.
4. wish to know more about personal finances and the economic factors that influence them.
5. have a healthy distrust of financial salespeople and wish to rely on their own well-informed judgment in financial matters.

Although we have designed this book to act as your consultant on personal finance, the goals you choose to pursue, the specific details of how you pursue those goals, and, of course, the rewards you reap for attaining them will be your own.

The Importance of Setting Financial Goals

We all have certain goals we wish to attain, but many people do not make the effort to articulate these objectives. When it comes to financial goals, you probably have at least a vague idea what you want ("I want to be rich." "I want to own a large house on the beach." "I want to retire with enough money to travel around the world."). But a general idea doesn't provide you with the specific focus around which you can make plans. That is one of the primary purposes of this book: to show you how to distill your wants and needs into achievable targets.

One lesson we hope to impress upon you is that it is a mistake to assume that there is a clear distinction between your financial and nonfinancial goals. Our experience shows that managing the financial side of life usually produces benefits on the nonfinancial side. A household that avoids financial turmoil is more likely to achieve its goals—financial and nonfinancial—than one that does not. Studies show that 75 percent of all domestic disputes are over money matters. Resolving those matters will allow you to devote more time to pursuing other, more entertaining interests.

Financial planning is much more than learning how to save. Just as important, and all too often overlooked, is the other side of the equation: how to spend. Most people are money makers and money spenders rather than money managers. If you want to move beyond the "What can I buy with what I have?" (living from paycheck to paycheck) approach, you need to know what you want—your life's goals. Only then can you focus your energies on satisfying your wants and needs.

A money manager would ask instead, "How much do I need to buy what I really want?" As you learn how to design your own Personal Profit Plan, you will see that it is really a plan for personal fulfillment rather than just a dollars-and-cents accounting of your money. Every dollar spent today or invested for tomorrow in accordance with a carefully constructed plan will return many times over in a happier, more secure, and more rewarding life.

The BB&K Way to Financial Fitness

The ideas and techniques presented in this book have been developed during our years of experience as financial advisors—serving such people as entrepreneurs, corporate executives, and retirees—and through our seminars, newsletters, and college textbook (*Personal Money Management* published by Science Research Associates).

You will find that the ideas and methods outlined in this book represent a unique approach to financial planning. While most financial planning books are oriented toward reducing everything to mere numbers, with numerous rule-of-thumb equations for determining the answers to your financial questions, we take a different approach.

We focus on you—your attitudes, values, financial profile, and the techniques that will achieve your goals. We then look at how economic trends and the vast array of financial products fit your situation. Financial products should be used to meet your plan's requirements, rather than forcefitting your plan around the latest trendy investment vehicles.

What a Financial Plan Is All About

Money management, the BB&K way, is called *Personal Profit Planning*. It is a process, not a static product to be used without alteration by everyone. We've found that successful money management is very much a case of applying on a larger scale the same instincts you probably already use in other areas of your life.

Personal Profit Planning is skill learning, not information passing. You can learn and apply the self-counseling skills to your unique circumstances.

If you have the desire and the time to commit to building and improving your financial physique, you won't have to rely on high-priced advisors or fall for the "free advice" that comes with undisclosed conflicts of interest.

The Personal Profit Planning method is flexible. You can learn and apply it at your own pace. In fact, we strongly recommend that you proceed slowly, taking each step only when you feel comfortable. The strength of Personal Profit Planning is that it allows for a wide diversity of individual preferences: different people will take different approaches. Some will devote time every day or every week to their financial affairs. Others will take a more passive approach, reviewing matters quarterly or annually. There is no right or wrong approach as long as you faithfully follow your plan's details.

An important, though admittedly nonquantifiable, virtue in the BB&K Personal Profit Planning technique is that it makes your financial planning an adventure in self-discovery and self-fulfillment rather than a boring mathematical exercise in money counting and changing!

How Personal Profit Planning Fits into Your Life

Financial planning can't, or at least shouldn't, be sold like the latest swimsuit fashions or the latest "in" toy at the local shopping center. And despite the claims in cleverly phrased advertisements of many financial salespeople—from stockbrokers to insurance salespeople to rare coin dealers—it requires more than simply knowing about a wide variety of financial products. As we've stated above, Personal Profit Planning goes beyond computerized number crunching in accordance with arbitrary standards. You can prepare your taxes that way, but not a comprehensive, individualized financial plan.

You should view your Personal Profit Plan as a framework for achieving financial well-being based on your individual goals and resources. It is a device for facilitating rather than forcing career and life development. It is a means for keeping money in its proper place: the servant, not the master, of a more rewarding life.

The major problem with many financial planning approaches is that they are product- or trend-driven. Typically, a salesperson is knowledgeable about a particular product and uses "financial planning" as an entree to sell that product.

Another sales approach is to focus on a trend, such as inflation, that is already familiar to most people. For example, in the late 1970s many salespeople were busy hawking tangibles such as gold, silver, diamonds, or collectibles as hedges against inflation. True financial planning (setting goals and designing methods for attaining them) was lost in the race to protect against the current problem.

Emphasis on the current trend of inflation proved costly to many investors. Gold and silver prices dropped sharply in the early 1980s, while other investment vehicles such as stocks and bonds, which had been out-of-favor, rose dramatically.

Personal Profit Planning is goal-driven. You focus on your personal and financial resources and how they can be employed to meet your wants and needs. Your Personal Profit Plan is a means of unifying your life to attain the things you want.

Most people think of their personal and financial lives as separate entities. You've probably heard friends, or even yourself, make statements like this: "I wish both my personal and business life would get in sync. When things are going well for me personally, business always seems to be at a low point. When things are going well at work, personal problems crop up." But when you stop to think about it, that distinction is artificial.

People tend to describe themselves by the personal and financial assets they possess. Personal assets are the "things you are" such as a singer, a manager, a writer, an actor, an entrepreneur. Financial assets are the "things that you have" like bank accounts, investment portfolios, autos, houses, and other possessions.

You can see then that important goals are achieved through the interchange of these resources. Personal assets are important in obtaining financial assets. These financial assets can then be reinvested in personal resources, for example, professional training via seminars, books, or education. In turn, increased personal assets can lead to earning more financial assets. Of course, the cycle can stop at any stage, with the additional financial assets being used to acquire more "things"—a new car, a larger house, a sailboat, and so on.

In some cases, material goods may also result in financial gain. For example, the house you purchase may appreciate. In fact, this has been a major element in the growth of net worth for many people. This additional gain can, and has, fueled another round in the cycle of personal and financial growth.

The important thing to remember is that goals, like personal and financial resources, don't just materialize out of thin air. They must be discovered and cultivated.

The Skills of Money Management

Personal Profit Planning is an important first step to a more fulfilling and rewarding life. There is, of course, more to effective money management than discovering and setting financial goals. You may know clearly what you want to achieve in life. But until you move beyond the money-making-and-spending stage to learn how to be a money manager, reaching those targets will prove a frustrating and elusive task. Effective money management can be broken down into three basic skills:

1. *Planning*. Find out about yourself and your resources. Design a Personal Profit Plan that will take you from where you are to where you want to be. The plan should act as a road map to your future.
2. *Influencing*. Find people who can implement your plan. Learn how to help them help you attain your goals.
3. *Controlling*. Know the techniques of effective money management that will keep your plan on track. Take control of your own financial destiny rather than sit back and leave your fate to the uncertainty of chance.

If your Personal Profit Plan is going to pay the dividends you expect, it is important to develop good money management habits. You must be consistent. For example, if you decide that you will review your investments quarterly, do it. Don't put it off.

It is vital to maintain certain financial records. This is critical not only to see how you are doing relative to your goals, but for legal reasons. The IRS requires that certain records be kept. In Chapter 6 we detail a record-keeping system that should serve most people's needs.

Discovering Your Financial Physique

Before you can know where you want to go, you must know where you are. Experience has shown us that everyone falls into one of four *financial physiques* (Figure 1–1). Your financial physique is the starting point from which you will pursue an individualized plan for financial fitness.

The Four Financial Physiques

The Type I, Light and Agile financial physique has few assets or possessions. This figure has a modest income. People in this category often are just starting a career. However, many people in this category simply do not place great value on money or the things that money can buy.

The Type II, Lean and Quick physique has plenty of current income but few assets. That dearth of assets hurts the potential for long-term financial fitness. The Lean and Quicksters often have great money-making talents but are usually enthusiastic money spenders as well.

The Type III, Strong and Sturdy people have numerous assets. However, they may run into problems with short-term cash flow. Because of previously inherited or acquired wealth, the Strong and Sturdy types have good long-term financial prospects. However, too often they run short of

FIGURE 1-1
The Four Financial Physiques

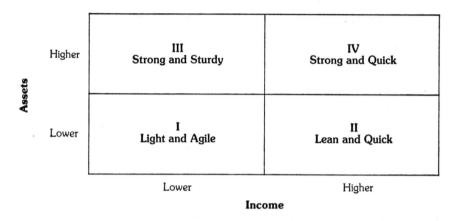

ready cash because they've tied up too much of their wealth in illiquid assets such as real estate, collectibles, or low-return investments.

Type IV, Strong and Quick individuals seem to have it made financially. However, most of them seek more satisfying ways to use their wealth and income. Accustomed to the good life, they want to ensure that their resources don't wither away before or during retirement. Strong and Quicksters are usually as concerned about preserving their resources as adding to them.

Determining Your Financial Physique

How fit are you financially? Which financial physique best describes your current circumstances? Which one reflects the way you'd like to see yourself in the future?

No one Personal Profit Plan is right for every financial physique. Even within a given category there are many variations in asset type, income resources, and career and life goals. These can all affect financial well-being. Some people may wish to move from one category to another—building wealth, income, and personal accomplishments in the process. Others will want to stay where they are—developing the money management skills that best preserve and exploit their current potential.

We believe that only you can and should be the star of your financial game plan. This book will show you how to get from where you are to where you want to be.

We've designed the following questionnaire to help you identify your

Taking Stock

Identifying Your Financial Physique

For each of the incomplete sentences below, circle the letter of the answer that best reflects your *current* financial attitudes and circumstances.

1. My salary is . . .
   a. barely adequate for, or doesn't meet, my needs.
   b. adequate for my needs.
   c. adequate for my needs but less than I would like.
   d. more than adequate for my current needs and desires.

2. Financially, I . . .
   a. often struggle to make ends meet.
   b. can meet my current expenses but have trouble saving for the future.
   c. am sometimes short of cash, but I have my share of possessions.
   d. can do almost anything I want to.

3. In terms of material possessions, I . . .
   a. own very little.
   b. have fewer possessions than most people with my income.
   c. have a good deal of real and personal property.
   d. have most of the material things I want.

4. When I think about *making* money, I . . .
   a. first think about the things I'd have to give up to get it.
   b. think about *spending* money too.
   c. think about the tangible things it can buy.
   d. feel a sense of accomplishment and satisfaction.

5. When I think about *losing* money, I . . .
   a. am not too worried because I don't have that much to lose!
   b. don't worry because I know I can make it back again.
   c. am fearful because it threatens what I have already gained.
   d. don't worry too much because there's more where that came from.

6. When I think of *spending* money, my thoughts turn to . . .
   a. watching every nickel.
   b. buying what I can right now.
   c. buying something substantial or an investment that will grow.
   d. attaining important goals.

7. If people envy me, it is probably because . . .
   a. I'm not preoccupied with money.
   b. I earn a good salary.
   c. they would like to have the things I own.
   d. they think I have everything I want.

8. If I had just a *little* more money, I would . . .
   a. be a *lot* better off.
   b. probably spend it as fast as I got it.
   c. invest it in something substantial.
   d. use it where it would do the most good.

9. When I think about *debt*, I . . .
  a. worry about mine a great deal.
  b. know I can pay mine off as I go along.
  c. know I could get a loan because of the property I own.
  d. think more about *lending* than borrowing.

10. Money is . . .
  a. a worrisome topic.
  b. an "easy come, easy go" proposition.
  c. valuable because of the tangible things it can buy.
  d. a potential source of personal fulfillment.

---

own financial physique. Your answers will also provide you with clues as to where your own Personal Profit Plan should take you. Take the time to complete it now. When you are finished, turn to the next page. The Measuring Your Financial Fitness section provides an interpretation of your answers.

Strategies for Financial Well-Being

Figure 1–2 on page 13 shows you how various needs can be addressed. You now know your financial physique and have an idea of where you want to go. Take a moment to review Figure 1–2.

Look down the left side of the chart to identify those needs that are important to you. Obviously, we cannot tally up all the options you have for each category. However, if you are very safety-conscious, the Protect What You Have row delineates the appropriate choices for your physique.

As you can see, if you are Light and Agile, you don't have the detailed estate-planning and management concerns of the Strong and Quick. That doesn't mean you won't have it in the future, but for the moment your time and efforts are best spent investigating different types of investing.

Knowing *what* to do is one thing, knowing *how* to do it is quite another. You must implement your financial fitness plan by learning how to counsel yourself through the goal-setting process. Then you must learn how to buy insurance effectively, allocate your financial assets efficiently, plan for your tax requirements, and finally, manage your investments wisely. Even with these diverse skills, you will still have to plan for retirement, build and transfer your estate.

At this stage, the task may seem overwhelming. However, as you progress through this book and others in the series, you will see that each step builds on the prior foundation. Once you've started to focus your attention on achieving specific goals, you will find that the rest falls into place.

| Taking Stock |

Measuring Your Financial Fitness

The questionnaire on pages 8–9 of this book measures the money-related attitudes and circumstances we've found most closely associated with the four basic financial physiques. To score your choices, count separately the (a) answers you picked, the (b) answers, the (c) answers, and the (d) answers and record the totals in the first row of spaces.

	Current	Desired
Total number of (a)s:	_____	_____
Total number of (b)s:	_____	_____
Total number of (c)s:	_____	_____
Total number of (d)s:	_____	_____

Finding Your Current Financial Physique

If you have more (a) answers than any other, you tend toward the Type I (Light and Agile) financial physique. Your income and assets are both relatively modest, and this may be a source of discomfort in your life. Even people with highly altruistic or nonmaterial values will probably find their lives enhanced by a more robust financial physique—one that provides more disposable income to spend on the things that really matter to them and that acts as a cushion to fall back on in adversity.

If you have more (b) answers than any other, you tend toward the Type II financial physique—long on income but short on accumulated wealth. You lack the asset foundation necessary to gain investment income or buffer you against economic adversity.

If you have more (c) answers than any other, you tend toward the Strong and Sturdy financial figure. Your values or circumstances have left you with more

things than cash and your financial flexibility may not be what you'd like.

If your (d) answers outnumbered all the others, you're probably a Strong and Quick financial athlete—an all-round competitor in the world of personal finance who may have already mastered many important skills of money management. Neither income nor wealth is a particular problem for you, but you may be finding that financial well-being means more than money in the bank.

On Figure T1–1, write the word "current" in the space provided below your current financial physique.

Finding Your Way to Financial Fitness

Now go back to the questionnaire and put a check beside each answer that best reflects *how you would like to see yourself in the future.* You may discover that your current situation suits you very well or, as is more often the case, that a new financial physique will provide a better vehicle for fulfilling your wants and needs. When you've finished, compute your new score by totaling your answers (by letter) as you did before and entering the results in the second set of spaces. The letter with the highest count is your *desired* financial physique. This is the general direction in which your career and life goals will be taking you. In the accompanying diagram, write the word "desired" in the space provided below your desired financial physique.

FIGURE T1–1
Your Financial Physique

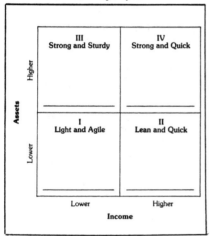

If You Want to Be Light and Agile Financially

As the name implies, the Type I financial physique enjoys the fewest commitments and encumbrances. Despite the ever-present risk of insolvency (if not outright poverty!), certain people may prefer it— as witnessed by the counterculture movement of the late 1960s and early 1970s. Type Is have fewer insurance needs and, because of their lower in-

come, lower needs for tax deductions, tax shelters, and tax credits.

A financial fitness program for these individuals requires a disciplined money management strategy that will support a mobile, rewarding lifestyle with minimum financial energy. The emphasis here is on knowing what's *really* important to you and adapting your lifestyle to the limitations your financial resources will impose.

If You Like the Lean and Quick Physique

Many young people (and quite a few impulsive older ones!) aspire to what they perceive to be the jet-set glamour of high-income, high-expenditure living. The Type II physique is sometimes all of this —but it can be much more. Many talented money makers are simply unskilled (or too enthusiastic) money spenders and would really like to hold on to some of the cash that slips too easily through their fingers—building wealth and alternative income sources through wise investments. Of course, not all lean-and-quicksters are voluntary money spenders. Many of them have to spend more than they like because of medical or family circumstances.

Regardless of their motivation, most Type IIs will benefit from learning more efficient ways to use their excess income as well as how to shelter it from excessive taxes and protect it against loss due to unforeseen events. For these people, financial well-being means cultivating long-range goals and acquiring the money management skills needed to reach them.

For the Strong and Sturdy Types

In our experience, the Type III physique is usually the most sought after (and achieved) of the financial physiques dis-

---

Measuring Your Financial Fitness (*concluded*)

---

cussed so far—mostly because assets (the possessions you can buy) are the traditional signs of success in our society. Too often, however, these people acquire nonproductive properties (taxable, repair-hungry residential real estate, for example) or try to live off investments that supply insufficient cash. Either way, these Strong and Sturdy types need to find other ways to stretch their financial muscles, such as investing for yield (as well as growth) and learning better resource allocation skills. They also discover that *self-insurance* becomes a practical alternative to paying others for protecting what they have—a real advantage to those with considerable holdings on the asset side of the ledger.

Goals for the Strong and Quick

Although people with more than adequate wealth and income may be spared the perplexities the other physiques can suffer, preoccupation with making and keeping money can devalue even the most affluent lifestyle.

For these financial competitors (from the merely well-off to the super-rich) we recommend a program of introspection, goal setting, and personal development —as well as enhancement of certain wealth-protecting skills. Tax shelters, careful resource allocation, and asset diversification all play a role in developing this physique to the fullest. In addition, since most Strong and Quick money managers tend to be at the senior end of the career and life spectrum, estate planning and transfer of accumulated wealth become more important and immediate issues.

Whichever financial physique you decide to develop, we hope you'll take the time to get to know yourself better—through introspection, self-evaluation, and a thoughtful review of your personal and financial resources.

How This Book Is Organized

This book begins with a discussion of how to go about discovering and setting your financial goals. You will learn how your place in the life cycle affects your planning. You will learn to identify and plan for your specific needs and wants.

Exercises and questionnaires throughout this book will give you an increasingly clear picture of your current and future financial and personal values and goals.

You will learn how to use tools to understand the environment and the economy. You will see how these external forces relate to your personal situation. If you are working with a partner, you will discover many different ways to work together to achieve common goals.

You will learn what type of spenders you and your partner are. You

FIGURE 1–2
The Strategies for Financial Well-Being

Your Financial Physique

General Need	Light and Agile	Lean and Quick	Strong and Sturdy	Strong and Quick
Protect what you have	Insurance Life Health Disability Automobile Renter's	Insurance Life Health Disability Liability Property Automobile	Insurance Health Liability Property Automobile Self-insurance	Insurance Health Liability Property Automobile Self-insurance
Spend more effectively	Basic budgeting	Cash flow planning Income/ tax planning	Income/ tax planning Resource allocation	Cash flow management Tax planning Resource allocation Goal getting
Build for the future	Goal setting Fixed-dollar investments Investing for growth	Goal setting Wealth building Tax shelters	Goal setting Investing for after-tax yield	Goal setting Estate planning and management
Get more of what you want	Goal getting Money management Skill building	Goal getting Money management Skill building	Goal getting Money management Skill building	Goal getting Money management Skill building

will learn that different people spend for widely varying reasons. Understanding those motivations will help make a happier household!

We show you a variety of methods for developing your own individualized Personal Profit Plan. You will choose and create the system that will work for you. Once you've set your goals, you will learn how your Personal Profit Plan will help you attain them.

Taking responsibility for your financial future does require time and effort. You have already taken the first step by opening this book. Now, read it and complete the Taking Stock questionnaires and the End Papers and Action Papers found in Appendixes A and B. You will be rewarded.

CHAPTER 2

ASSESSING YOUR CAREER AND LIFE RESOURCES

SETTING PERSONAL AND FINANCIAL GOALS

In this chapter you will learn the role money plays in career and life development. You will learn how financial fitness is affected by your stage in life and by the resources and limitations you bring with you from your cultural, economic, vocational, and family background. You will also learn the importance of defining financial and personal goals for a happier, more fulfilling life. You will understand how to distinguish valid goals from wishful, wrongheaded thinking. You will see that sound financial goals emerge only from a thoughtful survey of those background factors. And finally, you will reduce your vague desires to a list of specific needs and wants.

Your ability to make money depends on a variety of things. Personal skills such as athletic or artistic talent play a part. But we all know talented people who are not financially or personally successful. Education, motivation, and skill in applying knowledge also play a big part. But not all ambitious, educated people succeed where they want. Since big earning opportunities often develop unexpectedly, even someone who is in the right place at the right time still needs the skill and desire to take advantage of those opportunities.

While starting with substantial financial assets, such as an inheritance or a winning lottery ticket, may be an advantage; it is certainly no guarantee of long-term financial success or even personal happiness. Later generations can and often do fritter away a family's wealth. As the advertisement for *Barron's* laments, money does not come with instructions!

Your financial goals are an integral part of your Personal Profit Plan. But they are not the only part. Arriving at those goals is a process that involves much more than determining the amount of money you need to be financially independent. You bring to the project an aggregate of personal and financial assets.

Personal assets—your education, talents, and unique experience—are as much a part of your potential earning power as the dollars in your bank account. The ability to write, draw, build, or analyze are all assets that you take with you wherever you go, whatever your financial circumstances. Most people, including too many financial planners, tend to undersell the significance of these assets.

Financial assets are much more easily quantified. They are possessions such as your home, car, stocks, or cash that have marketable value. These assets have a definite monetary value that can be reduced to numbers. Sometimes there is nonmonetary value to possessions such as a family heirloom that is not quantifiable but must be considered when determining your assets.

Increasing personal assets are usually associated with increasing financial assets, though that is not always the case. Some Light and Agile people choose that financial physique for their ideal lifestyle. Their asset growth is more personal than monetary.

A college education, however, is a personal asset that typically carries with it the expectation of increased lifetime income. That's why people commit financial assets to obtain a degree. They see it as an investment in themselves.

The key point to remember is that this interaction between personal and financial assets is what career and life development is all about. Each builds on the other. Figure 2–1 shows a simplified example of this interaction.

A college education results in a higher starting salary. That salary can

FIGURE 2–1
The Goal-Setting/Goal-Getting Process

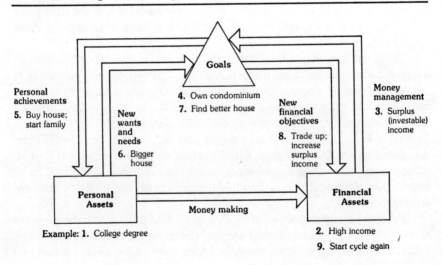

produce a surplus through careful money management. That surplus can be used to secure a financial asset such as a condominium. But owning the condominium may make starting a family more practical. You may then need a bigger house. The combination of personal and financial circumstances results in a new financial goal—finding and paying for a larger home. The cycle can begin again with savings for a child's college education.

Life-Cycle and Age-Stage Issues

This ongoing process of converting personal assets to financial assets, and vice versa, doesn't take place in a vacuum. In Chapter 4 we show you how different people view money in sharply contrasting ways. Your values, wealth, earning potential and opportunities, and your place in the life cycle all affect how you personally view money.

To show you how these factors interact, we've divided a typical lifetime into four phases we call *the stages of career and life development.*

Ages 18 to 28: The Strangers in Paradise Stage

This is when most people complete their formal education, through either college or vocational training. The initial career steps are often taken here. This is the time when people first begin to experience responsibility for many of their own expenses. Paying for school, renting or buying a place to live, buying a car and major appliances all require attention to allocate limited resources. Attention to financial details plays a key role in establishing credit.

Responsibilities grow in the personal sphere too. Young parents have to cope with arranging schedules for day care so both can work. Increasingly, one or the other parent often winds up with the responsibilities of single parenting because of separation or divorce.

In no other stage of life are so many diverse, powerful, and unfamiliar forces at work. Each situation and each problem must be met and dealt with by individuals who have little experience as successful money managers. For many people coping with these problems, financial maturity is one of the last skills of adulthood they acquire.

The financial physique most closely associated with this stage is Light and Agile. Sometimes, talented and fortunate money makers move quickly to the Lean and Quick physique when they settle into their careers.

Ages 25 to 45: The Sow and Reap Stage

During these years most people are concerned primarily with refining their careers. At this stage, people become more focused on getting their financial affairs in order. They prepare their first wills, make long-term decisions about insurance, tax planning, wealth building, and providing a desired lifestyle for themselves and their dependents.

For people with children, these are often the years of peak expense. Money spenders who have not learned to be money managers develop the habit of living from paycheck to paycheck regardless of how fast income grows. It is also the time when the need for Personal Profit Planning becomes evident. Parents face the reality of college education for their children. Retirement becomes a more pressing concern.

This stage is often characterized by growing household assets. Lean and Quick physiques can see their extra income absorbed as they slip into the Strong and Sturdy category. Sometimes the transition is not what was intended. Mortgage, car, and installment payments can mount up faster than expected or desired if you don't practice good money management.

Ages 40 to 65: The Consolidate and Share Stage
During this period most people wind up their full-time working careers. More and more, though, individuals in this stage leave one career to pursue another endeavor that is more personally rewarding. For many people these years are a time to consolidate their wealth. They look to enhance their financial foundation by investing in second homes, investigating other investment avenues including buying a wider variety of stocks, bonds, and/or other securities, and securing other tangible personal property such as a sailboat, a classic car, a coin collection, or other items of interest.

Having accumulated some business experience and perhaps some savings or at least a good credit rating, some people at this stage are willing to try their hand as entrepreneurs. Experience builds the confidence necessary to take some risks.

However, most people tend to wind down their lifestyles, traveling or channeling resources into cultural or community activities. For those with maturing children, these years can be rewarding in their efforts to assist their children in launching their own careers, buying their first home or car, or completing their education.

It is usually in this stage when people first begin to feel urgency about the problem of financial security in later life. For those who have not yet started their retirement planning, this stage is when they take an active interest in building and protecting a retirement income.

Financial fitness is possible with any financial physique. It depends largely on individual values and motivations. Those who target the Strong and Quick physique as part of their financial goals usually achieve it during this phase. Lean and Quick physiques complement their earning power by acquiring a broader asset base. Strong and Sturdy types who make the effort through good money management find ways to make their assets pay off with more income.

Age 55 and Beyond: The Torch-Passing Stage

People's retirement years can vary widely. Some merely change details but stay very active. Others pursue more leisurely interests. But regardless, by this time most people begin to address the issue of passing on their wealth to subsequent generations. This is the period when people begin to order their estates, sometimes establishing trusts or annuities for a spouse, relatives, children, or grandchildren. It is the time when taxable estates can be reduced through gifts to beneficiaries.

Their concern over personal financial security, with an emphasis on preservation rather than growth, is heightened. The prospects of peak earning years are gone. Medical expenses not covered by government or private insurance can create problems.

Although your physical prowess may decline in these years, your financial physique should not. Careful money management and adherence to the details of the plan you've created can make this stage the most rewarding of all. Goal setting and the sense of accomplishment through goal getting is a self-renewing, lifelong process that makes life more fulfilling, more interesting, and more rounded at each stage in life's cycle.

Finding Out Where You Are

As you may have already noticed, there are no clear-cut boundaries between each stage in the life cycle. Instead there are overlapping periods. As you will see in the next chapter, people have widely varying attitudes about money. Your psychological makeup, your cultural background, and your upbringing all influence how you tackle life's financial dilemmas.

The above categories are very general divisions. You may be in the Strangers in Paradise age group, but already concerned about retirement planning. Others, who are 55 to 60 years old, have a zest for living today and still are not concerned about taking precautions for tomorrow.

Only you can know what is right for you. Of course, if you have a life-partner, you work together to maximize your ambitions. Figure 2–2 illustrates the breakeven point between income and expenses. That point can occur anywhere in a typical life cycle. Most of us start out lamenting that with just a little more money all our problems would be solved. Experience shows, however, that needs tend to grow right along with income. Except for brief periods when your income and your desires are well matched, you will either be contending with too little money for too many wants, or wondering just how to employ your extra cash.

FIGURE 2–2
"When Am I Free from Money Worries?"

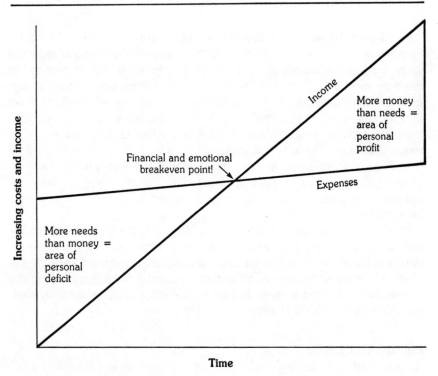

Increasing costs and income

Income

More money
than needs =
area of
personal
profit

Financial and emotional
breakeven point!

Expenses

More needs
than money =
area of
personal
deficit

Time

Determining What You Want

In the next chapter we lead you through completing specific accounting-type information in order to zero in on your exact starting point. However, it makes sense to review the goal-setting process in general terms before proceeding to the specific. You have heard people express unhappiness with their current circumstances only to conclude that they are locked into their situation (say an unsatisfactory job) and can't change a thing.

Let's begin with a clean slate. In this initial preplanning phase of your goal setting, direct your attentions to what you really want out of life. Don't be concerned with your current working circumstances. We will deal with that shortly.

We've designed Action Paper No. 1, "Your Career and Life Inventory," (One copy is for you, the second is for your spouse or life-partner) to provide an organized process for reflecting on your desires and resources. Complete the worksheet in Appendix B as you read the following pages.

Assessing Your General Financial Condition (Part I)

At this point it is not necessary for you to develop a detailed accounting of your personal finances. This first step is designed to get you thinking about how you relate to money. Are you a "money maker/money spender" as most people reading this book? Or are you already a competent money manager who simply seeks more meaningful goals?

Your answers to the questions in this part will help you focus on the things we've discussed so far. Do you barely make it from paycheck to paycheck? Are you able to put aside enough money to make some investments for the future? How are you spending your income? Are you acquiring an inventory of tangible assets—a home, a car, or an investment portfolio? Or have you cornered the latest in fashion but have little to show when styles change? Do your debts pose a problem?

Your financial fitness is made up of two separate components: your financial assets and your income. For example, people with a Strong and Sturdy financial physique have relatively small income compared to the assets they possess. On the other hand, high-salaried Lean and Quick individuals have accumulated very few assets.

In regard to your income, the connection between short-term income and short-term expenses will be an important element in your financial flexibility. At this stage you should distinguish those short-term expenses over which you have some control from those that are fixed. For example, entertainment expenses are more controllable than mortgage payments or insurance premiums.

Your future goal-getting activities rely to a great extent on the amount of surplus income, however modest, you generate and the saleable assets you possess. You should be aware of the necessity for emergency reserves. No one expects to be in an accident or suffer a debilitating illness, but these things do happen.

To reemphasize: you don't need to ferret out exact numbers from your bank account at this juncture. This exercise is meant to get you thinking about your financial condition. It gives you a chance to produce an honest, qualitative assessment. Are you comfortable or is there a sense of impending doom over your finances? Feelings like these will be important guideposts when you begin to set real, achievable financial goals.

Your Personal and Vocational Resources (Part II)

Your vocational and avocational accomplishments and interests are powerful factors in the ever-changing balance between your personal and financial assets. For example, some of us accept employment in fields that offer more financial than psychological rewards. To compensate, we often choose personal activities that provide the missing psychic benefits.

There is no fixed mix between the two that is best for everyone. However, we do believe that there is an optimal mix of these factors for each individual in any stage of life. Discovering the mix that is right for you is the purpose of this section.

To get the greatest value out of this exercise, observe the following two points:

1. *Pay attention to cause and effect.* Don't settle for a glib, quick response. For example, we've heard people complain that their jobs did not have enough responsibility or sufficient pay for the work. But on further inquiry, it turned out that their real complaint was about office politics or personality clashes.

2. *Know where the fun leaves off and the work begins.* Even the most pleasant hobbies have competitive, social, or technical components. For example, if you notice that your hobbies emphasize the pursuit of trophies, you might consider whether your current occupation offers the kind of personal recognition you require.

Take a moment to reflect on those things that have given you the greatest personal reward—emotionally and financially. Are there common themes? Do you prefer working with people, things, or with abstract concepts? Do you consider your basic approach to an important task to be that of an entrepreneur (the one who gets things started), a manager (the one who keeps things going), a worker (the one who gets things done), a craftsperson (the one who does things right), or an artist (the one who does things creatively)? Are there elements of your job, such as public speaking, that give you great personal satisfaction? Do you pursue outside interests that may have economic value?

We want you to move beyond a simple résumé of your education and experience. Instead, this review should bring out a qualitative statement of things you like, things you do not like, things you do well, and things you do poorly. Finally, and directly related to identifying your life's goals, your answers will help you focus on those pursuits you may not feel free to choose, but which, if the choice were left to you, might lead to a more fulfilling life.

Your Cultural and Economic Attitudes and Values (Part III)

Here we want you to reflect on those elements of your background—family, ethnic heritage, money-related issues—that have shaped you as a person. Are there strengths and weaknesses in your background that have affected your career and life development?

When you look at the worksheet questions in this section you may be bewildered about their connection to setting goals. Your effort here though will be well rewarded. As we've said before, knowing yourself is the most important single factor in structuring your Personal Profit Plan. The goal is a fulfilling, happy, secure lifestyle, not simply enough money in the bank to pay for shelter, food, and clothing! This section will help you focus on the following issues:

1. Have you had to struggle to get ahead or have your life accomplishments come more easily?
2. Have career challenges energized you to tackle challenges with zeal, or have they left you fatalistic and discouraged?
3. Do you see your life as a playing field for positive accomplishments or as a minefield of dangers?
4. Are you generally satisfied with your social and economic standing, or do you have a long way to go before you feel you've "arrived"?
5. Do you view money-related decisions in your household as a collaborative effort, or are they the sole prerogative of the principal breadwinner?
6. Is all fair in love, war and money, or are there ethical considerations that ought to shape our behavior?
7. Is each person responsible for his or her own economic well-being or are we all our brother's keeper?

What does all this have to do with organizing your life to meet personal and financial goals? Many needs and wants have their roots in our cultural and economic heritage. Some people who have suffered hardships in their childhood believe they can never be secure enough financially. They may tend to work on accumulating great wealth without really enjoying the benefits it can bring. These people lose sight of the fact that money is a means to happiness, not the end itself.

On the other hand, people from more privileged backgrounds may pay little attention to life's rougher edges. They assume that the good times will always roll. To them, it's perfectly acceptable, even expected, that each new discretionary dollar will be spent on more luxuries and fun.

And then there is the age-old question of material versus spiritual values. For some people, material success itself is an affirmation of their worth as individuals. Others view such acquisitive behavior as mere selfishness. A fulfilling life for them is achieved through human relationships and charitable works.

Everyone's cultural and economic experiences influence their expectations and goal-directed actions. The fact that these experiences act subconsciously for most people doesn't change their importance. Making the effort to examine these influences will pay you many dividends—emotional and financial. Though it may seem a bit esoteric at this point, these factors will play an important role in the goal-setting process covered in the next few chapters.

Uncovering Your Goals

Once you have completed your career and life inventory, the next step is to discover more specifics. Action Paper No. 2, "Your Needs/Wants Assessment," is located at the back of the book.

Action Paper No. 2 is designed to help you use the information you've put together in your inventory worksheet to spell out your needs and wants in three categories: (1) your general financial condition, (2) your personal and vocational resources, and (3) your cultural and economic attitudes and values. The sections below will assist you in identifying those wants and needs.

Wants versus Needs

Although there are many potentially satisfying ways to use your time and money, you should seek to do those things that not only bring pleasure but overcome some current or anticipated dissatisfaction. Once you have identified the areas of discomfort in your life and the means you have or will have to relieve them, you can begin to think about valid financial goals.

How can you tell bona fide, worthy goals from pipedreams? In our experience, most successful goal-directed actions are motivated chiefly by feelings of dissatisfaction. The power of dissatisfaction as a motivator applies to positive things as well. You may want to be president of your company, but it should become a goal only if the thought of not being president is very dissatisfying.

This is not just some theoretical nicety, but a very real test for establishing true financial wants and needs. For example, you might find it satisfying to own a vacation home, have a sports car, or take a Caribbean cruise, but personal and financial goals should derive from things that bring both satisfaction and the elimination of dissatisfaction.

With this understanding you can reduce a universe of satisfying possibilities to a relative handful of truly meaningful financial and personal needs and wants. Just ask yourself these two questions to narrow down your choices:

1. Do I truly feel some dissatisfaction about a current or anticipated situation?
2. Is that level of dissatisfaction strong enough to make me do something about it?

We will call a dissatisfier/motivator that passes this test and relates to a basic economic necessity, such as security, a *need*. A motivator that relates to an economic luxury (something you could do without), we'll call a *want*. This will help you both to identify your financial goals and to rank them in order of their importance.

Figure 2–3 is a Needs/Wants Assessment for a typical Lean and Quick married couple in their 30s. This form, along with the questions and hints that follow, will help you complete your own Action Paper No. 2.

Deriving Your Financial Needs and Wants
Your financial condition is the foundation of all your other goal-getting activities. The following questions will aid you in completing Part I of "Your Needs/Wants Assessment":

1. How comfortable is your current income? Do you have any surplus each month for savings? Do you have to constantly dip into reserves to meet your short-term expenses?
2. Do you have an emergency fund?
3. Are those financial assets not used for day-to-day living expenses earning income or appreciating?
4. Does your debt load exceed the value of your financial assets?
5. Do your long-term commitments limit your flexibility to meet new financial goals?
6. Do any of your financial assets (heirlooms, collections, etc.) have sentimental value that exceeds their financial value?

Separating wants and needs in the financial sphere is usually easy. Legal debts, insolvency, and absence of emergency funds are real financial needs. Note your intention to overcome these negative conditions in the financial needs section of the worksheet.

Your financial wants may include specific financial desires such as buying a home, stocks, bonds, gold coins, or other tangible assets. Or they may be more general such as building surplus funds for future investment. Note the example in Figure 2–3 for more ideas on typical financial needs and wants.

FIGURE 2–3
Sample Action Paper No. 2, Needs/Wants Assessment for a Lean and Quick Household

---

Action Paper No. 2

Your Needs/Wants Assessment

Name *Lean and Quick*
Date *January*

From Action Paper No. 1	Needs	Wants
Part I Your General Financial Condition	*Emergency fund* *Create monthly surplus*	*New car* *Own home*
Part II Your Personal and Vocational Resources	*Get professional certificate*	*Small business*
Part III Your Cultural and Economic Attitudes and Values	*Secure retirement* *(Financial Independence)* *College for daughter*	

Deriving Your Personal and Vocational Needs and Wants

For Part II, look again at Figure 2–3, and use the following questions to help you complete this section.

1. From your "Career and Life Inventory" (Action Paper No. 1), select your three most rewarding career and personal accomplishments. What do they have in common? These may be factors such as independent action, problem solving, leadership, communication ability, or even high-financial return. How are they different (teamwork or individual action, high return or psychologically satisfying, written versus verbal communication)? If you have a partner, how do your responses compare? What are the most rewarding activities on the individual and household levels?

2. How would a brief classified ad for your ideal career position read? (You may even want to write it down.) What personal strengths can you identify in your inventory that would satisfy the requirements of your ideal job?

3. Do you see yourself refining your skills in one or two activities or developing abilities in new directions?

4. What educational objectives would assist you in obtaining your desired new opportunities?

5. If you could start your career over again, what would be your first three vocational choices?

Divide your desires into needs and wants. For example, in the category of Personal and Vocational Resources, you might identify something that relates to maintaining your current job or income level. This would be particularly important if your job is threatened by a changing economy.

Most people will have many more wants than needs here. These may include more meaningful or remunerative employment that requires additional education or a change in careers. You may want to write a book. Others may want to make a contribution to society through teaching or volunteer work.

You will find that wants and needs relate to your stage of the life cycle. Younger people tend to emphasize career and family-building activities. Those near the end of their professional careers may look more to charitable or leisure-time pursuits.

Deriving Your Attitude and Value-Related Needs and Wants

Keeping your previous responses in mind, move on to Part III, Your Cultural and Economic Attitudes and Values. The following questions will help you in this review:

1. What sorts of activities, past or present, are mentioned most often as sources of satisfaction?
2. Do your answers show a greater sensitivity to the needs of others, or to personal, self-directed interests?
3. Is there any pattern of advantages from your background? Contacts with influential people, an entrepreneurial zeal, or unique family resources are only a few possibilities.
4. Which limitations you've identified are a result of external forces? Which are self-imposed?
5. How would you revise the percentages in your answer to item III-9 to be your ideal use of time? How do the ideal and the actual percentages compare? What do they tell you about your attitudes toward work, play, and family activities?
6. What are the three key words you'd like to hear used in a speech describing you upon retirement? How do they compare to the way you've described yourself in this section? Do you need to alter your behaviors and beliefs to move in the desired direction?
7. What was the worst mistake you ever made? Did this mistake occur because of or in spite of the attitudes and beliefs you've listed? How would you change your behavior in this matter if you had to do it all over again?
8. Which attitudes and values you've listed have been inherited from others? Which were adopted on your own?
9. Is there any way to employ the attitudes and values you like least in a positive manner? For example, if you are too critical of others, could the powers of observation and high standards that often accompany such characteristics be applied as a troubleshooter or auditor for your company? Don't make excuses for yourself, but give yourself and your values an even break. Use your imagination.

The desires that emerge from this section will usually take the form of *lower-order* needs. These may include things like desire for shelter, personal safety, or basic health care. On the other hand, your wants often take the form of *higher-order* accomplishments: wider social acceptance, community leadership, or political aspirations.

In the first column of your worksheet, under Needs, briefly summarize the more basic needs. For example, if you listed "living in the inner city" or "living in a high-crime area" as negative aspects of your childhood, you might consider "living in a quiet suburb" an important cultural need.

If you listed "running for the school board" as a highly satisfying experience, you might put down "holding political office" as a possible cultural want.

Now try to identify changes to your existing attitudes and values that would be crucial to obtaining your other wants and needs. For example, you may decide that your responses reveal a stoic, impersonal side to your emotions. Perhaps you think it is important for your success as an executive or for a more satisfying family life to get more "in touch" with your feelings. If you think this change is crucial, you might list "be more honest and open about my feelings" under Needs.

Or perhaps you border on being a workaholic. You'd like more leisure time, but it is not crucial to your success. Listing "cultivating a more laid-back attitude" under Wants would be appropriate.

Goal setting is more an art than a science. Our purpose here is to induce you to uncover as many of your hidden needs and wants as possible through honest introspection and your own creative thinking.

Wrapping Up

If you are having problems completing "Your Needs/Wants Assessment," look back at Figure 2–3. Throughout this book we will feature sample forms as though completed by a typical Lean and Quick married couple in their 30s. As you can see from Figure 2–3, this couple has a child they need to plan for. You will learn more about this family through the completed sample Action Papers in the balance of the book. By the end, you should have a fairly good picture of their current circumstances and their hopes, desires, and plans to achieve them.

For that matter, you too will have a clearer picture of how to achieve the things *you* really want in life. As you can see, it's more important to be honest and straightforward than specific or grammatically correct! You don't have to complete every box. However, a blank section may signal a need to review your inventory once again to see if any dissatisfier/motivators have been overlooked.

At this point you may be dubious about the value of this fairly esoteric, general, nonmathematical approach to developing a workable Personal Profit Plan. But as we told you at the beginning, our approach differs from the computerized, grind-out-the-numbers spreadsheet formula. Not everyone fits into a formula. If spending more time with your family and doing community and charity work is personally more satisfying than rolling up dollars in a bank account, your financial plan should, and will, be different from the ambitious, career-oriented corporate climbers.

You've already accomplished more than most people ever attempt. You have a comprehensive assessment of your true wants and needs, unlike most people who go through life with only a vague idea of what they

are doing and why they are doing it. With no clear idea of where they are
going, it is no surprise that many become dissatisfied and discouraged without being able to explain exactly what is wrong.

You've completed a significant first step. You now have a set of career
and life targets—the foundation of your Personal Profit Plan. In the next
chapter, you will begin to develop specific strategies for achieving your financial goals.

CHAPTER 3

ANALYZING YOUR FINANCIAL STARTING POINT

THE NECESSITY FOR ACCURATE RECORD KEEPING

In Chapter 2 you completed a general analysis of the relationship between your personal and financial assets as the preplanning phase of the goal-setting process. In this chapter you will begin the actual goal setting. To do an effective job, you have to know exactly where you stand now. You also need a method for measuring your progress. This is accomplished through the two basic administrative functions of Personal Profit Planning:

1. *Financial record keeping* is the recording and preservation of your relevant financial data.
2. *Financial score keeping* is the preparation and analysis of your financial statements.

These are both crucial elements in assembling and implementing an effective Personal Profit Plan.

Financial records are nothing more than receipts, invoices, tax forms, paycheck stubs, canceled checks, and other records of your financial transactions. For most people these important documents are scattered about haphazardly in large envelopes, boxes, or just plain piles on desks. And then, when tax time rolls around, they rush madly to locate records only to find that the one or two documents they really need have "disappeared."

Other people have such a fetish for saving every little slip of paper for eternity that they become inundated with piles of paper, most of which are useless. And important items are difficult or impossible to find in the mess!

One reason you need to keep financial records is to prepare financial statements. Financial statements enable you to "keep score" of your personal economic progress. You may have already run into one type of financial statement if you've applied for credit. The bank or credit card company wants to know where you stand, both in terms of income and assets.

In the last chapter you learned the distinction between income and wealth. You will need two different financial statements to track these areas. The *balance sheet* lists your financial assets and liabilities. The difference between your assets and liabilities is your *net worth*. That is the measure of your wealth. The other statement you will need is an *income statement* that delineates your income and expenses for a given time period. It shows your ability not only to meet current expenses but also to save and invest for the future.

It is important to understand that financial records and financial statements are interdependent. You certainly will not be able to prepare accurate statements—which you will need for things like securing a home mortgage as well as for keeping track of your financial progress—if your data storage system is faulty. On the other hand, it is difficult to maintain usable records if you don't know what to keep or why to keep it.

The Requirements for Good Financial Record Keeping

The following general guidelines will help you keep accurate and effective financial records:

1. *Always keep a personal information sheet.* This is the key to your financial records. It consists of an updated list of your checking, savings, and brokerage accounts. In addition, keep a list of your credit cards, with account numbers and customer service phone numbers. You should also identify the location of financial documents such as stock certificates, deeds, wills, insurance policies, and other important papers.

Since this list will frequently change as you add a new credit card, or open a different type of account with your bank, make sure the list is kept handy so you can update it quickly. Also, *be sure the members of your household know where to locate the list in an emergency.*

If a financial crisis occurs, such as the death of a breadwinner, an unexpected legal action, or an accident, the presence of such a list will aid greatly in easing confusion and minimizing costly errors. Neither you nor your family should have to guess where your important financial records are located.

Action Paper No. 3, "Your Personal Information Sheet," is included at the back of the book. You should complete the documentation along with the other exercises in this chapter.

2. *Keep only those records that have a specific future use.* Many of us keep poor records because we are not sure which items are worth keeping and which should be thrown away. Save only those documents which show legal entitlements (for example, tax-deductible items or veterans' benefits), contractual obligations, disposition of debt, legal ownership, and the purchase and sale price of fixed assets and investments.

All these items represent facts that may be contested at some time in the future. For example, you may need the data to support insurance claims, new loans, tax deductions, and other financial affairs.

Most bills that have already been paid and credited with payment can be thrown away except when doing so would violate one of the requirements listed above. For example, keep those bills that show tax-deductible expenses.

3. *Keep your financial records for a specific length of time only.* There are few areas in personal finance as fraught with misinformation and misconceptions as the length of time you should hold your financial records. No single time period is applicable to all financial records.

One year is appropriate for most financial records. Every year you should review your financial files and remove those items that may be needed for tax documentation. Keep those records in long-term storage. The IRS can audit your return up to three years after it is filed, so you need to keep your annual tax-related information at least that long. And remember, sales of assets may not take place for years. Only at that point will your tax calculations come into play.

The IRS can audit you up to six years after your return is filed if an item representing more than 25 percent of your reported income is omitted. There is no statute of limitations on fraud. If your income varies widely from year to year, or is derived from unusual or varied sources, you may be more subject to audits than people with salaried positions. Let your CPA or tax attorney advise you on what would be most appropriate for your tax-related records.

An effective record-keeping system is one that ties your financial assets to the relevant records that support them. Your system should be logical, accessible, and compatible with its most important function: providing data for your personal financial statements.

At the back of this book we've included an End Paper No. 1 that details a variety of record-keeping systems. What works for one person or household may not work for another. We recommend that you review the different approaches to see which one makes the most sense to you and your lifestyle. You may even want to combine some features, though you must be sure your final system includes all the necessary elements. The important thing is to be consistent once you've set up your system.

Organizing Your Financial Data

Your balance sheet gives you a snapshot of your financial assets and liabilities on a given date. The difference between those assets and liabilities is your net worth.

Creating your financial statements can be a time-consuming and frustrating task, especially at first. We've designed Action Paper No. 4, "Your Supporting Financial Schedules," to provide you with a checklist of the items and figures needed to complete both your balance sheet and your income statement. When you have completed Action Paper No. 4, you can put aside your financial records and use the Action Paper as the basis for completing your two financial statements.

Completing Your Personal Balance Sheet

Action Paper No. 5, "Your Personal Balance Sheet," is located at the back of the book. It is structured to help you compute your total assets (things you own) and your total liabilities (what you owe) to arrive at your net worth (the difference between them).

If your liabilities exceed your assets, you have a negative net worth. In other words, if you sold all your assets, you still would not have raised enough money to pay off all your outstanding debts.

As you can see, the balance sheet is designed to "balance" on the bottom line. Net worth can be viewed as a "fudge factor" to make it balance. It is a very good indicator of your real financial health. Your net worth can be increased by adding to your assets, paying off liabilities (out of your income, not your assets), or by increasing your assets' value.

Figure 3–1 shows a completed balance sheet for our typical Lean and Quick family. Below we address the details of the worksheet to help you fill out your own. The amounts shown represent market value of the assets on one particular day, January 10.

The first category on the balance sheet is Monetary Assets. These are assets that can be quickly converted to cash. Refer to Action Paper No. 4, "Your Supporting Financial Schedules," for a complete discussion of where to show various assets and liabilities on the balance sheet.

Fixed assets are those that take more time to convert to cash. Real estate (other than REITs and some limited partnerships) often takes weeks or months to sell. Even when a buyer is found, escrow procedures can take further weeks. Note that the Lean and Quick couple owns some raw land listed at the last appraised value. Ownership interests in small businesses are notoriously illiquid. For this reason it is best to list a very conservative valuation. This risk of selling an asset at less than its current value or the problem of finding a market for your asset at all give fixed assets their "fixed" quality. It is better to be conservative than to delude yourself into thinking you have more than you really do.

To derive a value for your car, either consult the *Kelley Blue Book* in your library, or simply look through the classified ads to find prices for comparable vehicles. Your personal property includes things such as appliances, furniture, and other tangible objects. For particularly valuable items (antiques, jewelry, or others) you may want to get an appraisal. The appraisal

FIGURE 3–1
Sample Balance Sheet for a Lean and Quick Household

Action Paper No. 5

Your Personal Balance Sheet

Name *Lean and Quick*
Date *January 10*

ASSETS			LIABILITIES		
Monetary Assets			**Short-Term Liabilities**		
1. Cash and Equivalents			14. Unpaid Bills		
Cash/checking/savings	4,850		Taxes	500	
Money market funds	0		Insurance premiums	0	
Certificates of Deposit	0		Rent	750	
Bonds (< 1 yr. maturity)	0		Utilities	130	
Total Cash and Equivalents		4,850	Charge accounts	600	
			Credit cards	1280	
2. Notes Receivable		0	Other	0	
3. Investments			Total Unpaid Bills		3,260
Stocks	3000		15. Installment Loans (balance due)		
Bonds (>1 yr. maturity)	0		Automobile	3,320	
Real estate (REITs, partnerships)	0		Other	0	
Cash value of life insurance	680		Total Installment Loans		3,320
Cash value of annuities	0		16. Total Short-Term Liabilities (14 + 15)		6,580
Retirement plans	2,000				
Total Investments		5,680	**Long-Term Liabilities**		
4. Total Monetary Assets (1 + 2 + 3)		10,530	17. Non-mortgage Loans (balance due)		
			Bank	0	
Fixed Assets			Educational	0	
5. Home and property	0		Other	0	
6. Automobiles/vehicles	12,500		Accrued capital gains tax liability	462	
7. Other personal property	20,000		Total Non-mortgage Loans		462
8. Total Personal Assets (5 + 6 + 7)		32,500	18. Mortgage Loans (bal. due)		
			Home	0	
9. Other real estate	8,000		Other	0	
10. Ownership in small business	0		Total Mortgage Loans		0
11. Total Fixed Investment Assets (9 + 10)		8,000	19. Total Long-Term Liabilities (17 + 18)		462
12. Total Fixed Assets (8 + 11)		40,500	20. Total Liabilities (16 + 19)		7,042
13. Total Assets (4 + 12)		51,030	21. Net Worth (13 minus 20)		43,988
			22. Balance (21 + 20)		51,030

can be valuable not only in arriving at a correct balance sheet figure, but also for insurance purposes.

Under Personal Property in our Lean and Quick example, we estimated $20,000 for clothing, utensils, furniture, jewelry, and other such items.

Now move to the other side of the ledger. We've found that people generally have a good idea of their assets, but tend to underestimate their liabilities. Liabilities are also divided into short-term (more liquid), and long-term (less liquid) categories. To be considered short-term, the liability should fall due within one year. A long-term liability is anything that falls due *after* this period.

Item 14, Unpaid Bills, comprises those debts for which you have been invoiced or that you know are due within 12 months. Include here your current month's rent if it has not been paid by the date you prepare the balance sheet. Other items here would include unpaid debts to your dentist, physician, or optometrist. List taxes if you have an unpaid balance or are self-employed and pay on the quarterly voucher system. Be sure to include the outstanding balance on your credit cards. You may have more or fewer categories than are listed. Include *only* those bills you have already received and expect to pay.

Item 15 will catch the balance of unpaid short-term liabilities. Include here the balances of your installment loans. In our example, one of the family car loans will be paid off in six months. The $3,320 entry represents the total outstanding balance.

Add items 14 and 15 to get your total short-term liabilities. The Lean and Quick example shows total short-term liabilities are $6,580. That is the amount they would have to raise out of monetary assets to stay solvent over the short term.

Long-term liabilities may be conveniently thought of as claims against fixed assets. The additional time needed to liquidate these assets tends to support the multiyear nature of long-term debts. For example, in the case of a home mortgage liability, the fixed asset itself is collateral for the borrower.

Too often people fail to consider the tax consequences of their capital gains transactions. The 1986 Tax Reform Act simplified things by eliminating the distinction between long-term and short-term capital gains. Now all gains from the sale of assets are taxed at your ordinary income rate.

However, because there is no withholding of capital gains taxes, you need to calculate what that liability will be. Look to the asset column, item 3, Investments. The purchase price of the stocks was $1,600. On January 10 their value was $3,000. If sold on that day there would be a $1,400 capital gain. Figuring a combined federal and state tax rate of 33 percent, there is a resulting tax liability of $462.

This liability can escalate quickly if the value of your portfolio is high. The same holds true if you sell a house or other real estate that has appreciated substantially. It is important to carefully compute the value of your investment holdings each time you revise your financial statements.

To find your total liabilities, add items 16 and 19 ($7,042 in our example). To compute your net worth, subtract item 20 from item 13. In our example that value is $43,988. The net worth figure is the amount you would have left over if you liquidated all your assets and paid off all your bills on the day you prepare your balance sheet.

The balance sheet is structured to double-check your calculations. Simply add back your net worth (item 21) to your total liabilities (item 20). The resulting figure, item 20, should equal item 11 (your total assets). If it doesn't, there is an error somewhere. Recheck your math until the two figures match.

Our Lean and Quick couple certainly seems financially well-off according to this statement. But remember, the balance sheet tells you only part of the story. It says nothing about your income or living expenses. Nor does it tell you anything about the way your assets and liabilities may have changed over time.

At this point you do not have enough information to construct a definite plan for building net worth or achieving particular financial goals. You also need to break down your income and expenses to see what ammunition you have to pursue these goals.

Creating Your Personal Income Statement

Find Action Paper No. 6, "Your Personal Income Statement," at the back of the book. You will plug the numbers from Action Paper No. 4 into the respective categories in Action Paper No. 6.

We start, logically enough, with income. Since income and social security taxes come off the top, they are the next entry. Subtracting taxes from income leaves you with your take-home pay or, more formally, *the Amount Remaining for Living Expenses, Savings and Investments.*

An important concept to understand in completing your income statement is the difference between *fixed* and *variable* costs. A fixed cost, like a fixed asset, is one that takes time to change. For example, a monthly mortgage is fixed for many years into the future. Changing it requires complicated, often time-consuming arrangements such as refinancing or selling your property. Other examples of fixed costs include monthly rent, insurance premiums, and installment loans.

Variable costs, on the other hand, are those over which you exercise some discretionary power on a month-to-month basis. Your food budget, for example, can vary depending on the quantity and type of food you buy. Entertainment expenses are perhaps the best example of a purely variable expense (you do *have* to eat). Entertainment expenses are the first things most families cut when economic pressures mount. In reality, fixed and variable costs depend on your circumstances and motivation. You *can* cancel an insurance policy if you need the money badly enough. An installment loan *can* be paid off in a lump sum if you have the resources. Ask yourself, "How committed am I to maintaining the status quo?" If the fixed cost still plays a valid role in your overall financial strategy, it should not be considered a variable expense.

You can also split any particular expense into its fixed and variable components. For example, gas expenses for your car can be broken down between those that are work-related, and those incurred for personal transportation. Work-related expenses are probably crucial to your income, but if the need arose, you could cut back expenses by limiting personal mileage.

Figure 3–2 is a sample income statement for our Lean and Quick couple. Most of the items are self-explanatory. Total up all sources of your income and deduct taxes to get the total of your discretionary funds. In this case it is $38,608.

Most of the living expenses are also straightforward. However, the next to the last entry under Living Expenses, Outlays for fixed assets, needs to be calculated. Our couple used the rule of thumb explained in Action Paper No. 4. The total value of their appliances—washer, dryer, kitchen appliances, televisions and stereos—was figured at $8,500. Ten percent of that total is the $850 entry on this line. This amount represents the cost to replace failed items, not upgrade to better models or add new equipment. Once this fund is set aside, you do not need to duplicate it on subsequent income statements unless it is depleted by use or outdated by the addition of new appliances.

At this point you can total up both your fixed and variable expenses. Subtract that total from item 5, Amount Remaining for Living Expenses, Savings and Investments, to get item 8, Amount Remaining for Savings and Investments.

Interpreting Your Financial Statements

There are three tests of financial fitness:

1. Liquidity.
2. Leverage.
3. Diversification.

Liquidity refers to your ability to convert your assets into cash on short notice. Do you have enough money to meet emergencies or capitalize on

FIGURE 3–2

Sample Income Statement for a Lean and Quick Household

Action Paper No. 6

Your Personal Income Statement

Name *Lean and Quick*

For the Year Beginning January 1, 19_____ and ending December 31, 19_____

1. Income

Spouse or Partner A	*34,500*	
Spouse or Partner B	*20,000*	
Total wages or salaries		*54,500*
Dividends and interest		*420*
Rents		*0*
Other _____		*0*

2. Total Income — *54,920*

3. Taxes

Personal income taxes	*11,684*
Social Security and disability taxes	*4,628*

4. Total Taxes — *16,312*

5. Amount Remaining for Living Expenses, Savings and Investments — *38,608*

6. Living Expenses

	Fixed	Variable
Housing		
Utilities	–	*2,100*
Repairs	–	*460*
Insurance	*250*	–
Taxes	–	–
Rent or mortgage payments	*9,000*	–
Other _____	–	–
Food		*5,300*
Clothing (including laundry, dry cleaning, repairs, and personal effects)		*2,000*
Transportation		
Gas, tolls, parking	*1,250*	–
Repairs	*1,300*	–
Licenses	*280*	–
Insurance	*1,100*	–
Auto payments or purchase	*3,320*	–
Fares		*3,200*
Recreation, entertainment, and vacations		–
Medical		
Doctor	*230*	–
Dentist	*160*	–
Medicines	*320*	–
Insurance	–	
Personal	*2,200*	
Life insurance (term)	*340*	
Outlays for fixed assets	*850*	
Other expenses _____	*800*	
Subtotal	*21,400*	*13,060*

7. Total Annual Living Expenses — *34,460*

8. Amount Remaining for Savings and Investment — *4,148*

new opportunities? If you did have to liquidate some assets, would you have to accept steep discounts from their value to get cash quickly?

A good rule of thumb is: *have 30 to 60 percent of your net worth in monetary assets.* If your income level is high and relatively secure, the lower part of the range is acceptable. If your income is not stable or predictable, stick with the upper end of the range.

If you have more than the recommended percentage in monetary assets, you may be missing out on capital growth opportunities. In times of inflation, you may be losing the purchasing power of your dollars to the erosion of inflation.

To figure your percentage, divide your total monetary assets (item 4 on the balance sheet) by your net worth (item 21 on the balance sheet). In our example, item 4 is $10,530. Item 21 is $43,988. The liquidity factor is 24 percent. A quick look at the balance sheet shows that the large raw land element probably accounts for a lower liquidity ratio than you would expect from a Lean and Quick physique.

Leverage refers to the extent that debt or other liability was used in acquiring assets. Liabilities incurred to acquire assets are the lever you use to increase your wealth. Virtually all homes are purchased with up to 80 percent of the price being borrowed. Because of the long-term upward trend of real estate prices since the 1940s, this common practice has come to be considered safe, provided the borrower's monthly cash flow covers the interest and principal payments on the debt. However, there have been extended periods of weak real estate prices in the past. Especially in today's uncertain and volatile economic environment, do not assume there is any guarantee of any single investment being safe.

Misuse of leverage is very dangerous even here. If the asset purchased with debt drops in value, you may be left with a loan that is worth more than the asset it secured. Your net worth would be reduced rather than increased.

Our rule of thumb on leverage is: *if your nonmortgage debts are more than half of your nonrealty assets, be very careful about borrowing more money.*

Our Lean and Quick couple does not own a home and their raw land is unencumbered with debt. Their only loan is the installment debt for their car (item 15 on the balance sheet). This represents less than 7 percent of their total assets of $51,030. Obviously they are well below the maximum ratio of 50 percent. Debt does not represent a problem for them at this juncture. In fact, they may be underusing leverage as a wealth-building strategy.

Diversification is the distribution of your financial resources over a number of different investment vehicles. While one or two asset classes may do well over a short period of time, our research shows that a diversified set of assets held over the long-term outperforms individual classes.

For example, in the late 1970s real estate and gold were sterling performers while the stock market lagged far behind. Later, from 1982 to the summer of 1987, the stock market surged over 300 percent while gold prices fell over 50 percent and real estate prices were stagnant in many parts of the country. If your investment portfolio had been diversified over a number of asset classes, including stocks, bonds, real estate, international securities, and gold, you would have experienced less overall volatility and better performance than any single asset class over that time.

We will cover this concept in relation to your specific goal-getting steps in Chapters 6 and 7. Diversification over different asset classes will play an important part in the actual implementation of your Personal Profit Plan.

For the moment, take a look at your monetary and fixed assets (excluding your home). If any single asset class such as stocks, bonds, money market funds, or real estate constitutes more than 30 to 50 percent of your net worth, you may be overly concentrated in that area.

To figure your cash percentage, divide item 1, Total Cash, on your balance sheet by item 13, Total Assets. Our Lean and Quick example shows about a 9.5 percent cash ratio.

We know the stocks portion of the balance sheet for our Lean and Quicksters is concentrated in only a few high technology stocks. That is a very volatile sector of the market. Their other stock investments are in mutual funds, which provide some diversification.

Counterbalancing the exposure to stocks is the cash and, to some extent, the raw land. Cash and equivalents tend to run counter to stock market developments. This is called *negative correlation*. It serves to dampen overall portfolio volatility. Raw land real estate investments perform independently of stock market developments, further reducing the volatility of this portfolio.

However, there is still at least one hole in this Lean and Quick couple's diversification program. There are no bonds—something a fully diversified portfolio would surely include.

Once you have completed your own Action Papers 4, 5, and 6, you will use this information to start an effective goal-setting plan.

Setting Your Financial Goals

In Chapter 2 you completed Action Paper No. 2, "Your Needs/Wants Assessment." You will need that form and your income statement and balance sheet to begin to make your Personal Profit Plan fall into place.

Ensuring a desired future is what goals analysis and planning is all about. Your wants and needs assessment is as important as the information you produced for your financial statements. The financial data gives you your economic starting point, but your assessment of your needs and wants provides the direction you want to pursue. You need to know both to formulate an effective plan.

Goals versus Objectives

You know by now that you don't reach your life's goals simply by identifying them. *Goals* are the desired future conditions you hope to achieve. *Objectives* are the specific, incremental steps you will take to reach your goals.

You achieve your goals by realizing the intermediate objectives that comprise them. This is more than a simple semantic distinction. You need a clear definition of the differences between your current situation and your desired future condition in order to appreciate the size of the task that lies ahead. You need specific benchmarks by which you can measure your progress or lack of it. Otherwise you won't know how well your plan is moving you toward your ultimate goals.

Though the difference between goals and objectives is critical to our program, there are also a number of things they have in common:

1. *They both must be specific.* For example, merely targeting a "college fund" is not going to achieve it. You need to specify the details such as tuition, books, room and board, transportation, and even spending money for a specific type of institution (private or public university, for example). To make accurate financial projections you need to target a particular time in the future.

2. *They both must be quantified.* You need a clear idea of what your goals will cost. Relying on vague, ballpark figures may result in your winding up in the wrong ballpark at just the wrong time!

3. *They both must be timebounded.* In order to design an investment program to meet your goals and objectives, you must know how long your money will have to work. Only then can you calculate how much your investment will grow at specific rates. Remember the "time value" of money. Compounding works, but to forecast its effect, you need to know how long you can let your money work. The targeted timeframe will influence the type of investments you can make with reasonable expectation of achieving the returns you need. The time horizon of a financial goal or objective is that point in the future when you will take the cash from an investment to spend on needs and wants.

4. *They both must have tangible results.* Think of it this way: How would someone else decide whether or not you've hit your target? Your objectives and goals must be specific enough that there is no doubt, even to an outsider, that they have been accomplished. To say, "I'm going to write a book someday" does not qualify. With no time limit or other details specified, no one can say you've failed to reach your goal, yet you've accomplished nothing.

5. *They both must be attainable.* If you are five feet tall and weigh 90 pounds, there is not much chance you will be a starting linebacker in the NFL. If hand-eye coordination has always presented a problem for you, it is unlikely you will erase the memory of Chris Evert from the minds of tennis buffs! Dreams are great. Dream as big as you wish but make sure your goals are appropriate to your resources.

Classifying Goals and Objectives

Classifying your goals and objectives helps you work more effectively with them. Following are several useful ways to categorize yours:

1. *By time.* How long will it take you to reach each goal? Different goals obviously take different amounts of time to accomplish. Short-term goals, such as buying a car, can be done in days or weeks. Long-term goals, such as financing retirement, normally require years.

2. *By frequency of attainment.* How often will each goal recur? Your car will have to be replaced eventually. That is a recurring expense that gets more costly all the time. Other things, such as a college degree, are normally once-in-a-lifetime accomplishments.

3. *By type of purchase.* As we've mentioned before, much of money management is really *spending management.* You will find it handy to classify your goals by the kind of purchase they represent. Goods and services can either be short-term *consumables* such as food, or longer term (over three years) *durables* such as cars.

4. *By purpose.* What desire does each goal satisfy? Some things, such as a new refrigerator, have tangible benefits. Others, such as art classes, have a strong intangible element. Most goal-related expenditures are a mixture of both. For example, a new home provides both shelter and satisfaction.

You will find these classifications helpful when you set priorities among your needs and wants. This is especially so when your priorities differ from those of your spouse or partner. Knowing the purpose and expected benefit of an expenditure can boost understanding and cooperation.

Preparing Your Goals Priority Worksheet

On Action Paper No. 7, "Your Goals Priority Worksheet," in the back of the book you will: 1) list the goals you've identified on Your Needs/Wants Assessment, 2) prioritize them, and 3) price them.

When you completed your financial statements, you evaluated them in terms of liquidity, leverage (use of debt), and diversification. Take another look at your goals (needs and wants) listed on Action Paper No. 2. Are you in a financial position to jump right into pursuing new goals? Or do you need a little "economic therapy" before you begin?

Establishing solvency, reducing excessive debt, and redistributing dangerously concentrated assets *all* must take priority in financial goal setting. If these actions apply to you, be sure that you make the appropriate entry ("reduce installment loans," "create emergency cash reserve,") on Your Needs/Wants Assessment.

Can you describe your general needs and wants in specific, quantified, time-bounded, results-oriented, and attainable terms? For example, if you listed "buy a home" as a want, can you define that home more specifically? What size do you want? What features do you have in the back of your mind? How much will such a house cost in the area in which you want to buy? What is your timeframe for being able to afford this home? These are only a few of the variables you need to consider.

Now that you have defined your goal more specifically, does it still hold the same appeal? Will buying the house still provide the benefits you expected? These may be anything from providing shelter, to pride of ownership, to tax benefits. But the key is whether the end result is worth the intermediate effort.

Has any one of the elements—price, timeframe, that "tied down" feeling—rendered the goal impractical? If so, go back and change your assumptions until you can honestly say that you have described an attainable goal.

You need to define each want and need in this manner. Then you will be ready to restate and rank them as bona fide goals on Action Paper No. 7.

Pricing Your Goals
There are numerous ways to price each of your goals. All costs should be shown in today's dollars (current year prices). In Chapter 6 we will show you how to account for the effects of inflation. For the moment, keep it simple. For those items that represent a single purchase or accrual of a particular sum of money, enter a single-dollar amount. For goals that require a recurring annual or monthly investment, enter the amount as dollars per year. For recurring purchases, but at irregular intervals, (antiques or art, for example) show the dollars as *per occurrence*.

Everyone prefers good surprises to bad ones. Therefore, make your "current year" dollar estimates as accurate and conservative as possible. You can get direct quotes from dealers for most anticipated purchases. A real estate agent can give you a pretty good estimate for housing. A quick call to the university admissions office will yield details on college tuition and other expenses.

FIGURE 3–3
Lean and Quick's Sample Goals Priority Worksheet

Action Paper No. 7

Your Goals Priority Worksheet

Name *Lean and Quick*
Date *January*

Priority	Goal	Price
① {	Emergency fund, 2 months reserve	6,000
	Get professional certificate	800
②	New car, Firestorm 5000	10,000
③	Buy home in La Ritz district	120,000
④	4 years at Learnmore College	28,000
⑤	Partnership share in furnishings boutique	25,000
⑥	Secure retirement / financial independence	2,000/yr.

The Lean and Quick Priority Worksheet

Figure 3–3 is filled out for our Lean and Quick couple. Look at Figure 2–3 to see the completed Needs/Wants worksheet. Not surprisingly, the needs were the highest priority. Since getting a professional certificate was a method to increase income, that shares the top priority slot with establishing an emergency fund.

Usually, your needs will be the top of your priority list. However, as you can see from Figure 3–3, age-cycle factors are also important. Since our Lean and Quicksters are still in their 30s, retirement concerns are not pressing at this time. That will be dealt with later.

For the moment, getting to work reliably advanced "a new car" up the priority list. Since home ownership affords tax benefits as well as offering reliable long-term capital appreciation, "buying a house" was close behind on the priority list. If their home appreciates, it could play an important role in the other goals: college education for their child, opening their own business, and eventually, contributing to their retirement nest egg.

As you can see, this is not a pure number-crunching process. Sit back and give yourself a little time to think over the implications and potential interrelationships of your chosen goals. As you can see with our example, combining or deferring goals and viewing them in light of the changing life cycle is integral to the goal-setting process.

Wrapping Up

You now have a comprehensive picture of your financial starting point. When combined with the insights you have into your specific needs and wants, you are well on your way to devising a workable Personal Profit Plan.

As we have told you, this whole process is threefold. First, there is identifying where you are. Second, you must establish where you want to go. Third, and most important, is the work you did in this chapter on prioritizing your goals. It is quite easy to run down a list of things you want—we all have virtually unlimited wants.

But the difference between your position now and that of most people working on their personal financial plans is that you have taken that extra step to identify what is most important and when you need to accomplish it. The balance of this book will deal with using this information in devising a workable plan for achieving those goals.

Take a minute now to congratulate yourself. You have already completed a major step in improving your financial prospects.

CHAPTER 4

UNDERSTANDING AND WORKING WITH PARTNERS

FINANCIAL PLANNING—FAMILY STYLE

You now have a good foundation for creating an individualized financial plan. However, before you can move on to putting together a workable Personal Profit Plan, you need to address day-to-day financial affairs. As we alluded to in Chapter 2, spending habits are too often overlooked when people examine their financial affairs. In this chapter you will learn how financial decisions are made in your household. You will also gain insight into the individual spending styles of yourself and your family members. Working together to understand and optimize your spending behavior plays a critical role in the overall success of your financial plan. You can't set realistic goals and plan an effective goal-getting program without getting honest input from your spouse or partner(s). Breaking down communication barriers will enhance the prospects for fulfilling your Personal Profit Plan.

To implement a successful Personal Profit Plan, you will need to consider not only *your* feelings, desires, and ideas; but also those of the people who share your life. For many of you, that will be your spouse. But there may be others to consider. Family members will be affected by the decisions you make. In fact, as your children mature, it is appropriate to include them as participants in your financial planning.

In Chapter 3 you completed financial statements that pinpointed your current financial situation. In this chapter you will learn more about your and your partner's psychological makeup. It is important to learn how to work out differences to the mutual satisfaction of all parties. Such differences need not remain a cause of conflict. Recognizing the strengths and weaknesses of each partner can be a source of real strength.

Most people tend to concentrate on income and earning power when they deal with financial affairs. But as we indicated in Chapter 2, recognizing your spending habits is crucial to understanding your current financial condition. People have many diverse attitudes toward money. In fact, most domestic disputes are occasioned by financial differences.

Financial discord may stem from differences in tolerance for risk, or even in widely varied spending habits. Some people are born risk takers:

fighter pilots, rock climbers, white-water rafters. Others prefer the tried and true: accountants, bankers, insurance agents. Neither approach is right or wrong; they are just different. It is as important to your long-term success to understand your partner(s)'s financial personality as it is to know your own.

Even if you do not currently have a spouse or life-partner, complete the questionnaires in this chapter for yourself. Take time to read about the characteristics of other financial decision makers and spending types. The insights will prove valuable to you in everyday transactions with people and money.

Spender Profiles

While you may have never made an investment, you can learn a lot about your attitudes toward money by examining your spending habits. This is an important step in linking goal setting and goal getting with the day-to-day skills of cash management. Dealing with such mundane matters won't make as exciting cocktail conversation as talking investments. However, your approach to allocating, spending, and controlling your financial resources is integral to your eventual investment (goal getting) plans.

There are two levels of concern: 1) your family's spending system, and 2) how individual spenders act within that system. When we refer to a *household's spending system*, we mean the different ways that families make spending decisions. There are three common approaches: competitive, collaborative, and compromising.

If you usually agree on the how, why, and what of household spending, your household tends toward the collaborative spending method. If you usually disagree, your household tends to compete for its resources. If you solve your spending conflicts by a cooperative method that falls short of full consensus, your household tends to compromise about your spending.

To find out your household's spending system, complete the following questionnaire, "Taking Stock of Your Household Spending Type." Have your spouse or partner complete the second form. Then score your questionnaire by following the directions on the form, "Evaluating Your Household Spending Type."

Understanding the Role of Spending Motivations in Your Household

People spend money for many reasons besides the simple economics of the transaction. For example, the decision to buy a home usually is motivated by much more than a desire to build wealth in real estate. One partner may feel that home ownership affords greater credibility among his/her peers. Or

Taking Stock

Taking Stock of Your Household Spending Type

This questionnaire has been designed to let you and your spouse or partner measure your household spending type. Two copies of the questionnaire have been provided to allow you both to answer the questions independently. After reading each question, fill in the figure on the right that best reflects your agreement with the statement. If you think the statement is *very true* for you and your partner, fill in the largest figure. If the statement seems only *somewhat true* for you as a couple, fill in the middle figure. If it is *not true at all*, fill in the smallest figure on the right.

Partner A (Partner B on page 50)	Very True	Somewhat True	Not True at All
1. My partner and I share equally in planning how to spend our money.	○	○	○
2. My partner and I have similar attitudes about saving for the future.	○	○	○
3. My partner and I rarely disagree about how much to spend on our vacations.	○	○	○
4. My partner and I agree about how much we should spend on gifts for each other and other members of our family.	○	○	○
5. In choosing between the least expensive and most expensive versions of a product, my partner and I almost always have similar values.	○	○	○
6. My partner and I have similar ideas about spending money to impress our friends.	○	○	○
7. My partner and I rarely disagree about money.	○	○	○
8. In our family, our motto is "share and share alike."	○	○	○
9. A frequent cause of arguments in our family is spending too much money to impress our friends.	☐	☐	☐
10. My partner and I sometimes spend money in reaction to something the other has done, almost as if we were in a contest.	☐	☐	☐
11. My partner and I frequently disagree about how much money to spend on having a good time.	☐	☐	☐
12. When we make major purchases, my partner and I sometimes disagree about whether to buy the highest quality product available or the least expensive one.	☐	☐	☐

Your Household Spending Type (*concluded*)

	Very True	Somewhat True	Not True at All
13. In our family, one partner likes to save and the other likes to spend.	☐	☐	☐
14. We sometimes argue about the amount of money we spend on gifts and activities for friends and family members.	☐	☐	☐
15. My partner and I frequently argue about money matters.	☐	☐	☐
16. In our family, one partner usually controls the purse strings.	☐	☐	☐

| Taking Stock |

Taking Stock of Your Household Spending Type

This questionnaire has been designed to let you and your spouse or partner measure your household spending type. Two copies of the questionnaire have been provided to allow you both to answer the questions independently. After reading each question, fill in the figure on the right that best reflects your agreement with the statement. If you think the statement is *very true* for you and your partner, fill in the largest figure. If the statement seems only *somewhat true* for you as a couple, fill in the middle figure. If it is *not true at all*, fill in the smallest figure on the right.

Partner B	Very True	Somewhat True	Not True at All
1. My partner and I share equally in planning how to spend our money.	○	○	○
2. My partner and I have similar attitudes about saving for the future.	○	○	○
3. My partner and I rarely disagree about how much to spend on our vacations.	○	○	○

	Very True	Somewhat True	Not True at All
4. My partner and I agree about how much we should spend on gifts for each other and other members of our family.	○	○	○
5. In choosing between the least expensive and most expensive versions of a product, my partner and I almost always have similar values.	○	○	○
6. My partner and I have similar ideas about spending money to impress our friends.	○	○	○
7. My partner and I rarely disagree about money.	○	○	○
8. In our family, our motto is "share and share alike."	○	○	○
9. A frequent cause of arguments in our family is spending too much money to impress our friends.	☐	☐	☐
10. My partner and I sometimes spend money in reaction to something the other has done, almost as if we were in a contest.	☐	☐	☐
11. My partner and I frequently disagree about how much money to spend on having a good time.	☐	☐	☐
12. When we make major purchases, my partner and I sometimes disagree about whether to buy the highest quality product available or the least expensive one.	☐	☐	☐
13. In our family, one partner likes to save and the other likes to spend.	☐	☐	☐
14. We sometimes argue about the amount of money we spend on gifts and activities for friends and family members.	☐	☐	☐
15. My partner and I frequently argue about money matters.	☐	☐	☐
16. In our family, one partner usually controls the purse strings.	☐	☐	☐

becoming a homeowner may be primarily an attempt to curry favor with a relative, in-law, or important business associate. Too often, a spending decision, such as buying a home, is made merely because it is perceived as the "right thing to do." After all, we learn from an early age that home ownership is part and parcel of the "American dream."

The motivations behind spending decisions vary widely. The most common motivations include:

| **Taking Stock** |

Evaluating Your
Household Spending Type

Like groups of any kind, families tend to develop personalities of their own, separate from, but dependent on, the motivations of their members.

The Taking Stock questionnaire on page 49 and 50 of this chapter measure your household's spending behavior in a number of typical financial situations. Since these behaviors are the product of individual motivations, you were asked to answer the questions "on behalf" of your spouse or partner as well as yourself. If you usually agree on the how, why, and what of household spending, your household tends toward the Collaborative spending model. If you usually *disagree*, your household tends to compete for its resources. If you solve your

FIGURE T4–1
The Range of Household Spending Types

Competitive Compromising Collaborative
household   household   household
└──────────────┴──────────────┘

spending conflicts by some sort of cooperation that falls short of a full consensus, you tend to compromise about your spending. Figure T4–1 shows these three basic household spending types on a scale ranging from highly competitive to highly cooperative. Here's how to score your questionnaire and determine your household spending type.

Computing Each Partner's
Household Spending Perceptions

Count the number of large circles you filled in on the questionnaire. Enter this number on the first line of the first column below for calculating Partner A's collaboration score. Next, count the number of medium-sized circles you filled in and enter the total below the previous number. Do not count any small circles you may have selected. Now multiply the numbers by the factors shown and add the products. This grand total is Partner A's collaboration score.

Repeat the above procedure for Partner B's questionnaire.

Partner A's collaboration score

_____ x 3 = _____
_____ x 1 = _____
Grand total = _____

Partner B's collaboration score:

_____ x 3 = _____
_____ x 1 = _____
Grand total = _____

Now count the number of large squares you filled in and put that total below on the first line of the first column for calculating Partner A's competition score. Next, count the number of medium-sized squares you filled in and place

Partner A's competition score

_____ x 3 = _____
_____ x 1 = _____
Grand total = _____

that total below the previous number. Now multiply those totals by the factors shown and add the products. This grand total is Partner A's competition score.

Repeat the above procedure for Partner B.

Partner B's competition score:

_____ x 3 = _____
_____ x 1 = _____
Grand total = _____

Now inspect the grand totals you computed for each category. If your total was 8 or higher in the competition score,

you perceive your household to be the Competitive spending type. If your grand total was higher than 8 for your collaboration score but lower than 8 for competition, then you believe your household spending type to be Collaborative. If your competition and collaboration grand totals are within 10 points of each other *or* if neither grand total is greater than 8, then your household spending type is usually Compromising.

Now perform a similar analysis for the totals of your spouse or partner. Are his or her conclusions the same or different from your own?

If your perceptions are the same, go back to the text and learn how individual spending motivations have led you to the household spending patterns you've observed. If your perceptions are different, the discussion in the text will show you why those perceptions may have diverged, and give you the insights you need to recognize the hidden realities of your household spending habits.

Notes

_____
_____
_____
_____
_____
_____
_____
_____
_____
_____

---

1. *Spending for pleasure.* People derive pleasure from different things. To a book collector, buying a rare volume in excellent condition yields returns far beyond simple investment potential. A wine connoisseur is inspired by ownership of fine wines. Some people like to stage great parties.

Couples with similar high-pleasure spending needs may enjoy life in the fast lane. However, financial problems can develop if the high-priced pleasure seeking continues unabated. On the other hand, couples with different pleasure spending needs (for example, a book collector and a party giver) may wind up competing for the financial resources to obtain them.

2. *Spending to acquire power and control.* Money usually means power, even for people who don't intend to use it that way. When power over others is consciously sought by two control-motivated people, the emotional toll can be high. Often the quest for power by like-minded individuals winds up being used against each other. However, when one spouse has a high need for control and the other's need is low, a very compatible partnership may develop. In this case, the differing needs complement each other.

3. *Spending to enhance prestige.* The expression "clothes make the man" typifies the prestige-motivated spender. Prestige-motivated spenders are driven more by what others think of their possessions, than by the personal pleasure derived from them. For example, they may be perfectly content for their own use with their American-made car, but feel the need to impress others with an expensive foreign automobile.

Couples who share common status symbols will share in the joys of prestige spending as well. However, like the pleasure-motivated spenders, if the symbols are different, competition for resources may result. That is a frequent source of conflict.

4. *Spending to show affection.* A common motivation is to spend money on a loved one to show affection. This spending motive can have many causes—an inability to express one's emotions in words or through other means, a desire to show one's affection in tangible ways, or a belief that such largess is required to ensure that affection will be returned.

Although spending money on loved ones can be very rewarding, it can also become a substitute for other forms of personal communication. Carried to the extreme (that is, spending so much that it affects money for necessities), this motivation can endanger rather than strengthen the very relationship it tries to nurture.

5. *Buying security with money.* Once one satisfies the basic necessities that money is used for—food, shelter, clothing, health and safety needs—other goals, such as a store of emergency cash or a retirement plan, loom large. The need for security tends to increase as we get older.

If both partners are mature, they may be more willing to forego other types of consumption spending to achieve their common goals. Sometimes, though, the security motivation becomes obsessive. This can lead to Scroogelike hoarding of assets or to buying more insurance than is needed. Perhaps the best combination of motivations occurs when the partner with the lower security need balances the higher security needs of the other.

6. *Spending to retaliate.* Spending to assuage anger is a common occurrence. The "I'll show him (or her)!" attitude toward spending money can be every bit as strong as spending to show affection. Retaliation, by definition, takes place only when some injury (real or imagined) has been done. The source of this spending motive is more emotional than economic. Money becomes a substitute battlefield for acting out feelings.

Typically this motivation will be clouded by focusing on the spending itself, rather than what motivated it. For example, the spouse who intentionally flouts the budget to buy new clothes rationalizes the expenditure: "My old coat is too worn." or "The sale was simply too good to pass up." Meanwhile the real problem—hurt feelings, frustration, or depression—is glossed over. This is an excellent illustration of the importance of working on effective communication with your partner.

7. *Spending for value.* Value, in this case, is the ratio of benefits received to the resources spent to obtain them. *Value* is the reason people comparison shop among stores and products. The degree to which these people shop before spending is a measure of their value motivation. You probably know people on both ends of the spectrum. There are the impulsive buyers who generally buy without investigating prices or features at all. At the other end is the shopper who never makes a purchase without checking the latest opinion in *Consumer Reports*, the current prices charged by at least three different shops, and the relative warranties on each item.

Though the latter approach seems to be just economic common sense, problems will certainly occur if a couple does not share the same notion of "utility." In other words, what is important to one partner (for example, price or independent recommendation) may not impress the other who thinks color or convenience (for example, neighborhood store a friend owns) is the most significant factor in the buying decision.

Even though partners may both be "value-driven," the fact that values are subjective means there is no single sure answer. As a result, disputes among value-driven spenders can be some of the most acrimonious!

UNDERSTANDING YOUR HOUSEHOLD SPENDING TYPE

A family's spending habits, viewed collectively, take on their own personality. The unique motivations of individual family members often result in spending behavior quite independent of any one member. Spending money is all about people—not cash, products, or financial services.

But keep in mind that spending motivations vary from person to person. They also vary with time. It is impractical to depend on simply recognizing your own spending motivations as a path for improving your financial health.

A better approach is to determine how the mix of motivations in your particular family has led to specific, observable, collective financial decisions. This behavior, your household spending type, is what you learned from completing the questionnaire "Taking Stock of Your Household Spending Type" and reviewing your responses with the form "Evaluating Your Household Spending Type."

Assessing Your Personal Spending Style

Now that you have seen how various spending motivations combine to create a separate and distinct household spending type, it is important to identify your own and your partner's *personal spending style*. The manner in which your household allocates, spends, and accounts for its resources on a day-to-day basis is dictated by the characteristics of its individual members.

The Taking Stock questionnaire, "Measuring Your Personal Spending Style," which follows will help you determine the spending styles of your spouse, partner, and other household spenders. (We've provided two copies. If there are more spenders, make copies so each can fill one out without being influenced by someone else's responses.) By comparing the needs and abilities of each household member, you will be able to create a financial management system that is emotionally satisfying as well as financially effective.

After you have completed the questionnaire, be sure to follow through with the interpretation of your answers on the worksheet, "Evaluating Your Personal Spending Style." Individual spending habits are determined largely by confident or anxious feelings about money and by impetuous or careful spending behavior. We've observed four distinct personal spending styles: Assertive, Protective, Active, and Impulsive.

| Taking Stock |

Measuring Your Personal Spending Style

In our experience, certain personal traits greatly influence why, how, and on what people spend their money. If your Personal Profit Plan is to suit not only your household's spending type but also the needs of its individual members, you must learn more about your personal spending attitudes and behaviors.

For each of the following statements, indicate your agreement or disagreement by circling the letter (A) or (D). Two copies of the questionnaire have been provided, but you should make as many copies available as there are spenders in your household. Each questionnaire consists of two parts, and you and your partner(s) should complete both of them before going to the scoring and evaluation discussion that follows.

Part I

1.	I rarely balance my checkbook.	A	D
2.	I enjoy spending money.	A	D
3.	I like buying presents for my friends and loved ones.	A	D
4.	I get a kick out of impressing my friends with a special new purchase.	A	D
5.	I believe that "life is short, so enjoy it while you can!"	A	D
6.	I often buy—or think about buying—something foolish.	A	D
7.	I seldom pass up a chance to have a good time, even if it costs a lot.	A	D
8.	I believe in saving for the future.	A	D
9.	I keep track of what I spend.	A	D
10.	My motto is "Be prepared!"	A	D
11.	I believe that buying the best quality product is the most economical choice in the long run.	A	D
12.	I seldom spend money foolishly.	A	D
13.	Compared to others my age and with my financial physique, I have a well thought-out investment program.	A	D
14.	I prefer to save for tomorrow rather than spend money today.	A	D

Measuring Your Personal Spending Style (*concluded*)

Part II
1. I have not had serious financial problems for a long time.   **A   D**
2. I rarely worry about money matters.   **A   D**
3. Compared to other people with my financial physique and at my stage of life, I am well informed on money matters.   **A   D**
4. I don't buy things simply because they're on sale.   **A   D**
5. When it comes to spending money, I'm nobody's fool.   **A   D**
6. I sometimes feel as though other people take advantage of me in financial dealings.   **A   D**
7. When it comes to important money matters, I sometimes feel as if I'm "in over my head."   **A   D**
8. My money never seems to go as far as it should.   **A   D**
9. I just can't resist a sale.   **A   D**
10. I worry a lot about money matters.   **A   D**

---| **Taking Stock** |---

Measuring Your Personal Spending Style

In our experience, certain personal traits greatly influence why, how, and on what people spend their money. If your Personal Profit Plan is to suit not only your household's spending type but also the needs of its individual members, you must learn more about your personal spending attitudes and behaviors.

For each of the following statements, indicate your agreement or disagreement by circling the letter (A) or (D). Two copies of the questionnaire have been provided, but you should make as many copies available as there are spenders in your household. Each questionnaire consists of two parts, and you and your partner(s) should complete both of them before going to the scoring and evaluation discussion that follows.

Part I
1. I rarely balance my checkbook.   **A   D**
2. I enjoy spending money.   **A   D**
3. I like buying presents for my friends and loved ones.   **A   D**
4. I get a kick out of impressing my friends with a special new purchase.   **A   D**
5. I believe that "life is short, so enjoy it while you can!"   **A   D**
6. I often buy—or think about buying—something foolish.   **A   D**
7. I seldom pass up a chance to have a good time, even if it costs a lot.   **A   D**
8. I believe in saving for the future.   **A   D**
9. I keep track of what I spend.   **A   D**

10. My motto is "Be prepared!"   **A   D**
11. I believe that buying the best quality product is the most economical
choice in the long run.   **A   D**
12. I seldom spend money foolishly.   **A   D**
13. Compared to others my age and with my financial physique, I have a
well thought-out investment program.   **A   D**
14. I prefer to save for tomorrow rather than spend money today.   **A   D**

Part II

1. I have not had serious financial problems for a long time.   **A   D**
2. I rarely worry about money matters.   **A   D**
3. Compared to other people with my financial physique and at my stage
of life, I am well informed on money matters.   **A   D**
4. I don't buy things simply because they're on sale.   **A   D**
5. When it comes to spending money, I'm nobody's fool.   **A   D**
6. I sometimes feel as though other people take advantage of me in
financial dealings.   **A   D**
7. When it comes to important money matters, I sometimes feel as if I'm
"in over my head."   **A   D**
8. My money never seems to go as far as it should.   **A   D**
9. I just can't resist a sale.   **A   D**
10. I worry a lot about money matters.   **A   D**

Taking Stock

Evaluating Your Personal Spending Style

The questionnaire on page 57 of this chapter measures the two most important dimensions of your spending personality:

1. Your tendency toward impetuous (versus careful) spending habits.

2. Your level of anxiety (versus confidence) about the spending process.

Part I of the questionnaire measured your position on a scale ranging from highly impetuous spending to highly careful (or methodical) behavior. Count the number of (A) responses you circled for items 1 through 7 and record your total in the space provided in Figure T4-2. This is your impetuousness score.

Next, count the number of (A) responses you circled for items 8 through 14. This is your carefulness score, and you should enter it in the space provided on the figure.

Now subtract your carefulness score from your impetuousness score and enter the difference in the space provided. If your carefulness score was greater, your answer will be a negative number. If your impetuousness score was greater, your answer will be positive. We'll use this

Evaluating Your Personal Spending Style (*continued*)

number in a moment to plot your composite spending type.

Part II of the questionnaire measured your position on a scale of very anxious to very confident spending behavior. Count the number of (A) responses you circled for items 1 through 5 of Part II and write the total in the space provided in the figure. This is your confidence score.

Next, count the number of (A) responses you circled for items 6 through 10 of Part II and write the total in the space provided. This is your anxiety score.

Now subtract your anxiety score from your confidence score and enter the difference in the space provided. If your confidence score was greater, your answer will be a positive number. If your anxiety score was greater, your answer will be negative.

Repeat this procedure for your spouse or partner, entering the results in the spaces marked "Partner B."

Finding Your Personal Spending Style

Now go to the figure below your scores and plot the *totals* for each dimension you measured. If your total impetuousness/carefulness score was a positive number, your score will fall somewhere along one of the vertical lines on the right half of the chart. Similarly, if your confidence/anxiety score was a positive number, it will fall along one of the horizontal lines in the top half of the chart. Thus a partner with positive numbers for *both* of these totals would find the point of intersection somewhere in the upper right quadrant of the chart. A partner with two negative totals would find the composite

score in the lower left quadrant. Someone with a negative carefulness score and positive confidence score would be in the upper left; and someone with a positive impetuousness score and negative anxiety score would be in the lower right. If your total score was zero for either (or both) dimensions, plot your score along the "0" reference lines that separate the quadrants.

When you've located the intersection of the lines representing both totals, make a heavy dot and label it with your name. Repeat this step for your spouse or partner and other household spenders who have completed the questionnaire.

Interpreting Your Personal Spending Style

As you can see from the chart, your personal spending style depends on your position on both the confident/anxious and careful/impetuous scales. The higher your total score on either dimension, the more committed you are to those attitudes and behaviors. Here's the way to interpret your position.

The Assertive Money Manager

If your composite score fell in the upper left quadrant, you show what we call the *Assertive* personal spending style. Your spending attitudes tend to be confident and your spending habits orderly and directed toward the future. Although your methods are usually logical and well thought out, you tend to judge others by your own self-critical standards and may come across as something of a taskmaster in day-to-day money management. In businesses, these traits are sometimes associated with financial managers

FIGURE T4–2
Your Personal Spending Style

	Partner A	Partner B
Impetuousness score	_____	_____
Carefulness score –	_____	– _____
Total (+ or –)	_____	_____
Confidence score	_____	_____
Anxiety score –	_____	– _____
Total (+ or –)	_____	_____

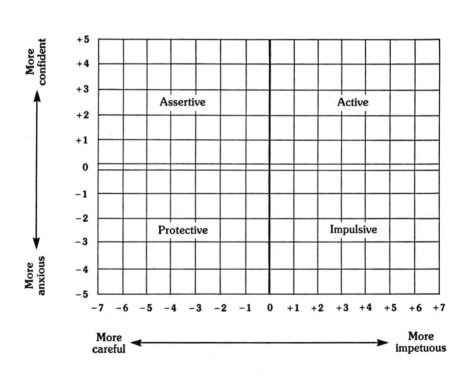

Evaluating Your Personal Spending Style (*concluded*)

and accountants, scientists and engineers, production supervisors, and other responsible executives—although we've found Assertive spenders in almost every walk of life.

The Active Spending Style

If your composite score fell in the upper right quadrant, you manifest the *Active* personal spending style. You tend to have the same confident money attitudes as the Assertive spending type but show more flexibility and spontaneity in actual spending behavior. Because of this, you may experience bigger financial payoffs but often at the price of bigger risks. Active spenders are frequently seen as colorful, generous people who spend a good deal of their time bailing themselves out of the sticky situations their enthusiastic spending created. Outside the home, entrepreneurs are often tagged as exemplary Active spenders, since they seem to thrive as much on the risks as on the rewards of each new business venture.

Those Careful, Protective Spenders

If your composite score fell in the lower left quadrant of the chart, you show the *Protective* personal spending style. Unlike the Assertive spender, your methodical ways have not been accompanied by a growth of self-confidence and your tenacious money-management skills are sometimes undone by misdirected or circuitous spending. Although your friends and family tend to admire your energy and capabilities, you fault yourself (sometimes too much!) for the lengths you take

to hedge your financial and emotional risks. In the workplace, we sometimes associate this strong sense of fiscal responsibility with institutional administrators, the leaders of social or community organizations, and a wide variety of skilled or professional employees who have simply learned about money "the hard way."

Spending Your Money Impulsively

If your composite score fell in the lower right quadrant of the chart, you tend toward the *Impulsive* personal spending style. Your spontaneous, sometimes mercurial spending habits are often directed at pleasing others but the results sometimes leave you hurt, insecure, or dissatisfied. Of all the personal spending styles, you are the most sensitive to the needs and feelings of others—often at the expense of your own financial well-being. While you are receptive to new ideas and better ways of doing things, you have trouble sticking with them and are first among the critics of your own unfocused money habits. An extreme example of the Impulsive spender was Lucille Ball's zany housewife in "I Love Lucy"—a woman whose ill-considered spending often got her into situations that, at least in TV land, always had a happy (if not completely logical) ending. Outside the home, Impulsive spending is sometimes associated with theatrical personalities, high-scoring salespeople (with the urge to splurge big bonuses), lottery winners, philanthropists, and a variety of big-hearted but sometimes regretful spenders.

Assertive spenders tend to be confident, self-disciplined, and accepting of delayed rewards. These traits, though, often lead to autocratic money management. Other Assertive spenders may become absorbed with the technical details of financial decision making. Their spending habits are orderly and directed to the future. They tend to be judgmental, holding others to their own standards.

Active spenders have the same confidence as the Assertive type, but are more flexible and spontaneous in their actual spending behavior. They usually overlook the financial details, concentrating on making the bottom line turn out well. Active spenders tend to be risk takers. They may spend almost as much time bailing themselves out of trouble as they do planning for the future.

Protective (anxious and careful) spenders tend to lack self-confidence, even though they are disciplined and methodical. They go to great lengths to hedge their financial and emotional risks. Overcautious, overprotective spenders sometimes see their efforts turn out poorly as they go in circles trying to divine a better approach but unwilling to risk it!

Impulsive spenders tend to be confounded by spending and investment choices. Often their spending habits are directed at pleasing others at the expense of their own financial well-being. Energetic, curious, and anxious to please, they are frequently taken advantage of in the financial product marketplace. Impulsive spenders are too willing to try the latest "in" thing without taking the time or making the effort to educate themselves.

The Household Dynamics of Money Management

At this point you should have a clear idea of how the personal spending styles in your family meld into a household spending type. Perhaps there have been conflicts over financial matters that weren't resolved to everyone's satisfaction. A lingering resentment in your partner or other household member can complicate future financial affairs. While there are no guarantees for resolving every potential financial dispute, your knowledge of the personal spending types within your household can help alleviate problems.

Below we have detailed suggestions for dealing with different personal spending styles within each household type. Using these suggestions in conjunction with the general communication hints in the next section of this chapter will ameliorate household financial deliberations.

The Competitive Household
Competitive households are created when the principal partners differ in their spending motivations or disagree about which things will satisfy similar wants and needs. The competitive atmosphere develops when each at-

tempts to monopolize the resources that will satisfy those needs. This behavior typically takes the form of spending contests, preemptive spending, and other kinds of noncooperation. Your goals will be to channel that competitive spirit into productive avenues rather than devolving into a destructive "me first" environment.

Competing with Assertive Spenders.   Assertive spenders tend to be very orderly and detail oriented. They usually make good money managers. They prefer well-documented spending figures as the foundation for decision making.

But they have their problems too. Often Assertive spenders lose sight of the reason for making such detailed plans and records. The elaborate record keeping may itself become a bone of contention if things don't work out as well as planned. Assertive spenders do best in households where their detail orientation is complemented by a different spending personality who injects vitality and perspective. Otherwise, what is supposed to be a fruitful, exciting venture in goal-getting can become a boring, rote financial scheme that engenders little enthusiasm.

When it comes to competing for resources, Assertive spenders will fall back on their ability to reason and use logic. Because their actions are typically taken only after careful consideration of the issues, they don't question their own opinions or systems. They assume fault must lie elsewhere and tend to reject out of hand suggestions that their own program may be at fault.

The best way to get Assertive spenders to listen to another perspective is to speak their language. Listen to their presentations and ask meaningful questions that they should have considered. If they've gone astray in their reasoning or are trying to mask arbitrary decisions with a show of dispassionate logic, this process will allow them to see it themselves. Remember, Assertive spenders are characterized by strong self-confidence. Try working with them to trigger a bit of self-analysis. Confrontation will only result in a fall back on records, the written plan, the logical thing to do.

Assertive spenders will work best with *negotiated* rather than *delegated* spending decisions. Delegating decisions to Assertive spenders gives them an opportunity to complain later that the decisions were not the ones they would have chosen. Negotiation, on the other hand, gives Assertive types the degree of control they need to maintain a commitment to their decisions.

Competing with Active Spenders.   Active spenders are also marked by strong confidence. Less record oriented than Assertive spenders, they tend to be a bit more impetuous. They believe that money is earned in order to be spent and sometimes lose sight of the fact that spending can occur many years in the future, not just now! Not detail oriented, they thrive on implementing a Personal Profit Plan rather than formulating its details.

Active spenders don't hesitate to make their preferences known. They are puzzled when others fail to share their faith in their intuitive decisions. Active spenders are most likely to say "It's only money." That attitude is the key to getting this impetuous spender under control.

When their free-wheeling spending gets them into trouble, they will belatedly realize that their financial affairs deserve more care and attention. A good way to work with an Active spender is to divide the *whats* and the *hows* of household spending. The term *hows* merely refers to the methods and allocations of doing the spending. Active spenders certainly know what they want; they get in trouble by not being organized in what they have and how to get what they want!

Competing with Protective Spenders. Protective spenders have the same aptitude for logical money management as Assertive spenders. However, they lack the confidence. They tend to worry about every little detail. "Will things work out as planned?" "Maybe I should have done it differently?" They tend to be very anxious over their financial affairs.

This anxiety often results in Protective spenders doubting whatever system they have adopted for organizing their financial affairs. Even if the Protective spenders' decisions are good ones, any challenge to them may trigger a helter-skelter search for new and better systems, investments, or alternate products. Their response to criticism is the exact opposite of the Assertive spender. They tend to accept financial criticism as always valid rather than tending to reject it outright.

Protective spenders have good money management skills: a propensity for detailed record keeping and a logical approach to planning. Bringing their records into a negotiated approach gives them the valuable role of exerting some practical influence over their more impetuous partners. Protective spenders need feedback and numbers-supported arguments to ease their anxiety.

Competing with Impulsive Spenders. Impulsive spenders are not usually systematic in their thinking. But that doesn't stop them from taking on the most Assertive spender's methods. Though they lack confidence in their own decisions, they will argue about the "calculated risks" of their Active partners. The secret of the Impulsive spenders' strength is their need to react to others and their ability to seek out and welcome beneficial changes.

Impulsive spenders invite a good deal of conflict simply by their own unfocused actions. What is really a trial-and-error search for good solutions to financial problems (from buying a car to investing for retirement) comes across to more confident or careful spenders as mere indecision or thoughtlessness. By trying to please everyone, they often please no one.

Their tendency to follow the trend into popular or heavily advertised investments comes from their need to reduce anxiety. Unfortunately, that tendency often means buying just when those investments have peaked or when the risk/reward ratios are deteriorating. In a competitive household, these efforts can result in more problems when the Impulsive spender is criticized by more analytical and confident spenders.

But Impulsive spenders' enthusiasm and willingness to seek out beneficial alternatives are valuable strengths for many households. In a competitive household, delegation of spending decisions may be the ideal solution for working with the Impulsive spender. The Impulsive spender will welcome an excuse to relinquish specific spending authority to bypass the heightened anxiety that comes from criticism.

The Compromising Household

There is something about compromise decisions (giving up something to gain something else) that tends to make family life a bit more legalistic and adversarial than it has to be. Compromise decisions also tend to unravel the longer they stay in effect. By definition, compromise implies *concession*, focusing as much on what you lose as what you gain. Spending compromises can get you by in a pinch, but your financial physique may suffer if they become a steady diet.

Typically, there is much more to compromise spending than meets the eye. Compromising households develop a language of their own for making decisions. The meaning is clear, at least in subliminal terms, to its users. While the language may be clear enough to allow for day-to-day spending decisions, it is vague enough to allow for willful misinterpretations and arguments when the compromisers decide they have had enough.

Household compromisers are adept at "getting by." They tend to avoid many of the knock-down, drag-out money battles of competitive households. They have learned to muddle through—neither reconciling their spending differences nor being overcome by them.

There are two ways to look at compromising decisions. The usual approach is the "win-some-lose-some" attitude. In order to win you have to lose. But often, this only aggravates the situation. Try to orient your compromises to a more "win-win" attitude. Use those something-for-something decisions on mutually beneficial outcomes rather than making them "win-lose" exchanges. As we stated above, in a win-lose environment, you will focus as much on the loss as on what you gained. No one likes to dwell on losses for any length of time.

Compromising with Assertive Spenders.   Assertive spenders are confident and careful. They are usually good planners and understand intuitively the necessity for balancing current spending with saving for future goals. This good sense is sometimes counterbalanced by a kind of closed-mindedness. They tend to reject the solutions of those they consider less rational and more impetuous. They also have a tendency to screen out data simply because they disagree with it. Their focus on form over substance sometimes results in missing out on the delights of spending money in a way their whole family enjoys. For example, they will ponder the details of a money decision for hours, but give short shrift to family members' emotional reasons for wanting something.

Obviously, Assertive spenders can be difficult partners in any compromise. It is important to let Assertive spenders be themselves. Use their talent for organization to the household's advantage: as bookkeeper or financial analyst. Turn your compromises toward these kinds of trade-offs. You will discover that your Assertive partner is less demanding in other areas and more receptive to your ideas.

Compromising with Active Spenders.   Active spenders can be generous to a fault, yet insensitive to other people's needs when things are less than rosy. These traits are barriers to effective compromise and cooperation.

As with other spending types, it is best to try to capitalize on Active spenders' strengths. Avoid challenging them on those things they do best. You need to organize your financial affairs so that Active spenders have the freedom they need to enjoy their spontaneous habits (e.g., "mad money" fund). At the same time though, structure things so that the balance of the family's finances are under control.

Compromising with Protective Spenders.   Protective spenders are sometimes the most successful money managers. They mix a healthy circumspection with a willingness to devote time and energy to developing and implementing a financial plan. Problems will arise, however, when their protective instinct takes the form of excessive worry. This fretting inhibits taking positive, problem-solving action.

On the plus side, Protective spenders have very good records as financial compromisers. They are pragmatic enough to see the value of win-win, cooperative rather than win-lose, competitive solutions. The problem is overcoming their insecurities long enough to give those new methods a chance.

We have found *structure* to be the Protective spender's best financial and emotional ally. Take advantage of their reliability and conscientiousness by delegating specific planning and spending tasks to them. This works better than constant negotiations over every spending decision. Negotiation over many items can arouse their insecurities. It is far better to identify the areas of family finances that Protective spenders can cope with on their own. Then stand back and let them do their thing rather than dredging up insecurities by dissecting every new decision.

Compromising with Impulsive Spenders. Impulsive spenders tend to be unfocused with money, unsure of where and how to proceed in the face of conflicting information. But while they may be anxious about their decisions and impetuous in their behavior, they are equally energetic when it comes to implementing a decision once it is made.

This is their principal strength in the compromising household. They are doers rather than talkers. When it comes to money they are deep feelers rather than deep thinkers. To develop a workable cooperative relationship, you must recognize the Impulsive's *realities.*

To the Impulsive spender, planning is something to do while waiting for the next good opportunity to come along. These spenders need to have a predictable source of funds for important spending. Organize your finances to accommodate this spending style. Just be sure that these funds have well-established limits.

Most Impulsive spenders have experienced sharp criticism of their financial decisions. Avoid this sensitive area by negotiating each major decision as it develops. Don't leave too much to their discretion. Once a decision has been made, the spender has a vested interest in defending it. Try to work things out agreeably in advance.

It is important to frequently reassure Impulsive spenders that their compromises are appreciated. Let the Impulsive know that family members are really being honest about the money situation.

The Collaborative Household

There are many different types of collaboration. Here, we are referring to true collaboration as distinct from other forms of cooperation, such as compromise. The distinction is important because cooperation in its other forms may actually promote unhealthy spending behavior. For example, compromising implies a loss in order to achieve a win. And that loss can be a long-term point of resentment.

Collaborative households are really *consensus-seeking* households. That consensus may be sought between two partners or a half-dozen people in an extended family. To better understand what we mean by true collaboration, it is helpful to take a look at forms of noncollaborative cooperation.

1. *Cooperating by majority rule.* This approach is what most people first think of when a cooperative method is mentioned. The family sits down together to discuss its spending options. They adopt the plan that wins the most votes. The problem is that for every winner, there is a loser. That is where majority rule differs from true collaboration.

While all family members may comply with the majority decision, that doesn't mean they are committed to it. The minority voters may find a way to undermine it. This effort is not necessarily vindictive. Passive resistance can take many forms—from neglecting duties to general grumpiness. And the resistance is often not even conscious!

2. *Cooperating by false consensus.* A collaborative decision implies that everyone involved understands and agrees on the course of action. The appeal of such consensus is easy to understand. In fact, it is so attractive an ideal that there is a tendency in some cases to pretend a consensus is present, even when it really isn't.

This most often occurs when one partner is more vocal or argumentative and simply outlasts the opposition. Eventually the less assertive participants find it easier to go along with the decision. Unfortunately, this false consensus rarely lasts. People who have not really been convinced will only carry out the decision half-heartedly. They may harbor resentment over being badgered into agreement.

3. *Cooperating by default.* Under this scheme, people cooperate by pretenting there is nothing to debate. Reliance on this form of cooperation will lead to a financial tyranny in which the most insistent spender gets used to having his or her own way. Eventually the skills of true consensus decision making will become completely lost.

In a true collaborative household, the consensus decisions can result in almost frictionless family finances. Resources are allocated to those areas that provide the greatest rewards for the family as a whole. The different spending styles act as checks and balances on each other. Money is understood as a tool to gain a better life, not an end in itself or the reward for winning a contest.

Collaborating with Assertive Spenders. Assertive spenders can play a very important role in orchestrating true consensus decisions. Their attention to detail and record keeping will provide accurate background for making proper spending decisions. Their problem, as in other household types, is the tendency to be rigid, uncommunicative, and intolerant of others' views.

In a collaborative household, focus on using the Assertive spenders' strengths. They are good at researching options. Have them lay the groundwork for most consensus decisions. They can lay out the issues surrounding the problems. Their passion for order makes them ideal as leaders or "parliamentarians" of the family.

Collaborating with Active Spenders. Active spenders are confident spenders who exhibit more impetuousness than structure with their money. These spontaneous types enjoy the dynamics of good collaborative decisions. However, their free-wheeling ways can undo their best commitments when it comes to putting your Personal Profit Plan into action. Your home financial program needs to be structured to allow Active spenders some freedom to pursue their spending pleasures. At the same time though, the rest of the family needs to be assured that other resources will be available when they are needed for other things. In Chapter 6, we detail a few options. One alternative is to set up a specific separate account to take into consideration the Active spenders' needs.

Active spenders need a scheduled opportunity to sit down and apply the rules of consensus decisions. They tend to be more comfortable with one-on-one conversations than with the detailed paperwork of an Assertive spender.

Collaborating with Protective Spenders. Protective or careful/anxious spenders make good collaborators because they appreciate consensus decisions. They will spend a lot of energy searching for and applying new solutions. Unfortunately, they tend to settle for false consensus quickly if it seems to lower tensions. Their tendency to comply without real commitment or acquiesce without acceptance needs to be guarded against.

Protective spenders need structure and security. That will help them take the personal risks necessary to increase the family's mutual trust and openness. Future-oriented and security-minded, Protective spenders will benefit psychologically from a separate money fund (a "Fun Fund"). It will lessen their worries over every little detail.

Collaborating with Impulsive Spenders. None of the personal spending styles is more willing to try consensus decision making than the Impulsive spender. Anxious and impetuous, these spenders will switch among different household money management systems as the mood hits. They tend to be very open-minded. ("What is the latest thing?") They work well in a harmonious group.

Impulsive spenders do have a few problems with the practicalities of consensus decisions. They are more emotional and enthusiastic than reasoned and logical. Their serious potential handicap is the tendency to be oversensitive to the needs of others and the emotions of the family. The ability to empathize with others is normally an aid in the consensus-finding process. Sometimes though, Impulsive spenders go even further and anticipate the other person's reactions. That makes their own actions suspect since they may be based on erroneous assumption.

Impulsive spenders, not surprisingly, are mercurial. Their feelings can change rapidly and often depending on how they perceive the feedback they are getting from their family. This leads to inconsistent, hard-to-predict spending habits. The frequent changes point up a lack of persistence when carrying out their end of the financial plans.

Impulsive spenders also tend toward inconsistent communications. One day they may offer a logical, analytical approach and the very next day react on gut-level intuition. The following section on improving communication pinpoints some of the barriers you may encounter when dealing with Impulsive spenders. They can be a great asset to your consensus decision making, if you are sure to include them in the communication loop of the family's system.

COMMUNICATING WITH OTHERS: RESOLVING DIFFERENCES

You have already taken a major step toward enhancing family communications. Just as you can't plan for your financial future without knowing where you stand, you can't hope to resolve problems arising from family spending patterns without knowing the spending personalities of each member.

As you learned from the questionnaire, "Evaluating Your Household Spending Type," there are three basic household spending types: competitive, compromising, and collaborative. When you combine them with the variety of personal spending styles falling on the grid from impetuous to careful and from confident to anxious you see that the "simple" spending decisions can indeed be complex. In fact, it is this wide variety that results in many of the conflicts arising in family finances.

Barriers to Family Financial Communication

Many people look at interpersonal communication as something that can be turned on and off, modulated like a radio signal and controlled at the pleasure of the sender. Nothing could be further from the truth—particularly when the subject of that communication is money. We have identified six of the most common barriers to clear and healthy financial communication:

1. *Differing perspectives.* Different people often view the same set of facts in entirely disparate ways. Our different backgrounds, experiences, and expectations influence our perceptions. For example, an accountant, businessperson, or manager will often view banking problems quite differently from a person whose skills run in other areas such as art, sports, or social work. It doesn't mean that either is right or wrong. It simply means that each will bring a different set of problem-solving perspectives to financial questions.

2. *Selective perceptions.* Most of us hear what we want—or expect—to hear even when the message is negative. Some people are so insecure that it takes a thousand compliments to erase one derogatory remark. Others will remember false compliments for years while they miss more constructive criticism. Especially when dealing with a spouse or family member, there is a strong tendency to interpret even neutral comments as supportive of your own perception.

3. *Source believability.* We are all familiar with the story of the little boy who cried wolf. By raising the alarm once too often without cause, he lost his credibility as a transmitter of important information. The same is true in our own communications. Intentionally or not, we tend to assign value not only to the information but to the person who transmits it. As a result, we can modify, skew, accept, or reject almost any message without really understanding it.

In financial matters, a partner who ranks another's credibility as higher than his or her own may avoid confrontation by displacing the blame on a third party. For example, you may have heard about "That stupid bank screwing up again" (that's why the check bounced) or "Joe Blow, our broker, didn't do it right" (that's why we missed that investment opportunity).

4. *Choice of words.* Unfortunately, we cannot directly transmit our understanding of a problem or situation. We can only use words to explain our understanding. Since most words have many nuances and alternative meanings, we must be careful not only which words we use, but how we say them. "I did it right away" may mean within 24 hours to one person; to someone else, it may mean within minutes. When *was* that check mailed, anyway?

Often, more aggressive personalities create defensiveness in others through their choice of words. "What gives?" at the end of a decision may seem combative to the listener when it is really more a reflection of the speaker's personality than a desire to intimidate the other party. Such a comment may inhibit effective communication because the person being spoken to immediately takes a defensive stance, volunteering nothing more than is absolutely necessary.

5. *Specialized terms.* Language is in a constant state of flux. You know how people's verbal expressions often "date" them. Dominant trends such as the technology revolution also affect language. Rather than giving information, we now "input data." We don't go through files, we "access" them.

Numerous such expressions are regularly added to our everyday vo-cabulary. Technical terminology, or jargon, is so pervasive in our lives that we often take it for granted. This influences our communication since one person's jargon is another's gibberish. Too often people resort to the use of technical terms as a substitute for communicating when dealing with a difficult topic. Family decisions must rest on a common understanding of specific financial terms. In talking over family matters, your highest priority must be clarity. Avoid adding to confusion by resorting to impressive sounding but obscure terminology.

6. *Communication speed and quantity.* Another barrier to clear com-munication is the sheer speed and volume with which information bom-bards us. Financial data comes to us from many sources: print media, radio, TV, by mail, and by word-of-mouth from everyone—from neighbors and friends to financial authorities.

When communication pressures become too great, we often react by reducing our own communications. Most of us have forgotten to remind a spouse about something (e.g., depositing a check or picking up the dry cleaning) due to the crunch of business, only to be disappointed when that something wasn't done in time.

Overcoming Communication Barriers

The underlying values leading to clear communication are mutual trust and openness. Even though we prize these values highly, they are not shared by every family. Some people strongly believe in certain traditional roles that inhibit the trust and openness that is necessary to good communication. This is particularly so when it comes to family finances. Our suggestions will not work for these people. These techniques will work however, for those people who believe that:

1. Partners should not be dependent, but *interdependent.* They should be self-directing in their actions. This means that one partner does not dominate the other in spending decisions. Each relies on the other's personal strengths for the benefit of the family.
2. Partners should move toward collaboration, rather than monopoly or competition in the use of their resources.
3. Manipulative behavior is counterproductive over the long run.

It is important that you deal positively with the issues. Of course, it is not always as easy as it sounds. Don't hesitate to bring up new ideas or of-fer new ways of looking at old problems. Seek and give information freely. Be sure to label your opinions as just that—opinions, not necessarily facts. Make concerted efforts to clarify complex issues. Don't fall prey to letting a decision get off-track. Try to bring things back to the central issues. When

How to Make Consensus Spending Decisions

Consensus decisions about spending are *unanimous* decisions, although this is not "unanimity" in the traditional sense, where everyone happens to vote the same way. A consensus decision is one that reflects (and results in) a unanimity of *purpose*, which still allows for conflicting views. In fact, true consensus decisions are even more important when those views are diverse and the issues at hand are complex and emotional. Here are the three basic rules for making effective consensus decisons:

> Consensus Rule No. 1:
> ## No votes allowed!

Although voting is a common procedure for deciding between two alternatives, it's fatal to consensus decisions. To have a winner, you have to have losers; and as we've seen, losers can be very uncooperative, despite their good intentions. But if the decision is truly unanimous (that is, by true mutual consent), everyone comes out on top.

> Consensus Rule No. 2:
> ## Everyone has a veto.

In consensus-finding discussions, you don't cast a vote—you cast an opinion. The discussion must continue, in fact, until either everyone's opinion becomes virtually the same—hence, unanimous—on the issue at hand, or everyone agrees on a common course of action, albeit for different reasons. An important part of this obligation to agree, however, is the freedom to object. If your partner seems (or other spending group members seem) close to a consensus and you alone are still unconvinced, it's your duty to the family to stick by your guns until sufficient reasons have been given to compel (by force of logic or appropriate emotions) your consent. Some people fear that this veto power will become a tool for the intransigent to block the consensus-finding process, but in practice this rarely happens. Simply by *knowing* they could veto any unsatisfactory decision, people tend to be more secure and open-minded, receptive to alternatives rather than defensive.

> Consensus Rule No. 3:
> ## All opinions
> ## must be heard.

Consensus decisions work best when they reflect the total knowledge, judgment, and experience of the partners or the group. Thus the right to disagree by veto brings with it the responsibility to make positive contributions as well. If you truly have no opinions on the matter, seek information from your partner (or others) until you do. Consent is an active, not passive, household spending technique.

In short, consensus spending decisions are possible only in an atmosphere of openness, mutual trust, clear communications, and personal initiative. It may take a little while to un-learn old ways of doing things and accept this new and better style, but when you do, you'll be rewarded with higher-quality decisions and more commitment from the people who must carry them out.

you feel that a consensus is near, "poll" your partner(s) to see if the agreement is genuine. Polling for a consensus is *not* the same as voting. You are merely soliciting opinions, not counting ballots for a course of action.

Enhancing the Consensus-Finding Process

As we've already mentioned, our diverse backgrounds and experience affect our communication skills. Many people are hesitant about expressing their views even when they have much to offer and are asked by their group (or partner) to contribute.

Encourage others to participate without prejudging their contributions. Mediate differences when they occur. Don't make the mistake of retreating from them. Work to set standards for acceptable solutions. Don't be afraid of humor. A well-placed joke can do much to relieve tension and promote communication. Be upfront about problems you and your partner may be having with your financial life. Suggest appropriate solutions.

Recognizing Communication Barriers

It is difficult for most people to recognize the common barriers to communication. Selective perception might be explained away as "discriminating judgment." A prejudiced viewpoint may be seen as a "professional opinion." The best way to lower these and other barriers is to recognize them in yourself and others when they occur. Here are some more rules to keep in mind:

1. *Don't go off on a tangent.* Keep your mind on the issues at hand. Distracting activities can only harm your financial decision making.

2. *Don't attack your partner(s) verbally.* Discussion about your financial affairs can often be frustrating. Resist making the easy cutting remark out of anger. Nothing is more certain to raise the communication barriers than sarcasm or hostile remarks.

3. *Don't strive for quick or extreme decisions.* Don't let time concerns push you into prodding or badgering your partner(s) into hasty, half-baked decisions. Give others room to maneuver, think, and respond. You will find that the quality of decisions will then be high.

4. *Don't dominate your partner(s) to get your way.* Monopolizing the floor, constantly interrupting or criticizing others will not expedite your decision. To arrive at true consensus decisions, all participants have the power to veto any decision. Agreement should be arrived at mutually, not by intimidation.

5. *Don't withdraw from the decision if you can't have your way.* Some people show their displeasure by acting indifferent to the subject being discussed or by withdrawing participation. This accomplishes nothing and works against the solution you may have in mind.

Techniques to Overcome Common Barriers

If you notice any of the above behaviors developing in your own family financial decisions, try one or more of the following suggestions.

1. *Restate a complex or confusing statement.* If your partner makes a proposal or statement that is unclear, simply restate it as you understand it. This will head off an extended decision in which both parties move further apart without realizing it. If your restatement is inaccurate, your partner will be sure to clarify the issue immediately. Don't be afraid to restate the message in your words as often as possible.

2. *Ask your partner to restate for you what you've just said.* If you suspect that your message is not getting through, try asking your partner to restate what you have said. Repeat the procedure until you are certain your message is being received as you intended it.

3. *Ask a third party to verify what is being said.* If there are more than two people in your household spending group, ask one of them to restate the comment that has just been made for everyone's benefit. This verification of message can be invaluable when barriers to communication are high and well established.

4. *Be sensitive to nonverbal forms of communication.* Look for nonverbal cues to the attitudes and meanings of your financial partners. This will take some practice but will be well worth the effort. But keep in mind that just as verbal communication is inexact, reading nonverbal language is more an art than a science. One problem is that people often act differently when they are ill or if under stress. In our culture, however, some behaviors are recognized as fairly typical for communication of certain attitudes and feelings. Here are a few gestures, postures, and signals we've observed and interpreted over the years:

1. *Touching someone else's arm or hand while speaking.* This indicates a strong desire to be believed and accepted. It is a sign of affection. The person may also be saying, "I just don't want to argue anymore!" regardless of the words you are hearing.
2. *Sitting unusually close* (within three or four feet). This is a sign of assertiveness or intrusion. Such behavior suggests a very confident negotiator.
3. *Leaning back in chair, hands behind head, legs crossed ankle to knee.* This posture indicates confidence or acceptance. The person does not feel threatened.
4. *Upright posture; fingers tented.* This indicates an evaluative stance, like a buyer considering some merchandise. The merchandise in this case would be your ideas. (Also suggested by resting chin on fingers or fist.)

5. *Rubbing eyes; knitted forehead.* This is a sign of doubt. This person has yet to be convinced of your case. (Also suggested by collar rubbing and face scratching.)
6. *Leaning forward, hands on legs or table.* This is a position of readiness. The person is prepared to act or react promptly.
7. *Speaking with hands in front of mouth.* This is a sign of distrust. It also signals dishonesty in some cases.
8. *Standing while others sit.* This is a strong sign of detachment. A person who is also speaking may be trying to increase his or her authority or to speed things up. Someone who is moving around may be agitated or impatient.
9. *Rubbing the back of the neck; clasping arm or hands behind back.* This signals frustration. The person is making a conscious effort at self-control.
10. *Folding arms across the chest.* This posture indicates defensiveness. There is a desire to withhold personal trust.

As you can see, there are many nonverbal signals people use to communicate. It is a good idea to add to this list through your own careful observations. By keeping alert to the coded messages of others, you can enhance your ability to communicate consistently and reliably.

Wrapping Up

In Chapters 2 and 3 you took very important first steps in creating your Personal Profit Plan by delineating your wants and needs, prioritizing them, and finally, defining your financial starting point. While most books on financial planning move right to the investment aspects of your plan, we feel it is critical that you fully understand how your spending habits—and those of your family members—influence the ultimate success of your program.

It is impossible to develop financial plans without knowing your starting point. It is equally necessary—if you are not single—to scrutinize your household's decision-making style. At this point it is more important to recognize what you are doing than to worry about changing things. The Taking Stock questionnaires in this chapter pinpointed both your household spending type and your personal spending style.

While the Collaborative household model would seem to operate with less conflict and rancor over the long haul, it simply may not be the way you prefer to do things. Our guidelines make it possible for any type of household to successfully fulfill its Personal Profit Plan.

Communication problems are the source of much misunderstanding. Overcoming those barriers will prove invaluable in helping to resolve disputes with family members or even business associates. Before you can hope to put the final pieces into your Personal Profit Plan, it is necessary to understand the spending motivations of your partner(s) and to be able to communicate among yourselves.

The key is thinking where you are, what you want, and how to get there. This chapter concludes the "where you are" part of the equation. In Chapter 2 you put into writing what you want. In the next chapter you will learn important financial facts that will determine your answers to the final part of the equation: how to get there.

CHAPTER 5

UNDERSTANDING THE
WORLD OF FINANCE

UNDERSTANDING ESSENTIAL FINANCIAL CONCEPTS

In this chapter you will learn about the time value of money. In these volatile economic times, the purchasing power of your money fluctuates almost as much as the stock market! You must make informed investment decisions to fulfill the goal-getting phase of your Personal Profit Plan. Future value calculations will show you how inflation can shrink the purchasing power of today's dollar. At the same time, you will learn the power of compounding for your investments.

You will also be introduced to *present value*. Before you can make informed decisions about achieving financial goals, you have to know what amount you need to start *earning* a specific return so you can actualize those goals. The time value of money: understanding this concept is an important part of putting together a realistic Personal Profit Plan.

Up to this point we have been working with information that only you can know: your wants and needs, your financial circumstances, your household spending type, and your personal spending style(s). Prior to setting out a specific plan for reaching your financial objectives though, you must become familiar with certain more technical financial concepts. This doesn't mean you need to try to become an expert in areas where full-time professionals ply their trade! But it does mean that in order to take advantage of the opportunities afforded by the wide variety of financial vehicles in today's markets, you need to understand key elements in the big picture.

The ideal investment would be the one that offers the highest possible return without any risk. Despite what you may be told by that anonymous voice at the other end of the telephone line, such an investment does not exist. While there are certainly exceptions, a reliable rule of thumb is: higher risk accompanies higher returns.

If an investment sounds too good to be true, it probably is. But you do not have to achieve spectacular 40, 50, or even 100 percent annual returns to significantly increase your financial nest egg. Take a lesson from the turtle and the hare: slow but steady works in the financial arena. The key is understanding the *time value of money.*

The Time Value of Money

In this day and age of instantaneous worldwide communication, we have a tendency to lose sight of the fact that there is a crucial connection between time and money. Indeed, time is a crucial element in any monetary matter. During periods of high inflation, such as the late 1970s, this connection was more readily apparent than in calmer economic environments. Then, people experienced the loss of the purchasing power of their money in short time periods. It was not unusual to see prices of staples, such as bread, go up in price almost every visit to the grocery store.

As you will see in Chapter 7 when you finalize your Personal Profit Plan, knowing how much you will earn or spend is only part of the equation. You must know *when* you plan to earn or spend it. The timeframe is every bit as important as the quantity. It determines what must be done today to ensure that you have what you require in the future.

Time can play a very positive role in your plans. When money is invested at compound rates, it can achieve very impressive returns. Of course, time can also work against you. Perhaps the best example of the negative role of time and money is inflation. Your money loses purchasing power at the rate of inflation. To understand the goal-getting steps we describe in the next two chapters, you will need to become familiar with the important concepts of present and future value of money.

Inflation: Invisible Thief

Inflation is a rise in the general price level of goods and services in the economy. Don't confuse inflation with the rise in price of a particular item. The free flow of supply and demand, people's changing needs and wants, and numerous other factors too complex to quantify can all influence the price of individual items.

When the Hula Hoop was the latest fad, prices were higher simply because people were willing to pay more. Once its popularity faded, prices fell. This phenomenon has been repeated many times with fads such as the Pet Rock or puka shell necklaces. In recent years the prices of personal computers rose and fell due to a variety of noninflationary causes.

Inflation refers to an average price rise for most items. The distinction is very important. The above examples show price fluctuations independent of inflation. During inflation it is possible for most consumer products to be rising in price, while a few items actually fall. For example, even in inflationary times, an overproduction of potatoes may result in falling prices.

This discussion of inflation's influence must be prefaced with the caution "all other things being equal." All other things could include factors such as production volume, new technology, and the availability of raw materials.

To understand how inflation wreaks its damage, suppose an item cost $1.00 in January. Assume that the annual rate of inflation is 10 percent. Assuming that all other things are equal, that same item would cost $1.10 in late December of the same year. Ten percent of $1.00 is $.10. That amount is added to the beginning price to represent the effect of inflation at year's end.

Another way of looking at the effect of inflation is to divide the starting value, $1.00, by the ending inflated value, $1.10. This calculation reveals that our hypothetical dollar ($1.00) has fallen to 91 percent ($1.00 divided by $1.10 = .91) of its original purchasing power. If we calculate the next year's effect if inflation continues at 10 percent, that $.91 dollar would be worth $.83. (.10 × $1.10 = .11. Add that to the $1.10 price at the end of the first year. You get $1.21. Divide that figure into the original $1.00 to get .83). Clearly, at a 10 percent inflation rate, the original $1.00 loses purchasing power quickly.

You can see that the increased profits earned through the inflated prices of goods and services are hollow indeed! If you simply look at the year-end tallies, it would look like the seller of the item which goes up in price 10 percent every year is doing well. The problem is that the numbers look good only in the absence of knowledge about the deleterious effect of inflation. Profits may look as though they are improving, but in reality they are flat since most other prices will also move up by the 10 percent average inflation rate. The seller is no better off.

What typically happens is that these "phantom" inflation profits are not recognized as such at first. Producers who do not adjust their books for inflation think they are suddenly making more money. They may then expand capacity to maximize what they see as increasing profits. When it becomes apparent later in the inflation cycle that the higher numbers are not greater *real* profits, the problems begin.

This is what happened in the 1970s. The first flush of inflation was seen as boosting business. Economists became enamored with the *Phillips Curve*, an economic theory which stated that some inflation would actually lead to greater enployment. Unfortunately, after a few years of false profits, the subsequent damage to employment and the economy as a whole was devastating. Unemployment soared, economic growth fell sharply, the dollar collapsed, and interest rates shot to record high levels as the economy struggled to regain a sound noninflationary foundation.

The sharp recession in the early 1980s was the price the U.S. economy paid for wringing inflation out of the system. The strong noninflationary foundation that resulted from this painful experience was sufficient to support the longest post-World War II peacetime economic expansion.

How can such a thing occur in this modern age of high technology and professional financial management? How can we tolerate such conditions? Space limits us to only brief answers to what are really very complex questions.

Too Much Money Chasing Too Few Goods. If the output of the economy stays the same while everyone gets more money, then each consumer would have more cash to bid up prices for the same amount of goods and services. More money is injected into the financial system by the Federal Reserve Board (the Fed). The Fed is our country's central bank. It controls the amount of money in circulation (both credit and currency) through various technical procedures beyond the scope of this book.

If inflation is such a bad thing, you probably wonder why the Fed would ever allow more money into the economic system than is needed. This is a difficult question to answer. There are many forces influencing the Fed. These include unions that try to get higher wages for their members, Congress which tries to ensure a better standard of living for its constituents, government contractors who want ever more work to keep their labor force employed, and many others.

Different people and organizations have different perspectives as to what is best for the economy. What this means is that there are many conflicting forces, all adamant in the belief that their solutions are the right ones. While low interest rates and generous wages would seem to be the ideal situation, such an "easy money" policy (the Fed increasing the money supply) can quickly switch from benefit to burden when it kindles the fires of inflation.

Inflation affects different groups at different times. Those who are at the head of the line in receiving the "new" money created by the Fed (government contractors, for example) are able to reap the benefits of higher income before that money has percolated through the economy and raised the general level of prices. Groups who must live on fixed incomes (e.g., those who have retired) tend to be the biggest losers in inflationary environments.

Government Spending. Government spending has a *multiplier effect*. This simply means that for every federal dollar spent, it multiplies its effect throughout the economy several times. One dollar may result in many additional dollars being created in national income. This is what is known as *fiscal stimulus*.

This is fine when there is high unemployment and overall prices are falling. However, such policies can be disastrous in more prosperous times when the private sector is generating new jobs and steadily producing more products and services. An overheated economy, "too many dollars chasing too many goods," will result in higher interest rates, higher prices, and strained productive capacity. Eventually the very stimulus that seemed so beneficial in a recession or depression will lead to a sharp reversal of the economic expansion.

Slow, steady economic growth is preferable to volatile swings in the rate of growth. Slow and steady means you can make plans with some degree of reliability. If the economy constantly fluctuates from very slow growth and low employment to rapid growth and employment strains, it is impossible to make reliable plans.

Foreign Shock.   International cartels like OPEC have played a role in spurring domestic inflation through real and threatened price hikes. In the early 1970s OPEC arbitrarily tripled oil prices. As a result, the Fed was confronted with the choice of maintaining the money supply at a static level or increasing money in the financial system to help ease the shock of the price increase.

If the money supply had not been increased, certain prices would have risen more than others. Consumers would have had to make choices between paying for energy and going without other items, or cutting back on energy usage to maintain the balance of their standard of living. Either way, other sectors of the economy would have been severely effected. The steady-money school of thought would trade for recession, or depression in this case, as the method for restructuring the economy. They would avoid inflation at all costs.

What actually happened was that the Fed expanded the money supply aggressively. This enabled the economy to absorb the shock but escape the depression that many analysts expected. At the same time it ignited inflation as there was suddenly much more money to chase essentially the same number of goods and services.

Another factor widely viewed as contributing to inflation is the status of the dollar. In the late 1970s, the very weak dollar accompanied the sharp increase in inflation. It was a "chicken-and-the-egg" question. Some economists argued that the falling dollar exacerbated the inflation problems. Others asserted that the falling dollar was a direct result of the high rate of U.S. inflation.

From 1985 until the end of 1987, the dollar also fell sharply. However, this time inflation was not a major factor. While many explanations were advanced to explain its fall (the huge trade deficit, the huge budget deficit, aggressive foreign policy moves, the replacement of Federal Reserve Board

Chairman Paul Volcker, and numerous other explanations), inflation was not significantly affected.

Many economists argued that a weak dollar will eventually result in rising inflation because it will force foreign-made producers to charge higher prices to cover their costs. It was felt that when pressure from foreign price competition lessened, domestic manufacturers would be able to raise their prices. However, the whole incident just serves to illustrate the complexity of these many interrelationships.

The most commonly used measure of the prevailing rate of inflation is the Labor Department's Consumer Price Index (CPI). This percentage is based on a statistical sampling of a typical consumer's "market basket" of goods and services. These prices are compared to those of a base year. We will use this figure later when we compute the future cost of your goals.

Future Value: The Power of Compounding

The same *principle of compound interest* that works to build the CPI also works to increase the value of your investments. If you invest $1,000 today at 10 percent per year, next year you will earn $100 on your original investment. If the rate of inflation is zero that year, your *real* return in terms of purchasing power is 10 percent.

Leave that $1,100 invested for another year at the same rate with no inflation. You will earn 10 percent on the $1,100. That equals $110. That would increase the value of your principal sum to $1210 (the original $1,000, plus the first year's interest of $100, plus the second year's interest of $110).

Over the two-year period then, you would enjoy a 21 percent return on your original investment. That is more than the 10 percent per year because in the second year you earn interest on the interest you earned the first year.

This compounding is extremely powerful over a period of many years. For example, $1,000 invested once at 10 percent, compounded annually, would be worth $2,600 at the end of ten years. That is more than two and a half times its original value.

Of course, our inflation rate has not been zero for a long time. To figure the real rate of return on any investment, you must subtract the inflation rate from the nominal (quoted) rate of interest. If inflation were 7 percent, the real rate of return would be 3 percent (10% minus 7%).

The concept of the *future value* of a principal sum invested at compound interest is central to most investment decisions. It is equally important to calculate the reverse effect that a compounding rate of inflation has on determining the real rate of return to be earned. We will apply both of these concepts—future value of both investments and inflation—as you define the financial objectives that will help you achieve your goals.

The Concept of Present Value

The flip side of future value (what today's dollar will be worth at a future date), is *present value*. Present value is the value today of a desired future sum (for example, an anticipated bill like college tuition) discounted at an appropriate compound interest rate. In other words, if you have in mind a specific sum you will need in 10 years, the present value would be that sum discounted by the amount it would earn in interest over the next 10 years.

For example, $100 that you will receive 10 years in the future has a present value of $38.60 at a discount rate of 10 percent compounded annually. To get that figure, you use the Present Value Table, Figure 5–1. Find the column headed by 10%. Then look down that column to the 10-year row. The present value factor is 0.386 for $1. Multiply that by $100 to get $38.60.

The present value calculation is used to determine how much money should be invested today—at a given rate—to result in a specific amount at a future date. Present value tables are compounded interest tables in reverse!

Let's take one more example to ensure that you understand this important concept. Say you had a goal to take a world cruise in four years. If you established that the cost of that cruise would be $8,000 in four years, you have all the data (along with the Present Value Table) that you need.

If you are reasonably sure that you can make an investment that will yield 10 percent over the next four years, the Present Value Table will tell you how much you need to invest now in order to have that $8,000 when you need it. Enter the table at 4 Years—10%. The factor is 0.683. This number means that 68 cents invested today at 10 percent would yield $1.00 in four years.

But, you want to know how much you need to invest today in order to have $8,000 in four years. Multiply $8,000 by the present value factor of .683. You need to invest $5,464 today at 10 percent compounded annually to get $8,000 in four years.

While this may seem a bit confusing at first, it will prove worthwhile to try out a few exercises of your own. The heart of the goal-getting process involves establishing the future cost of your goals. You then need to calculate what you need today to reach those goals. Try running a few exercises on your own to be sure you understand how to use the table. This will be very important in the next few chapters when we get to planning your actual goal-getting activities.

FIGURE 5-1
The Present Value Table

Years Hence	1%	2%	4%	6%	8%	10%	12%	14%	15%	16%	18%	20%	22%	24%	25%	26%	28%	30%	35%	40%	45%	50%
												Present Value of $1											
1	0.990	0.980	0.962	0.943	0.926	0.909	0.893	0.877	0.870	0.862	0.847	0.833	0.820	0.806	0.800	0.794	0.781	0.769	0.741	0.714	0.690	0.667
2	0.980	0.961	0.925	0.890	0.857	0.826	0.797	0.769	0.756	0.743	0.718	0.694	0.672	0.650	0.640	0.630	0.610	0.592	0.549	0.510	0.476	0.444
3	0.971	0.942	0.889	0.840	0.794	0.751	0.712	0.675	0.658	0.641	0.609	0.579	0.551	0.524	0.512	0.500	0.477	0.455	0.406	0.364	0.328	0.296
4	0.961	0.924	0.855	0.792	0.735	0.683	0.636	0.592	0.572	0.552	0.516	0.482	0.451	0.423	0.410	0.397	0.373	0.350	0.301	0.260	0.226	0.198
5	0.951	0.906	0.822	0.747	0.681	0.621	0.567	0.519	0.497	0.476	0.437	0.402	0.370	0.341	0.328	0.315	0.291	0.269	0.223	0.186	0.156	0.132
6	0.941	0.888	0.790	0.705	0.630	0.564	0.507	0.456	0.432	0.410	0.370	0.335	0.303	0.275	0.262	0.250	0.227	0.207	0.165	0.133	0.108	0.088
7	0.933	0.871	0.760	0.665	0.583	0.513	0.452	0.400	0.376	0.354	0.314	0.279	0.249	0.222	0.210	0.198	0.178	0.159	0.122	0.095	0.074	0.059
8	0.923	0.853	0.731	0.627	0.540	0.467	0.404	0.351	0.327	0.305	0.266	0.233	0.204	0.179	0.168	0.157	0.139	0.123	0.091	0.068	0.051	0.039
9	0.914	0.837	0.703	0.592	0.500	0.424	0.361	0.308	0.284	0.263	0.225	0.194	0.167	0.144	0.134	0.125	0.108	0.094	0.067	0.048	0.035	0.026
10	0.905	0.820	0.676	0.558	0.463	0.386	0.322	0.270	0.247	0.227	0.191	0.162	0.137	0.116	0.107	0.099	0.085	0.073	0.050	0.035	0.024	0.017
11	0.896	0.804	0.650	0.527	0.429	0.350	0.287	0.237	0.215	0.195	0.162	0.135	0.112	0.094	0.086	0.079	0.066	0.056	0.037	0.025	0.017	0.012
12	0.887	0.788	0.625	0.497	0.397	0.319	0.257	0.208	0.187	0.168	0.137	0.112	0.092	0.076	0.069	0.062	0.052	0.043	0.027	0.018	0.012	0.008
13	0.879	0.773	0.601	0.469	0.368	0.290	0.229	0.182	0.163	0.145	0.116	0.093	0.075	0.061	0.055	0.050	0.040	0.033	0.020	0.013	0.008	0.005
14	0.870	0.758	0.577	0.442	0.340	0.263	0.205	0.160	0.141	0.125	0.099	0.078	0.062	0.049	0.044	0.039	0.032	0.025	0.015	0.009	0.006	0.003
15	0.861	0.743	0.555	0.417	0.315	0.239	0.183	0.140	0.123	0.108	0.084	0.065	0.051	0.040	0.035	0.031	0.025	0.020	0.011	0.006	0.004	0.002
16	0.853	0.728	0.534	0.394	0.292	0.218	0.163	0.123	0.107	0.093	0.071	0.054	0.042	0.032	0.028	0.025	0.019	0.015	0.008	0.005	0.003	0.002
17	0.844	0.714	0.513	0.371	0.270	0.198	0.146	0.108	0.093	0.080	0.060	0.045	0.034	0.026	0.023	0.020	0.015	0.012	0.006	0.003	0.002	0.001
18	836	0.700	0.494	0.350	0.250	0.180	0.130	0.095	0.081	0.069	0.051	0.038	0.028	0.021	0.018	0.016	0.012	0.009	0.005	0.002	0.001	0.001
19	0.828	0.686	0.475	0.331	0.232	0.164	0.116	0.083	0.070	0.060	0.043	0.031	0.023	0.017	0.014	0.012	0.009	0.007	0.003	0.002	0.001	
20	0.820	0.673	0.456	0.312	0.215	0.149	0.104	0.073	0.061	0.051	0.037	0.026	0.019	0.014	0.012	0.010	0.007	0.005	0.002	0.001	0.001	
21	0.811	0.660	0.439	0.294	0.199	0.135	0.093	0.064	0.053	0.044	0.031	0.022	0.015	0.011	0.009	0.008	0.006	0.004	0.002	0.001		
22	0.803	0.647	0.422	0.278	0.184	0.123	0.083	0.056	0.046	0.038	0.026	0.018	0.013	0.009	0.007	0.006	0.004	0.003	0.001	0.001		
23	0.795	0.634	0.406	0.262	0.170	0.112	0.074	0.049	0.040	0.033	0.022	0.015	0.010	0.007	0.006	0.005	0.003	0.002	0.001			
24	0.788	0.622	0.390	0.247	0.158	0.102	0.066	0.043	0.035	0.028	0.019	0.013	0.008	0.006	0.005	0.004	0.003	0.002	0.001			
25	0.780	0.610	0.375	0.233	0.146	0.092	0.059	0.038	0.030	0.024	0.016	0.010	0.007	0.005	0.004	0.003	0.002	0.001	0.001			
26	0.772	0.598	0.361	0.220	0.135	0.084	0.053	0.033	0.026	0.021	0.014	0.009	0.006	0.004	0.003	0.002	0.002	0.001				
27	0.764	0.586	0.347	0.207	0.125	0.076	0.047	0.029	0.023	0.018	0.011	0.007	0.005	0.003	0.002	0.002	0.001	0.001				
28	0.757	0.574	0.333	0.196	0.116	0.069	0.042	0.026	0.020	0.016	0.010	0.006	0.004	0.002	0.002	0.002	0.001	0.001				
29	0.749	0.563	0.321	0.185	0.107	0.063	0.037	0.022	0.017	0.014	0.008	0.005	0.003	0.002	0.002	0.001	0.001	0.001				
30	0.742	0.552	0.308	0.174	0.099	0.057	0.033	0.020	0.015	0.012	0.007	0.004	0.003	0.002	0.001	0.001	0.001					
40	0.672	0.453	0.208	0.097	0.046	0.022	0.011	0.005	0.004	0.003	0.001	0.001										
50	0.608	0.372	0.141	0.054	0.021	0.009	0.003	0.001	0.001	0.001												

EXAMPLE: Suppose you need $20,000 ten years into the future. How much must you invest today to achieve it assuming a 12% rate of return? First, enter the chart at "10 Years Hence", and move right until you intersect the column headed by the label "12%". The factor is .322. Multiplying $20,000 by .322, you will find that the present value of this amount (discounted at 12%) is $6,440.

Depreciating Assets

When you completed your personal income statement in Chapter 3, the only entry that was not really self-explanatory was Outlays for Fixed Assets. At that time we gave you the formula for calculating this figure. You may have asked yourself why an entry was made for fixed assets in your personal income statement.

The reason is that certain assets you own will depreciate with time. Your car, appliances, even your house (though rising real estate values may boost the price of your home) depreciate with time. *Depreciation* is the decline in dollar value of an asset over time and through use.

When you buy an asset such as a car or appliance, its cost is more than just its purchase price. There are three other cost factors to consider: operating cost, lost interest that could have been earned on the money spent (this is called *oppportunity cost*) and depreciation.

Since you will need to replace an important asset that wears out, depreciates, good financial planning requires that you take this ongoing cost into consideration. If you plan for depreciation and set aside money to replace the asset, you will be eliminating a major piece of the paycheck-to-paycheck existence that can be so frustrating and limiting.

You may be familiar with this problem of failing to account for depreciation on a national level. In recent years debate has raged over the continuing deterioration of the nation's "infrastructure." Roads, bridges, parks, and other public property have been allowed to deteriorate while money was spent on other endeavors. This deterioration means that the items are worth less simply because they are in poorer condition.

Government spending policies have failed to account for the depreciation of the assets they are charged with caring for. This mistake, on the national level, is similar to the mistake many consumers make in not preparing for replacing depreciating assets. When a bridge collapses, there is an uproar over the tragedy. Money is then taken from some other theoretically worthy project to "fix" the problem.

The same uproar happens when your washer breaks down and no provision has been made over time for replacement: "Oh no, now where are we going to get the money for a new washer?" While we all prefer to dwell on more pleasant subjects, like possession of appreciating assets, don't neglect this important concept in your financial planning.

Understanding Spending

As we've emphasized throughout this book, spending is too often neglected when it comes to financial planning. It is far more than a simple single act.

FIGURE 5-2
The Spending Cycle

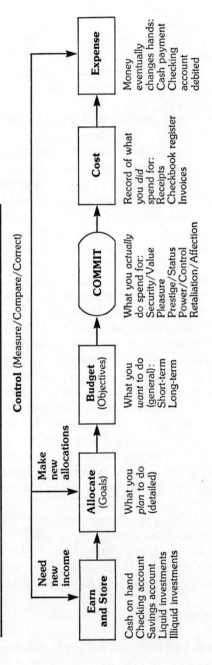

Control (Measure/Compare/Correct)

| Earn and Store | → Need new income → | Allocate (Goals) | → Make new allocations → | Budget (Objectives) | → | COMMIT | → | Cost | → | Expense |

Earn and Store
Cash on hand
Checking account
Savings account
Liquid investments
Illiquid investments

Allocate (Goals)
What you *plan* to do (detailed)

Budget (Objectives)
What you *want* to do (general):
Short-term
Long-term

COMMIT
What you *actually* do spend for:
Security/Value
Pleasure
Prestige/Status
Power/Control
Retaliation/Affection

Cost
Record of what you *did* spend for:
Receipts
Checkbook register
Invoices

Expense
Money eventually changes hands:
Cash payment
Checking account debited

In the last chapter we focused on helping you learn your household and personal spending styles.

Many of us are confused by the game of numbers that surrounds spending of any kind. For example, consider our own federal government. Some politicians claim that many millions are spent for one thing or another. Their opponents claim just the opposite. Both point to exactly the same event and the same congressional records. Who is right and who is wrong?

Chances are that both sides are right. They are simply focusing on different stages of the *spending cycle* to make their points. Understanding this cycle is the key to understanding how all spending works: how money is allocated, disbursed, and accounted for. Figure 5–2 illustrates this spending process graphically.

Money that is received must be stored, either as cash, a bank deposit, or in some other type of investment. From this perspective even unused credit can be viewed as money. Once you make a decision about spending the money, you are *allocating* it for a specific purpose. Congress makes allocations just as you might make them yourself: a general amount for a general purpose.

Your next step is to construct a more or less definite plan for how your allocated money will be spent. Since this plan is more specific, the "budgeted number" is sometimes different from the general allocation you first made. There may even be a surplus left over once your detailed plan has been designed. Of course, it also happens sometimes that you wind up spending more than you had originally allocated. How many times have you set a budget to buy a TV or car, and once you got to the dealer's, you couldn't resist that added cost feature?

Eventually, you will *commit* to a spending transaction. This commitment seals with actualities, not plans. Here again, numbers for the same spending activity can differ. For example, prior to buying a new car you may have allocated, "guesstimated," that it would cost $10,000. Once you investigated things more thoroughly you budgeted $11,500. But once you got to the dealer you managed to negotiate the price down to $10,800, almost $1,000 above your original allocation.

Finally, you will record the spending commitments you made. If you wrote a check, the record is the entry in your check register. If you used a credit card, the record is your copy of the sales slip. The one thing these specific cost records have in common is that they are all *after the fact*. They are useful only to remind you of the spending commitments you've made.

For these and other reasons, politicians (and household members!) can wrangle all day about the future cost of an expenditure. It all depends on where and when in the spending cycle they look for it.

As you can see from the discussion about the varied motivations of spenders in Chapter 4 and this explanation of the spending cycle, financial planning is more complicated than you may have thought at first. With or without written plans and records, it is a complex process undertaken and controlled by *people*. For you, then, the key to making money count in this process is to *control your commitments to spend*.

Borrowing brings up an important aspect of the time value of money. When you borrow, you have the use of someone else's money for a certain period of time. Basically, you pay a fee for immediate use of the money. The lender forgoes current use of the money in order to earn the fee.

In inflationary times it makes sense to borrow money when real interest rates are low, in order to buy things before their prices increase. For example, when inflation was over 13 percent in 1980, the real interest rate on a credit card charging 18 percent, was 5 percent or less. When prices were rising at double digit rates, it made sense to buy immediately before prices went higher.

A number of other factors combined to make borrowing the common-sense approach to handling financial affairs. At the time, the interest paid on credit cards and other consumer loans was tax deductible.

But things changed in the 1980s. Inflation dropped from double digit rates to under 5 percent. The 1986 Tax Reform Act reduced the deductibility of consumer interest in stages so as to eliminate it entirely by 1990. But despite these changes, lenders continue to push credit aggressively. And Americans continue to pile on debt.

By 1987 consumer debt payments absorbed 19.7 percent of the average American family's income. A Gallup poll indicated that 63 percent of American families were concerned that their debt levels were too high.

As a result of eliminating the tax deductions on consumer interest, the strongest push by lenders has been for *home equity* loans. Mortgage interest retained its deductibility within certain limits. Lenders have launched ad campaigns for home equity loans touting their use "for practically any purpose."

As we explained in Chapter 3, the use of credit itself is neither bad nor good. However, you need to be aware of the problems such *leverage* can create for your financial plans. A good rule of thumb is to calculate how much of your take-home pay must be used to pay off debt. If more than 30 percent goes toward mortgage payments and more than 20 percent goes to installment loans, you should cut back your use of credit.

Borrowing: Uses and Abuses of Credit

The experience of the 1970s and 1980s points up the importance of knowing the true cost of borrowing. In the 70s it made sense to borrow heavily.

In the 1980s the benefits of added credit were outweighed by the higher real costs.

When you apply for a loan you will find that interest rates are expressed in a number of different ways. Perhaps you are most familiar with *simple interest*. A $1,200 loan at 10 percent simple interest would cost $120 per year in interest.

But assessing the cost of loans is more complicated than merely comparing the stated interest rate. For example, if you paid off the loan in our example in 12 equal payments, the effective interest rate on the money you were actually able to use of the loan would be considerably higher. After all, you were able to use the $1200 for only the first month of the loan. After you paid the first month's loan payment of $110 ($1,200 × 10% = $120; added to the principal, you get $1,320. Divide that by 12 and each monthly payment will be $110). You only have effective use of $1,090 of the original loan once you've made the first payment. After the first six payments you have paid out $660. Yet you are still paying interest as though your balance was $1,200 (your monthly payment stays the same as it was when you had use of the full $1,200).

When you look at it this way, you see that your average balance for the entire period is closer to $600 not the $1,200 you started with. The $120 interest charge on the average outstanding balance of $600 is actually 20 percent per year. In other words, the *effective cost of borrowing* is twice as much as the stated simple interest rate. And the *effective* interest rate is what should interest you most.

The terminology used to describe different types of interest charges is quite complicated. To address this problem, Congress passed the Truth-in-Lending Act. This legislation standardized the method for calculating the effective cost of all loan proposals. Most lending institutions are required to advise borrowers the effective cost of borrowing before a contract is completed.

And don't forget to make the additional calculation of the real, inflation-adjusted interest rate. An interest rate of 21 percent may seem prohibitive when inflation is running under 5 percent. But if inflation is 15 percent, then a 21 percent rate is more tolerable.

Risk versus Reward: Finding the Right Balance

Risk in the financial sense means two different things. One is *economic risk*. That is the susceptibility of your investment to market, political, and other economic events beyond your control. The other kind of risk is *individual risk*. This refers to the sorts of chances you feel you can take given your age, current mix of assets, job stability, personal needs, psychological approach to risk taking in general, and the nature of your goals themselves.

Take a moment to complete the following Taking Stock questionnaire, "What Sort of Financial Risk Taker Am I?" Have your spouse or partner complete the form also. This questionnaire is designed to help you identify your risk-taking style. When you have completed the form and read the interpretation of your responses in the "Evaluating Your Financial Risk-Taking Style," you will have a better appreciation of the factors affecting individual risk.

Keep in mind that this is a self-discovery questionnaire. It is not a test. There are no right or wrong answers. There are only different ways to respond to common situations.

Taking Stock

What Sort of Financial Risk Taker Am I?

How willing are you to take financial risks? Just as your financial decision-making style is influenced by both emotional and rational factors, so your willingness to take financial risks depends on a variety of complex characteristics. To understand how these traits affect you and your household's risk-taking decisions, take a few minutes now to complete this questionnaire. After reading a statement, decide which number in the accompanying scale best reflects how well the statement describes you and write it in the space provided. Have your spouse do so as well in the appropriate column.

Very like me 5	Often like me 4	Occasionally like me 3	Seldom like me 2	Not like me at all 1

	Partner A	Partner B
1. Although I may consider them, other people's feelings seldom affect my financial decisions.	___	___
2. In dealing with money, I am usually calm and not easily upset.	___	___
3. I have no trouble concentrating on money-related tasks.	___	___
4. Reading the financial page of the newspaper relaxes me.	___	___
5. I am optimistic about my financial future.	___	___
6. I don't like doing the same thing over and over.	___	___
7. I prefer trying new restaurants to going back to the same one all the time.	___	___

8. I can't imagine myself in the same job for more than a few years at a time.   _____ _____
9. When things get boring, I get going.   _____ _____
10. I believe variety is the spice of life.   _____ _____
11. I enjoy being "where the action is."   _____ _____
12. I prefer doing work that has lots of excitement.   _____ _____
13. When waiting for a traffic light to turn green, I often get impatient.   _____ _____
14. I trust my "gut reaction" in most situations.   _____ _____
15. I agree that "actions speak louder than words."   _____ _____
16. When I'm involved in a group activity, I like to be the center of attention.   _____ _____
17. I like to be part of whatever is new and fashionable.   _____ _____
18. I value strong attachments to my friends.   _____ _____
19. I get very embarrassed if I make a mistake or "slip up" in public.   _____ _____
20. I often buy presents for my friends.   _____ _____

| Taking Stock |

Evaluating Your Financial Risk-Taking Style

Social science research has shown that our desire to take risks in important areas (such as money, sex, and politics) seems to depend on at least four major factors:

1. our tendency to worry (called *anxiety*)

2. our desire for change or need for variety

3. our general impulsiveness

4. our desire for social acceptance

The questionnaire on page 92 of this book measures the strength of these four factors in a way that will allow you to chart your risk-taking characteristics and compare them to those of other people and to an interesting array of typical risk-taking profiles. Here's how to evaluate your answers.

Your Tendency to Worry

Anxiety is a normal emotion and we all suffer from it at one time or another. Although seldom pleasant, a little healthy worrying can help protect us from ill-considered or dangerous activities. Excessive worry, however, is something else. It can rob us of our sunny dispositions and bring more risk, rather than less, to our decisions. Unfortunately, fast-paced modern living gives us many opportunities to feel anxious. Financial decisions sometimes must be made quickly with little information and inade-

---

Evaluating Your Financial Risk-Taking Style (*continued*)

quate time for reflection. In such an environment, your money-related problems may be among the most anxiety-provoking of all.

Add your answers to questions 1, 2, 3, 4, and 5. This value is your "anxiety score," and you should enter it in the space provided on the accompanying Figure T5–1.

Your Need for Variety

A desire for change (sometimes for the sake of change itself) is often associated with risk-taking tendencies. People who prefer to be good at many things, rather than really excellent at one, are sometimes thought of as "job hoppers." To them, the risk of lost income or seniority

FIGURE T5–1
Your Personal Risk-Taking Profile

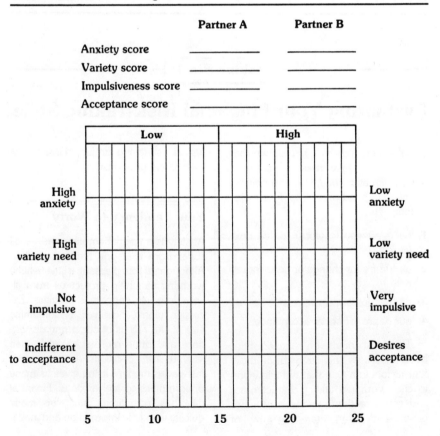

is clearly secondary to the promise of more variety in daily tasks. When it comes to spending money, people driven by a need for newness often become great collectors—of books, appliances, and gadgets of all kinds; or they may shop around for alternative products and services, even though their current needs are being met. For these people, variety is *truly* the spice of life, and it's worth a bit of risk to get it.

Add your answers to questions 6, 7, 8, 9, and 10. This value is your "variety score," and you should record it in the space below your previous entry on the figure.

Your Penchant for Impulsiveness

To some degree, all of us react emotionally to new situations, financial or otherwise. How well we control these feelings and allow our more rational faculties to operate is a sign of our impulsiveness. While impulsive behavior in one case may be "inspiration," in another it may be "foolhardiness." The ability to act quickly can lead to impressive financial gains, but a predilection for rapid action can also make even the most ordinary financial decisions more risky than they should be.

Add your answers to questions 11, 12, 13, 14, and 15 and enter this value —your "impulsiveness score"—in the space provided below your other answers.

Your Desire for Social Acceptance

Almost everyone wants to be liked by other people—by family members co-workers, friends, and community groups with which one wants to be identified. Even when there is no obvious social aspect to a financial decision, we tend to be influenced by how that decision will be received by the "in crowd" or how that decision will help or hurt us in our efforts to keep up with the Joneses. The use of money to realize social aspirations is as old as money itself and is a basic motivation in many consumer decisions. But taken to the extreme, it can lead anyone to high-risk investments and a spiral of wasteful spending.

Add your answers to questions 16, 17, 18, 19, and 20 and enter the results in the last space on the figure. This is your "acceptance score," and it completes the list of factors we'll use to chart your risk-taking profile.

Your Financial Risk-Taking Profile

Now transfer your scores in each area to the chart below them. Make a single, heavy dot where the score for each factor intersects that factor's reference line. For example, an "anxiety score" of 18 would be plotted on the intersection of the vertical "18" line and the horizontal line between "High Anxiety" and "Low Anxiety."

When you have plotted all four dots, connect the top dot to the dot immediately below it with a solid line of your own. Continue down your dots in this manner until all dots are connected by a single line, top to bottom. If your spouse or life partner has also completed the questionnaire, plot his or her dots and connect them with a separate dashed or colored line. The distinctive shapes formed by those lines are your own,

---

Evaluating Your Financial Risk-Taking Style (*continued*)

---

unique risk-taking profiles, and we think they can tell you a lot about how you approach—and make—risk-related decisions.

The "Straight Arrow" Profile

If the shape formed by your connected dots is a vertical (or nearly vertical) line, you have what we call the "straight arrow" profile. It means you tend to balance your risk-taking factors and apply them in a fairly consistent way.

If your vertical line is in the left half of the chart, the risk criteria you use are generally conservative. You know that you tend to worry about money decisions and tend to control your spending impulses, complementing that self-discipline with an acceptance of things you cannot (or do not want to) change. Despite your acceptance of the status quo, people still may tend to view you as an individualist—with the group but apart from it—and perhaps a bit "standoffish." If your line is very close to the left-hand margin, you may want to use the group's resources better to improve the quality of your money-related decisions and reduce your tendency to worry.

If your vertical line is in the right half of the chart, you tend to make higher-risk decisions and, if you are typical, may rationalize your lack of worry about them with a sense of fatalism about the outcome. You tend to be dissatisfied with the status quo and sometimes may try new approaches just to "shake things up" and see if they will work. In general, your financial risks tend to be based on how well the payoff will enhance your position within a valued group—your family, friends, co-workers, or community.

If your line falls exactly in the middle

FIGURE T5–2
Some Typical Risk-Taking Profiles

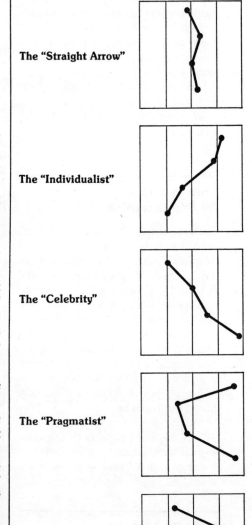

The "Straight Arrow"

The "Individualist"

The "Celebrity"

The "Pragmatist"

The "Adventurer"

of the chart, you probably tend to view each risk decision on its own merits—but beware. We've found that many "straight arrows" who shoot up the middle have either fudged on the questionnaire (chosen answer 3 to avoid committing themselves) or, if answering accurately, sometimes baffle those around them by reacting with apparent unpredictability to risky financial questions. If your line falls genuinely in the middle, you may want to take extra pains to communicate your money-related feelings to partners in your decisions.

The "Individualist" Profile

If your line slants generally upward to the right, you tend to show the "individualist's" characteristics when taking financial risks. You don't worry too much about how things will turn out, possibly because you seek mostly to please yourself, rather than others, with your financial decisions. If the upper-line segment extends very close to the right-hand side of the chart, you may, in fact, flirt occasionally with overconfidence. Similarly, if the lower segment goes too far to the left, you may be neglecting some important social norms or group resources that could improve your risk-related decisions.

The "Celebrity" Profile

If your line descends from upper left to lower right, you tend to exhibit the "celebrity" profile—so named because many people with this set of characteristics base their actions heavily on the opinions of their peers and other groups. They hope, nearly above all else, to be popular and accepted. If your line extends very close to the lower right-hand margin, you are probably willing to take some pretty big risks to gain or maintain this acceptance, even though you know you'll worry about the outcome after you've made your decision. Although you tend to value the status quo, your impulsiveness may give others the impression that you are a trendsetter as well as a fashion-follower—an impression that will usually enhance your reputation in the group.

If the upper part of your line extends very close to the left-hand margin, you may be worrying more than necessary about your financial risks. Your strong tendency to feel anxious will probably moderate your high-risk impulses. If your line extends far to the lower right, you may be placing group values too far ahead of your own good judgment.

The "Pragmatist" Profile

If your line forms a concave shape (dishing inward to the left, like the letter C), you have the classic "pragmatist's" profile. Even though you don't worry too much about your money and place great value on your social position, you tend to make lower-risk decisions than most. Some pragmatists even classify a decision as "high-risk" if it threatens the status quo—regardless of its financial safety. Extreme pragmatists like these (such as those whose curve extends very close to the left-hand margin) may be so averse to risk that their financial partners sometimes accuse them of sprouting roots and leafy branches while they ponder financial issues. On the other hand, if the "horns" (the upper and lower line segments) of the profile extend far to the right, you may be relying too heavily on group acceptance as a risk-decision criterion—and might well

---

Evaluating Your Financial Risk-Taking Style (*concluded*)

benefit from a little healthy anxiety about where and how your well-considered financial decisions are taking you.

The "Adventurer" Profile

As the name implies, risk takers with a convex (bowed to the right, or D-shaped) profile can lead very exciting lives indeed. Although their tendency to worry and sense of independence can keep their financial dealings from becoming too outlandish, their desire for change and impulsive habits can sometimes bring on an attack of rollercoaster economics. Confirmed adventurers, in fact, often experience "boom and bust" finances—going from big scores on complex or off-the-wall financial deals to losing their shirts on the next roll of fortune's dice. Although this sort of financial gamesmanship has great appeal for those who dream big and crave a lot of action, a significant spread between the horns of the curve (the points farthest left in the lower-risk zones) and the bow of the curve (on the higher-rolling, freer-wheeling right) can sometimes lead to many sleepless nights—as well as lost investments!

Interpreting Composite Profiles

If your line zigzags left-right-left (like the letter S) or right-left-right (like the letter Z) or forms some other shape not described above, you can analyze your risk-taking style by breaking the line into segments that contain one of the above patterns and assessing the relationship of the factors that compose it. For example, an S-shaped curve has two distinct regions: the upper part (dished left, like the letter C, between anxiety, variety, and impulsiveness); and the lower part (bowed right, like the letter D, between variety, impulsiveness, and acceptance). Thus you know that your higher-risk decisions tend to be based on your relative freedom from worry and/or your tendency to be impulsive and that these forces are balanced (held in check or complemented) by your desire to preserve the status quo and your relative insensitivity to pressures from the crowd—both risk-reducing qualities. Thus you tend to show the pragmatist's characteristics when faced with new or unusual situations, and the adventurer's when presented with an opportunity that is "just too good to pass up!"

Using this method, any combination of scores and patterns can be quickly and profitably analyzed.

Making the Most of Your Personal Risk-Taking Profile

Throughout these pages, we've tried to avoid any suggestion that one style is better than another for all situations. This is because risk (and all that it entails) is very situational. One year's risky decision (such as investment in IBM in the 1950s) may be next year's safest bet. Our aim has been only to help you find those areas of your personality that are more susceptible to the siren's song of gain and, conversely, those that might inhibit you unnecessarily when it's time to "pay your money and take your chances."

For couples, the areas of greatest divergence (points where your dots are farthest apart) can be both sources of conflict and of strength. For example, a Celebrity living with a Pragmatist will tend to share that Pragmatist's desire for social acceptance, moderate impulsiveness, and low need for variety. When it comes to anxiety about decisions, however, the Celebrity may suffer a sudden attack of sweaty palms. This can be doubly perplexing if the partners' other risk-taking variables are closely matched. On the other hand, the "not to worry" Pragmatist might benefit from listening to a few words of caution when those pressures to impress the group result in too many high-risk decisions.

Whatever your risk-taking profile, we hope you'll use this knowledge to make your goal-getting plan more rewarding and secure.

In general, there are three golden rules that govern any investment decision. These common-sense guidelines give you a frame of reference from which to consider your options:

1. *The highest returns usually require the highest risks.* If you want to aim for 30 percent to 40 percent per year returns, you have to be prepared to suffer substantial losses in the attempt. The best way to evaluate the risk of a high-return investment is to gauge the reasonableness of the *time* involved to receive it. Some lower-risk investments might return 15 percent or 20 percent, but only if you were lucky enough to buy them very early in their up cycle and sell them before they turned down.

2. *The more important the goal, the less risk you can afford.* The extreme example of this is your retirement fund. At age 60 or 65, financial security is of paramount concern. It is unlikely you could go back to work at this age and earn enough to rebuild your life's savings. Other goals, such as a trip around the world, may be worth taking a few speculative risks (with money set aside specifically for that venture) to achieve.

3. *The sooner you need the goal, the fewer risks you can afford.* Common sense tells you that the more quickly a job has to be done, the less opportunity you will have to repeat it to correct your mistakes if things go wrong the first time. For example, if retirement is 25 or 30 years away, you can afford more risks with your "nest egg" investment than if retirement is only 5 or 10 years away.

Wrapping Up

In this chapter you have learned basic concepts that are crucial to long-term financial planning. With today's constant ebb and flow of inflation, informed planning requires a knowledge of the time value of money. In the 1970s many businesses and individuals were led astray by the false prosperity that inflation can create. Some people thought they had far more money than they really did when inflation was factored out.

You now know how to calculate the injurious effects of inflation by using future value tables. You are striving to build additional purchasing power, not only higher numbers of dollars.

And of course, it is equally important to be able to project the future value of dollars invested today. Without access to present value tables or calculations, it would be difficult to set aside the correct amount of money to achieve those future goals.

And last, but certainly not least, a central element in any investment decision is risk. The Taking Stock questionnaire in this chapter will help you make decisions that you can sleep with. An old Wall Street saying goes: "Sell down to the sleeping point." This simply means that a primary consideration for any investment decision is your personal comfort level. If you can't sleep with it, don't do it!

CHAPTER 6

TARGETING YOUR FINANCIAL GOALS

IMPLEMENTING YOUR GOAL-GETTING PLAN

In this chapter you will finally see the culmination of all the worksheets and numbers you have been completing. You will learn how to apply the concepts of future and present value you learned in Chapter 5 to your own situation. You will discover that setting out specific goal-getting targets is not just a one-shot process. You will also learn how to put together a plan that combines the various elements of risk and reward you have learned about in previous chapters.

But a goal-getting plan is only as good as the method you use to activate it. Even professional investors have to contend with managing their day-to-day financial affairs. It is pointless to spend all your time working out an investment scheme and financial plan to achieve goals as many as 10 or 20 years away if you do not have a system for tracking your income and spending. After all, these two factors will ultimately determine the success of your carefully structured plan.

In this chapter we introduce some ideas on what we call *Resourcing*. Traditional budgeting tends to be static, forcing people into unnatural behavior patterns. With your own Resourcing system, your record keeping and day-to-day financial affairs are individualized to suit you. Rather than trying to force square pegs into round holes, or more accurately, impetuous spenders into security-conscious patterns, you will learn a variety of ways to implement a Resourcing system that fits your circumstances.

At this point you probably know more than most people about yourself, your partner, and your household spending style. However, even though you now have a clear picture of where you stand financially and your financial goals, you do not have a clear plan for getting "there" from here. That is the purpose of this chapter.

In Chapter 5, we introduced the important concept of the time value of money. Here you will see what present value and future value mean to you in concrete terms. In Chapter 5, you also learned about risk. Risk/reward equations are not usually reducible to pure numbers. There is an element of subjective judgment. Take a moment to review the three rules of thumb for risk/reward in the realm of investing.

Beginning Your Goals Achievement Schedule

Action Paper No. 8, "Your Goals Achievement Schedule" is the worksheet you will use to calculate the future value of the goals you ranked in Action Paper No. 7, "Your Goals Priority Worksheet" (Chapter 3). Now, complete Action Paper No. 8 in the back of the book by first listing your goals down the left side of the form under item 1, Goals, in the order of priority that you set earlier in Action Paper No. 7.

Under item 2, Goal Price, Current Value, enter the price for each item you had figured for Action Paper No. 6. Next enter the number of years into the future when you desire your goals to be realized. This is an important number. Some goals, such as buying a car or paying for your child's dental braces, may be only two or three years away. Others, like that world cruise or retirement, may be 20 or more years away.

You will need to time your goals realistically. Don't have too many expensive ones occurring in the same year. This is particularly the case in the short term. Remember, you want to design your plan to take advantage of the effect of long-term compounding rather than relying on high-risk speculations.

Some of your goals will require recurring annual contributions. For example, your retirement planning may depend on regular IRA contributions. To obtain an aggregate sum for these items, multiply the yearly amount by the number of years the contributions will take place. Put that amount under item 2 and use it when calculating item 6a.

Finding Your Inflation-Adjusted Costs

What looks adequate today to meet living expenses may prove woefully inadequate 10, 15, or 20 years down the road when it comes time to actually pay living expenses. During the late 1970s the inflation rate ran well over 10 percent. At that pace, you would lose half the purchasing power of your money in slightly more than seven years! Regardless of what the inflation rate is when you read this book, it is vital that you keep in mind the deleterious effects that resurgent inflation can have on your investment plans.

Making inflation adjustments is not an exact science. No one knows with certainty what the future holds. To make your own calculations you will need two tools: 1) the future value table (Figure 6–1), and 2) your own good judgment.

Figure 6–1 shows the effect of compounding on a sum invested or put at risk by inflation for the number of years shown. The numbers in each column are known as *factors*. These factors are multipliers that will correct any current amount to its future value at a particular rate of return or rate of inflation. To put it in to better perspective, see the discussion below of our sample Lean and Quick household.

A Sample Goals Achievement Schedule

Figure 6–2 shows our Lean and Quick example's goals adjusted for an anticipated 5 percent annual inflation rate. The actual inflation rate you use depends on your assessment of the long-term economic outlook. Regardless of how you make your forecast, take a single average value for your entire time horizon and apply it uniformly to all current year prices on your form. We have found this to be the best approach even though actual inflation will vary from year to year.

As you can see in Figure 6–2, our couple estimated that the high-priority emergency fund and professional certificate need to be available within two years. Taking the $6,800 current price (the price was set in Chapter 3 when Action Paper No. 7 was completed) and multiplying that by the 1.1 factor from Figure 6–1 (5 percent for two years) you get $7,480. That is the amount it will take in two years at 5 percent inflation to pay for something that costs $6,800 today.

Working down the list in the same manner, you can see how the effect of compounding inflation increases the cost of this couple's goals. A $10,000 car purchased five years from now will cost $13,000 ($10,000 × the 1.3 (we've rounded 1.28 to 1.3) factor from the table = $13,000). The cost of the college funds which will be due in 12 years, becomes a whopping $50,400! Of course, these calculations assume that all other things are equal. Even so, it clearly illustrates the importance of adjusting for the effects of inflation.

So far we have been working with set principal sums. However, your retirement fund probably requires periodic investments as well as taking advantage of compounding your investment returns. Our sample household planned to put away $2,000 per year in an IRA account. You will need to consult Figure 6–3 to get the appropriate multiplier for this periodic investment strategy.

Starting with a $2,000 investment, our Lean and Quick couple plans to invest the same amount each year. At the end of 20 years they will draw out the entire sum. This approach means that the eroding forces of inflation will have a small amount to work on initially, growing larger as the effects of compounding and year-end contributions become really significant.

Figure 6–3 gives you a multiplier to use when a fixed dollar investment is made at the end of each year for a given number of years. To see how the calculation was made for our Lean and Quick example, go to the 5% (the estimated rate of inflation) column of the table. Read down the column

FIGURE 6-1
Computing the Effects of Inflation or Rates of Return on Lump Sum Investments

Rate of Inflation or Rate of Return

Length of Investment (Years)	2%	3%	4%	5%	6%	7%	8%	10%	12%	14%	16%	20%
1	1.02	1.03	1.04	1.05	1.06	1.07	1.08	1.10	1.12	1.14	1.16	1.20
2	1.04	1.06	1.08	1.10	1.12	1.14	1.17	1.21	1.25	1.30	1.35	1.44
3	1.06	1.09	1.12	1.16	1.19	1.23	1.26	1.33	1.40	1.48	1.56	1.73
4	1.08	1.12	1.17	1.22	1.26	1.31	1.36	1.46	1.57	1.69	1.81	2.07
5	1.10	1.16	1.22	1.28	1.34	1.40	1.47	1.61	1.76	1.93	2.10	2.49
6	1.13	1.19	1.26	1.34	1.42	1.50	1.59	1.77	1.97	2.20	2.44	2.99
7	1.15	1.23	1.32	1.41	1.50	1.61	1.71	1.95	2.21	2.50	2.83	3.58
8	1.17	1.27	1.37	1.48	1.59	1.72	1.85	2.14	2.48	2.85	3.28	4.30
9	1.20	1.30	1.42	1.55	1.69	1.84	2.00	2.36	2.77	3.25	3.80	5.16
10	1.22	1.34	1.48	1.63	1.79	1.99	2.16	2.59	3.11	3.71	4.41	6.19
11	1.24	1.38	1.54	1.71	1.90	2.10	2.33	2.85	3.48	4.23	5.12	7.43
12	1.27	1.42	1.60	1.79	2.01	2.25	2.52	3.14	3.90	4.82	5.94	8.92
13	1.29	1.47	1.66	1.88	2.13	2.41	2.72	3.45	4.36	5.49	6.89	10.70
14	1.32	1.51	1.73	1.98	2.26	2.58	2.94	3.80	4.89	6.26	7.99	12.84
15	1.34	1.56	1.80	2.08	2.40	2.76	3.17	4.18	5.47	7.14	9.27	15.41
16	1.37	1.60	1.87	2.18	2.54	2.95	3.43	4.60	6.13	8.14	10.75	18.49
17	1.40	1.65	1.95	2.29	2.69	3.16	3.70	5.05	6.87	9.28	12.47	22.17
18	1.43	1.70	2.02	2.41	2.85	3.38	4.00	5.56	7.69	10.58	14.46	22.62
19	1.46	1.75	2.11	2.53	3.03	3.62	4.32	6.12	8.61	12.05	16.78	31.95
20	1.48	1.81	2.19	2.65	3.21	3.87	4.66	6.73	9.65	13.74	19.46	38.34

21	1.52	1.86	2.28	2.79	3.40	4.14	5.03	7.40	10.80	15.67	22.57	46.00
22	1.55	1.91	2.37	2.92	3.60	4.43	5.44	8.14	12.10	17.87	26.19	55.21
23	1.58	1.97	2.46	3.07	3.82	4.74	5.87	8.95	13.55	20.36	30.38	66.25
24	1.61	2.03	2.56	3.23	4.05	5.07	6.34	9.85	15.18	23.21	35.24	79.50
25	1.64	2.09	2.66	3.39	4.29	5.43	6.85	10.83	17.00	26.46	40.87	95.40
26	1.67	2.16	2.77	3.55	4.55	5.81	7.40	11.91	19.04	30.17	47.41	114.47
27	1.71	2.22	2.88	3.73	4.82	6.21	7.99	13.11	21.32	34.39	55.00	137.37
28	1.74	2.29	3.00	3.92	5.11	6.65	8.63	14.42	23.83	39.20	63.80	164.84
29	1.78	2.36	3.12	4.12	5.42	7.11	9.32	15.86	26.75	44.69	74.00	197.81
30	1.81	2.43	3.24	4.32	5.74	7.61	10.06	17.45	29.96	50.95	85.84	237.37
31	1.84	2.50	3.37	4.53	6.08	8.14	10.88	19.19	33.56	58.08		
32	1.88	2.57	3.50	4.76	6.45	8.72	11.74	21.11	37.58	66.22		
33	1.92	2.65	3.64	5.00	6.84	9.33	12.68	23.23	42.09	75.49		
34	1.96	2.73	3.79	5.25	7.25	10.00	13.69	25.55	47.14	86.05		
35	1.99	2.81	3.94	5.51	7.68	10.68	14.79	28.10	52.80	98.10		
36	2.03	2.89	4.10	5.79	8.14	11.42	15.97	30.91	59.14	111.83		
37	2.08	2.98	4.26	6.08	8.63	12.22	17.25	34.00	66.23	127.49		
38	2.12	3.07	4.43	6.38	9.15	13.08	18.63	37.40	74.18	145.34		
39	2.16	3.16	4.61	6.70	9.70	14.00	20.12	41.15	83.08	165.69		
40	2.20	3.26	4.80	7.04	10.28	14.97	21.72	45.26	93.05	188.88		

NOTE: The numbers at the end of the last columns are not supplied because they are not needed for financial planning. It would be unrealistic to expect such high returns over long periods of time.

EXAMPLE: Enter the chart at the rate of inflation or rate of return you're using and go down the column until you intersect the row corresponding to the length of investment (years) at the left. For $1.00 invested at 10% for 5 years the future value is $1.60.

FIGURE 6-2
Inflation-Corrected Goals Achievement Schedule for a Lean and Quick Household

Your Goals Achievement Schedule

Action Paper No. 8

Name _Lean and Quick_
Date _January_

1 Goals (in Priority) From Action Paper No. 7	2 Goal Price, Current Value	3 When Desired (Years From Now)	4. Future Value Factor From Figure 6-1 (or Figure 6-3) if using annual contributions at _5_ %	5 Future Value (at _5_ %) (2) x (4)
① Emergency fund/professional certificate	$ 6,800	2	1.1	$ 7,480
② New car	10,000	5	1.3	13,000
③ Own home (20% down payment on $120,000 house)	24,000	10	1.6	38,400
④ College	28,000	12	1.8	50,400
⑤ Boutique partnership share	25,000	13	1.9	47,500
⑥ Retirement fund ($2,000 per year for 20 years)	2,000 per year (40,000 total)	20	33.1	66,200
(6a) Total Goals Current Value	$133,800	(6b) Total Goals Future Value:		$222,980
(7) Total Investable Assets (Balance Sheet items 4 + 11)	18,530			
(8) Total Annualized Surplus Income (Income Statement item 8 times factor from Figure 6-5)	51,725			
(9) Total Investable Resources, (7) + (8):	70,255	(9b) Record item (9), from left, here:		70,255
(10) Current Goal Achievement Surplus (or shortfall), (9) - (6a)	(63,545)	(10b) Future Goal Achievement Surplus (or shortfall), (9b) - (6b)		(152,725)

FIGURE 6–3

Computing the Effects of Compound Interest or Deflation on Investments Made at the End of Each Year

					Compound Sums for Equal Annual Investment						
Number of Years						Rate of Return					
	3%	4%	5%	6%	7%	8%	10%	12%	14%	16%	20%
1	1.0	1.0	1.0	1.0	1.0	1.0	1.0	1.0	1.0	1.0	1.0
2	2.0	2.0	2.0	2.1	2.1	2.1	2.1	2.1	2.1	2.2	2.2
3	3.1	3.1	3.2	3.2	3.2	3.2	3.3	3.4	3.4	3.5	3.6
4	4.2	4.2	4.3	4.4	4.4	4.5	4.6	4.8	4.9	5.1	5.4
5	5.3	5.4	5.5	5.6	5.8	5.9	6.1	6.4	6.6	6.9	7.4
6	6.5	6.6	6.8	7.0	7.2	7.3	7.7	8.1	8.5	9.0	9.9
7	7.7	7.9	8.1	8.4	8.6	8.9	9.5	10.1	10.7	11.4	12.9
8	8.9	9.1	9.5	9.9	10.2	10.6	11.4	12.3	13.2	14.2	16.5
9	10.2	10.6	11.0	11.5	12.0	12.5	13.6	14.8	16.1	17.5	20.8
10	11.5	12.0	12.6	13.2	13.8	14.5	15.9	17.5	19.3	21.3	26.0
11	12.8	13.5	14.2	15.0	15.8	16.6	18.5	20.6	23.0	25.7	32.2
12	14.2	15.0	15.9	16.9	17.9	19.0	21.4	24.1	27.3	30.8	39.6
13	15.6	16.6	17.7	18.9	20.1	21.5	24.5	28.0	32.1	36.8	48.5
14	17.1	18.3	19.6	21.0	22.6	24.2	28.0	32.4	37.6	43.7	59.2
15	18.6	20.0	21.6	23.3	25.1	27.2	31.8	37.3	43.8	51.6	72.0
16	20.2	21.8	23.6	25.7	27.9	30.3	35.9	42.7	50.9	60.8	87.4
17	21.8	23.7	25.8	28.2	30.8	33.8	40.5	48.9	59.1	71.6	105.9
18	23.4	25.6	28.1	30.9	34.0	37.4	45.6	55.7	68.3	84.0	128.1
19	25.1	27.7	30.5	33.8	37.4	41.4	51.2	63.4	78.9	98.5	154.7
20	26.9	29.8	33.1	36.8	41.0	45.8	57.3	72.0	90.9	115.2	186.7
21	28.7	32.0	35.7	40.0	44.9	50.4	64.0	81.7	104.8		
22	30.5	34.2	38.5	43.4	49.0	55.5	71.4	92.5	120.4		
23	32.4	36.6	41.4	47.0	53.4	60.9	79.5	104.6	138.3		
24	34.4	39.1	44.5	50.8	58.2	66.8	88.5	118.2	158.7		
25	36.4	41.6	47.7	54.9	63.2	73.1	98.3	133.3	181.9		
26	38.5	44.3	51.1	59.2	68.7	79.9	109.0	150.3	208.3		
27	40.7	47.1	54.7	63.7	74.5	87.4	121.0	169.4	238.5		
28	42.9	50.0	58.4	68.5	80.7	95.3	134.0	190.7	272.9		
29	45.2	53.0	62.3	73.6	87.3	104.0	149.0	214.6	312.1		
30	47.6	56.1	66.4	79.0	94.5	113.0	164.0	241.3	356.8		
31	50.0	59.3	70.8	84.8	102.1	123.3	181.9	271.3	407.7		
32	52.5	62.7	75.3	90.9	110.2	134.2	201.1	304.8	465.8		
33	55.1	66.2	80.1	97.3	118.9	146.0	222.3	342.4	532.0		
34	57.7	69.9	85.1	104.2	128.3	153.6	245.5	384.5	607.5		
35	60.5	73.7	90.3	111.4	138.2	172.3	271.0	431.7	693.6		
36	63.3	77.6	95.8	119.1	148.9	187.1	299.1	484.5	791.7		
37	66.2	81.7	101.6	127.3	160.3	203.1	330.0	543.6	903.5		
38	69.2	86.0	107.7	135.9	172.6	220.3	364.0	609.8	1031.0		
39	73.3	90.4	114.1	145.1	185.6	238.9	401.4	684.0	1176.3		
40	75.4	95.0	120.8	154.8	199.6	260.0	442.6	767.1	1342.0		

NOTE: The numbers at the end of the last columns are not supplied because they are not needed for financial planning. It would be unrealistic to expect such high returns over long periods of time.

EXAMPLE: Enter the chart at the rate of inflation or rate of return you're using and go down the column until intersecting the row corresponding to the number of years at the left. For $1.00 invested at 10% for 15 years, with $1.00 annual contributions made to the principal at the end of each year, the future value is $31.80.

to the row for 20 years. The multiplier is 33.1. Multiply that number by $2,000—the annual contribution amount. The total ($66,200) is the future value that is entered in column 5 of Action Paper No. 8.

Now take a moment to complete your own Action Paper No. 8. You are now ready to prepare the last Action Paper of your Personal Profit Plan, "Your Investment Specifications."

Analyzing Your Investment Objectives

As you learned in Chapter 2, objectives must be specific, quantified, time-bounded, results-oriented, and attainable. Your goal-getting plan must be structured to let you see and understand the differences between "an emergency fund" and a "Caribbean cruise" even though they may both cost the same and occur in the same year.

This is where Action Paper No. 9, "Your Investment Specifications," comes in. When you have completed this form, you will have a detailed description of your financial objectives. The form classifies your goals in terms of risk, return, and the amount of money required for investment today to achieve your goals tomorrow.

This form incorporates the present value concepts we discussed in Chapter 5. To understand how to complete your own form, look at Figure 6–4 which shows how our Lean and Quick couple completed their investment specifications.

Completing the Investment Specifications Worksheet
Action Paper No. 9, "Your Investment Specifications," pulls together all the work you have done so far into a coherent, workable plan of action. But before you complete your own form, follow along while we show you how our Lean and Quick couple filled out theirs. Their example will help you deal with unfamiliar ground.

You will notice that this worksheet is designed to allow for a trial-and-error approach. The actual task of adapting and adjusting your goal specifications to the limits of your resources is a repetitive procedure. Just as we do for our sample couple, you will work down and across your form using the 6% return entries as your starting point.

Those with substantial resources or modest goals may find that a single pass through the form will be adequate. However, for most people, completing the entire matrix will enable you to more fully understand your investment objectives.

First carry over the data from Figure 6–2 to complete the left panel. Turn to the Present Value Table, Figure 5–1, on page 86. The present value factor for two years at 6 percent is .890. This number is entered to the

FIGURE 6-4
Lean and Quick Investments at 6 Percent

Action Paper No. 9

Your Investment Specifications

Name *Lean and Quick*

Date *January*

From Action Paper No. 8

Item (1), Goals (In Priority)	Item (5), Future Value (at _5_ %)	Year Needed
① Emergfund/ certificate	7,480	2
② New car	13,000	5
③ Own home	38,400	10
④ College	50,400	12
⑤ Boutique	417,500	13
⑥ Retirement	2,000/year	20

Present Value of Goals for Various After-Tax Rates of Return
(Factor from Figure 5-1 or 6-5/Present Value Tables)

	High Priority, Near Term				High Priority, Long Term
	6%	8%	10%	12%	14%
High Priority, Near Term	.890/6,657				
	.747/9,711				
	.558/21,427				
	.497/25,048				
	.469/23,277				
	11.46/22,920				
Low Priority, Near Term					Low Priority, Long Term

Final Investment Objectives (Selected from left)

Present Value Sum	% Return

(A) Total Present Value of Goals: 108,040

(B) Total Investable Resources (From Action Paper No. 8, Item 9): 70,255

(C) Final Goals Achievement Surplus (or Shortfall) (B) − (A) above: (37,785)

FIGURE 6–5
Present Value of an Annuity Table for Investments Made at End of Each Year

Length of Invest-ment. (Years)	Percentage Rate of Return or of Inflation								
	3%	4%	5%	6%	7%	8%	10%	12%	14%
1	0.9708	0.9615	0.9523	0.9433	0.9345	0.9315	0.9090	0.8923	0.8771
2	1.9134	1.8860	1.8594	1.8333	1.8080	1.7832	1.7355	1.6900	1.6466
3	2.8286	2.7750	2.7232	2.6730	2.6245	2.5770	2.4868	2.4018	2.3216
4	3.7170	3.6298	2.5459	3.4651	3.3872	3.3121	3.1693	3.0373	2.9137
5	4.5797	4.4518	4.3294	4.2123	4.1001	3.9927	3.7907	3.6047	3.4330
6	5.4171	5.2421	5.0756	4.9173	4.7665	4.6228	4.3552	4.1114	3.8886
7	6.2302	6.0020	5.7863	5.5823	5.3892	5.2063	4.8684	4.5637	4.2883
8	7.0196	6.7327	6.4632	6.2107	5.9712	5.7466	5.3349	4.9676	4.6388
9	7.7861	7.4353	7.1078	6.8016	6.5152	6.2468	5.7590	5.3282	4.9473
10	8.5302	8.1108	7.7217	7.3600	7.0235	6.7100	6.1445	5.6502	5.2161
11	9.2526	8.7604	8.3064	7.8868	7.4936	7.1389	6.4950	5.9877	5.4527
12	9.9540	9.3850	9.8632	8.3838	7.9426	7.5360	6.8136	6.1943	5.6602
13	10.6349	9.9856	9.3935	8.8526	8.3576	7.9037	7.1033	6.4235	5.8423
14	11.2960	10.5631	9.8986	9.2049	8.7454	8.2442	7.3666	6.6281	6.0020
15	11.9379	11.1183	10.3796	9.7122	9.1079	8.5594	7.6057	6.8108	6.1421
16	12.5611	11.6522	10.8377	10.1058	9.4466	8.8513	7.8237	6.9739	6.2650
17	13.1661	12.1656	11.2740	10.4772	9.7632	9.1216	8.0215	7.1196	6.3728
18	13.7535	12.6592	11.6895	10.8275	10.0590	9.3718	8.2014	7.2496	6.4674
19	14.3237	13.1339	12.0853	11.1581	10.3355	9.6035	8.3649	7.3657	6.5503
20	14.8774	13.5903	12.4622	11.4699	10.5940	9.8181	8.5135	7.4694	6.6231
21	15.4150	14.0291	12.8211	11.7640	10.8355	10.0168	8.6486	7.5620	6.6869
22	15.9369	14.4511	13.1630	12.0415	11.0612	10.2007	8.7715	7.6446	6.7429
23	16.4436	14.8568	13.4885	12.3033	11.2721	10.3710	8.8832	7.7184	6.7920
24	16.9355	15.2469	13.7986	12.5503	11.4693	10.5287	8.9847	7.7842	6.8351
25	17.4131	15.6220	14.0939	12.7833	11.6535	10.6747	9.0770	7.8431	6.8729
26	17.8768	15.9827	14.3751	13.0031	11.8257	10.8099	9.1609	7.8956	6.9060
27	18.3270	16.3295	14.6430	13.2105	11.9867	10.9351	9.2372	7.9425	6.9351
28	18.7641	16.6630	14.8981	13.4061	12.1371	11.0510	9.3065	7.9844	6.9606
29	19.1884	16.9837	15.1410	13.5907	12.2776	11.1584	9.3696	8.0218	6.9830
30	19.6004	17.2920	15.3724	13.7648	12.4090	11.2577	9.4269	8.0551	7.0026
31	20.0004	17.5884	15.5928	13.9290	12.5318	11.3497	9.4790	8.0849	7.0198
32	20.3887	17.8735	15.8026	14.0840	12.6465	11.4349	9.5263	8.1115	7.0349
33	20.7657	18.1476	16.0025	14.2302	12.7537	11.5133	9.5694	8.1353	7.0482
34	21.1318	18.4111	16.1929	14.3681	12.8540	11.5861	9.6085	8.1565	7.0598
35	21.4872	18.6646	16.3741	14.4982	12.9476	11.6545	9.6441	8.1755	7.0700
36	21.8322	18.9082	16.5468	14.6209	13.0352	11.7171	9.6765	8.1924	7.0789
37	22.1672	19.1425	16.7112	14.7367	13.1170	11.7751	9.7059	8.2075	7.0868
38	22.4924	19.3678	16.8678	14.8460	13.1924	11.8288	9.7326	8.2209	7.0937
39	22.8082	19.5844	17.0170	14.9490	13.2649	11.8785	9.7569	8.2330	7.0997
40	23.1147	19.7927	17.1590	15.0462	13.3317	11.9246	9.7790	8.2437	7.1050

EXAMPLE:
Suppose you plan on investing $1,000 at the end of every year for 5 years at a compound rate of return of 6%. What is the present value of the future sum you would earn? First, find the intersection of the 6% column and the 5 year row. This present value factor is 4.21. Multiply this number by your annual investment of $1,000. The present value of this investment plan, then, would be $4,210.

left of the "slash" under the column labeled 6%, in the top row for the highest priority goal. Multiply the future goal value of $7,480 by .890 to get the present value of $6,657. That number is recorded to the right of the slash in the same column. As you continue down the column you can see how similar calculations were done for each goal.

However, goal number six, Retirement, involved annual contributions as well as compounding. To calculate the proper present value for this situation you will need to refer to Figure 6–5, the Present Value of the Annuity Table. This table should be used only if you have a goal requiring regular annual contributions.

For this computation, multiply the annual contribution (in this case $2,000) by the factor of 11.46 (20 years at 6 percent). This yielded the $22,920. That is the present value of the $66,200 goal to be received in 20 years if $2,000 is contributed annually and 6 percent is the compound investment return earned.

Next, you need to total up the numbers in the 6% column to find the present value of all your goals. In our example, the Lean and Quick couple needs $108,040 currently to reach their goals, based on a 6 percent return. Subtracting that requirement from the total investable resources they had on hand, left them with a deficit of $37,785.

Obviously an average after-tax rate of return of 6 percent would not be enough to achieve their goals on time. But the process has just begun. You would indeed be lucky if one pass through these numbers at 6 percent proved sufficient to meet your goals!

As you can see, the next rate of return is 8 percent. In Figure 6–6, we have detailed the present value numbers for each goal assuming an 8 percent rate of return. You may want to double check your understanding of these calculations by working through the numbers in the example to see if you arrive at the same totals.

Once again you will note, however, that our Lean and Quick couple's total investable resources fall short of the needed amount. Though this time they are short much less, $19,895 versus $37,785, that is still a substantial sum in relation to their investable resources.

The figures for 10 percent are shown in Figure 6–7. At this rate of return our Lean and Quick couple fall short only $5,690. When you take into consideration that the entire process is subject to a certain degree of inaccuracy, this shortfall is easily within a standard margin of error (in the estimates made and the vagaries of a changing economy).

However, our Lean and Quick couple should not yet assume that their goals are assured. Even if they could structure their investment portfolio to earn a bit over 10 percent, the higher return usually carries more risk. It would be more prudent to accept a lower return and higher initial invest-

FIGURE 6-6
Lean and Quick Investments at 8 Percent

Action Paper No. 9

Your Investment Specifications

Name _Lean and Quick_   Date _January_

Item (1), Goals (in Priority)	Item (5), Future Value (at _5_%)	Year Needed	Present Value of Goals for Various After-Tax Rates of Return (Factor from Figure 5-1 or 6-5/Present Value Tables)					Final Investment Objectives (Selected from left)	
			High Priority, Near Term 6%	8%	10%	12%	High Priority, Long Term 14%	Present Value Sum	% Return
① Emergency fund/certificate	7,480	2	.890/6,657	.857/6,410					
② New car	13,000	5	.747/9,711	.681/8,853					
③ Own home	38,400	10	.558/21,427	.463/17,779					
④ College	50,400	12	.497/25,048	.397/20,008					
⑤ Boutique	417,500	13	.469/22,277	.368/17,480					
⑥ Retirement	2,000/year	20	11.46/22,920	931/19,620					
			Low Priority, Near Term				Low Priority, Long Term		

(A) Total Present Value of Goals: 108,040 90,150

(B) Total Investable Resources (From Action Paper No. 8, Item 9): 70,255 70,255

(C) Final Goals Achievement Surplus (or Shortfall) (B) − (A) above: (37,785) (19,895)

FIGURE 6–7

Lean and Quick Investments at 10 Percent

Action Paper No. 9

Your Investment Specifications

Name _Lean and Quick_   Date _January_

From Action Paper No. 8

Item (1), Goals (in Priority)	Item (5), Future Value (at _5_%)	Year Needed
① Emergency fund/certificate	7,480	2
② New car	13,000	5
③ Own home	38,400	10
④ College	50,400	12
⑤ Boutique	47,500	13
⑥ Retirement	2,000/year	20

Present Value of Goals for Various After-Tax Rates of Return
(Factor from Figure 5-1 or 6-5/Present Value Tables)

	6% High Priority, Near Term	8%	10%	12%	14% High Priority, Long Term
	.890/6,657	.857/6,410	.826/6,178		
	.747/9,711	.681/8,853	.621/8,073		
	.558/21,427	.463/17,779	.386/14,822		
	.497/25,048	.397/20,008	.319/16,077		
	.469/22,277	.368/17,480	.290/13,775		
	11.476/22,920	9.81/19,620	8.51/17,020		

Low Priority, Near Term   Low Priority, Long Term

(A) Total Present Value of Goals: 108,040 | 90,150 | 75,945

(B) Total Investable Resources (From Action Paper No. 8, Item 9): 70,255 | 70,255 | 70,255

(C) Final Goals Achievement Surplus (or Shortfall) (B) – (A) above: (37,785) | (19,895) | (5,690)

Final Investment Objectives (Selected from left)

Present Value Sum	% Return

ment for the more important goals. For their lower-priority goals, they could try for a higher return with lower initial investments. The important thing to remember is that our sample couple needs only an *average* return of 10 percent, not necessarily 10 percent for everything.

Targeting Higher Returns

Note Figure 6–8 where we have filled in the numbers for more aggressive rates of return: 12 percent and 14 percent. At these levels, the numbers in our example show strong surpluses. While it would not be prudent for our Lean and Quicksters to expect to achieve these high returns consistently with all their funds, these numbers do serve an important role. Note that at each corner of the center grid, there are labels which draw a kind of map of the possible ways the goals can be achieved.

For example, at the upper left are the high priority, near-term goals for which our Lean and Quick couple would not want to take much risk to achieve. At the lower right are the low-priority, long-term goals which will require greater risks to obtain. The overall mix of risk and return that is right for our Lean and Quick couple—as for most people—will lie somewhere between these two extremes.

Optimizing Your Investment Objectives

Once you have completed all the calculations for achieving your goals at the various rates of return, so your Action Paper No. 9 looks like Figure 6–8, you are ready to move to the final step of designing your investment program. This entails selecting and verifying the final investment objectives that will meet your goal-getting desires and risk-taking styles.

First divide your goals into two groups: 1) the highest priority, near-term goals that require little risk taking, and 2) the long-term, lower priority goals that allow for a higher risk.

Our sample couple judged that their two highest priority goals, the emergency fund/professional certificate and the new car, were too important to take any risks. These goals are circled in Figure 6–9. They are then entered on the panel to the right, Final Investment Objectives. The total of the first group's required present value was $16,368 ($6,657 plus $9,711) to be invested at a 6 percent rate of return.

The balance of this couple's goals fell into group two (low priority, long term). Since, as we have seen, 10 percent was too low an overall return for achieving the portfolio's goals and the initial goals were already committed to an even lower rate of return, the most logical target rate of return from those we have calculated would be 12 percent. Note that these four goals have been circled under the 12 percent column in Figure 6–9.

The present values were then entered on the panel to the right. The to-

FIGURE 6-8
Lean and Quick Investments at 12 Percent and 14 Percent

Action Paper No. 9

Your Investment Specifications

Name: *Lean and Quick* Date *January*

From Action Paper No. 8			Present Value of Goals for Various After-Tax Rates of Return (Factor from Figure 5-1 or 6-5/Present Value Tables)					Final Investment Objectives (Selected from left)	
Item (1), Goals (in Priority)	Item (5), Future Value (at 5%)	Year Needed	High Priority, Near Term / High Priority, Long Term 6%	8%	10%	12%	14%	Present Value Sum	% Return
① Emergency fund/ certificate	7,480	2	.890/6,657	.857/6,410	.826/6,178	.797/5,961	.769/5,752		
② New car	13,000	5	.747/9,711	.681/8,853	.621/8,073	.567/7,371	.519/6,747		
③ Own home	38,400	10	.558/21,427	.463/17,779	.386/14,822	.322/12,364	.270/10,368		
④ College	50,400	12	.497/25,048	.397/20,008	.319/16,077	.257/12,952	.208/10,483		
⑤ Boutique	47,500	13	.469/22,277	.368/17,480	.290/13,775	.229/10,877	.182/8,645		
⑥ Retirement	2,000/year	20	11.44/22,920	9.81/19,620	8.51/17,020	7.46/14,920	6.62/13,240		

Low Priority, Near Term / Low Priority, Long Term

	6%	8%	10%	12%	14%
(A) Total Present Value of Goals:	108,040	90,150	75,945	64,445	55,235
(B) Total Investable Resources (From Action Paper No. 8, Item 9):	70,255	70,255	70,255	70,255	70,255
(C) Final Goals Achievement Surplus (or Shortfall) (B) − (A) above:	(37,785)	(19,895)	(5,690)	5,810	15,020

Action Paper No. 9

Your Investment Specifications

Name *Lean and Quick*   Date *January*

From Action Paper No. 8

Item (1), Goals (in Priority)	Item (5), Future Value (at 5%)	Year Needed
① Emergency fund certificate	7,480	2
② New car	13,000	5
③ Own home	38,400	10
④ College	50,400	12
⑤ Boutique	47,500	13
⑥ Retirement	2,000/year	20

Present Value of Goals for Various After-Tax Rates of Return
(Factor from Figure 5-1 or 6-5/Present Value Tables)

	High Priority, Near Term 6%	8%	10%	12%	High Priority, Long Term 14%
	.890/6,657	.857/6,410	.826/6,178	.797/5,961	.769/5,752
	.747/9,711	.681/8,853	.621/8,073	.567/7,371	.519/6,747
	.558/21,427	.463/17,799	.386/14,822	.322/12,369	.270/10,368
	.497/25,048	.397/20,008	.319/16,078	.257/12,952	.208/10,483
	.469/22,277	.368/17,480	.290/13,775	.229/10,877	.182/8,645
	11.46/22,920	9.81/19,620	8.51/17,020	7.46/14,920	6.62/13,240
	Low Priority, Near Term				Low Priority, Long Term
(A) Total Present Value of Goals:	108,040	90,150	75,945	64,445	55,235
(B) Total Investable Resources (From Action Paper No. 8, Item 9):	70,255	70,255	70,255	70,255	70,255
(C) Final Goals Achievement Surplus (or Shortfall) (B) − (A) above:	37,785	19,895	(5,690)	5,810	15,020

Final Investment Objectives (Selected from left)

Present Value Sum	% Return
6,657	6
9,711	6
12,364	12
12,952	12
10,877	12
14,920	12
67,481	
70,255	
2774	

tal for the second group's required present value was $51,113. The total present value required for both groups was $67,481. Since our Lean and Quick couple had previously determined that they had $70,255 in investable resources, this arrangement left them with an anticipated surplus of $2,774.

Matching Your Objectives with Specific Investments

If you have filled out Action Paper No. 9, "Your Investment Specifications," along with our example, you have completed a major part of your Personal Profit Plan. But there is still one last element. You will need to match your risk/return and present value objectives with specific investment instruments that will do the job you have in mind. To do this effectively, you will need to gain at least a little knowledge of investment vehicles and markets.

You may want to refer to another book in this series, *How to Be a Successful Investor*, for more complete information about detailed investment planning. Here, we can only suggest a general strategy.

Cash Equivalent Investments

Cash equivalents are liquid, short-term (maturing in less than one year) investments. Examples include passbook and time deposit accounts at banks or thrift institutions, money market mutual funds, and short-term paper issued by corporations, commercial paper, or by the Treasury Department, Treasury Bills.

If you have limited cash or inadequate time to work on improving the return on your investments, cash equivalents may be your most suitable avenue. You can buy these instruments from your local bank, savings and loan, or from a full service brokerage firm.

Stock, Bond, and Mutual Fund Investments

Stocks represent ownership shares in corporations manufacturing goods or performing services. Bonds are loans to companies or government entities at fixed interest rates for specified time periods (maturities). Mutual funds are professionally managed pools of individual investor monies that invest in stocks, bonds, and other investment vehicles. When you buy shares in a mutual fund, you are buying a proportionate share of the fund's investment portfolio.

If you have $5,000 to $10,000 to invest, you may want to add capital market vehicles to your portfolio. These investments offer not only diversification, but also higher real returns. At the same time, they are subject to more volatile price swings. They lose as well as add dollars to your portfolio.

If you are adequately capitalized, this drawback is outweighed by their diversification value and appreciation potential.

You should consider combining your goals and pooling your resources to obtain the minimum amount recommended for these investments in order to take advantage of these valuable features. Returns of 8 percent to 12 percent are not uncommon for a well-designed stock and bond portfolio.

Real Estate Investments

Owning your own home has long been an important part of the American dream. You can buy land through direct ownership, partnership interests, or owning shares of a Real Estate Investment Trust (REIT) to name a few of the most common ways.

If you have a reasonable surplus of investable funds over and above your fixed dollar and capital market assets, you should consider investing in real estate. Real estate investing is, however, a long-term proposition. Don't plan on quick in-and-out trading here.

Minimum investments in limited partnerships are typically fairly high: $5,000 to $10,000. If you can wait the 6 to 10 years necessary for most of these programs to mature, you can often expect to receive a payback of 9 percent to 12 percent per year on your investment.

High-Flying Speculations

While it is possible to earn more than 14 percent per year on your investments, those returns are more in the realm of professional speculation than personal money management. And it should be noted that most professional investors fall short of those returns over a long period of time. Few managers outperform the stock market average of about 10 percent per annum. The part-time investor would be well-advised to heed the gambler's warning, "Never bet more than you are prepared to lose!" Amateur speculators often pay another nonmonetary price: sleepless nights and increased stress.

Make no mistake: targeting your investment objectives is more an art than a science. All the mathematical tables and techniques you have learned here can only serve to improve your odds of success. They are not a guarantee of success in themselves.

As you progress through life, many factors will cause you to revise your numbers—and even your goals. Inflation may be more or less than you expected. That will change the present value requirements of your investments. On a more positive note, your income will probably rise faster than inflation, giving you more investable resources than you had expected.

For these and other reasons you will want to *control* your goal-getting plan with the same degree of care you used to create it.

IMPLEMENTING YOUR PERSONAL PROFIT PLAN

In Chapter 4 we touched on the importance of spending in making your Personal Profit Plan workable. We delineated the different types of spenders and how they work together. In understanding the dynamics of household financial affairs, it is important to adopt a system that allows for varying individual spending motivations and styles, while still maintaining control.

You have already spent hours completing forms and working out details of a financial plan that is individually tailored for you. But all that work, all that time, and all that effort will go to waste if you fail to develop and use a system to organize and track your household's financial affairs.

Resourcing is our term for the day-to-day cash management program that is the vital link between your goal-setting and goal-getting. In the balance of this book we will outline a plan for allocating, spending, and controlling your financial resources. As you will see, it is a step beyond traditional budgeting methods.

Resourcing Your Financial Choices

In Chapter 4 you learned about your household spending type. With so many different personal spending styles and alternative household spending types, no single Resourcing System can be right for everyone. More careful spenders want orderly plans and records. But these bookkeeping systems tend to drive their more impetuous partners crazy. On the other hand, impetuous spenders tend to make their more methodical partners very nervous. And you should realize by now that if you have problems on the day-to-day level of finances, it will be next to impossible to follow the discipline necessary to carry out your Personal Profit Plan.

While keeping track of your financial affairs is important to the success of your plan, don't become so future oriented and overly methodical that you sacrifice your current quality of life. All planning and no doing *can* make Jack and Jill a dull couple!

To allow individuals to enjoy their natural spending style while accommodating the styles of their partners and their households, we have developed the menus of Resourcing techniques shown in Figure 6–10. While at first glance the chart may appear overwhelming, you will only be concerned with the one or two squares in which you and your partner's personal spending styles intersect with your household spending type.

For example, if your household is Collaborative, and your spending style is Active while your partner's is Impulsive, you will be concerned only with the second and last squares under the Collaborative column. To interpret the shorthand notes, use the following explanations.

FIGURE 6–10
Finding the Resourcing System that's Right for You

Household Spending Type

		Competitive	*Compromising*	*Collaborative*

Personal Spending Style	*Assertive*	**A -** Binder
		B - Flexible
		C - Negotiate
		D - Written
		  Round table
		E - Fun fund
		  Fixed rewards
			A - Binder
			B - Flexible
			C - Delegate
			D - Round table
			E - Fun fund
			  Mad money
			  Fixed rewards
				A - Binder
				B - Flexible
				C - Share
				D - Written
				  Round table
				E - Fun fund

	Active	**A -** Jar
		B - Intuitive
		C - Negotiate or
		  mediate
		D - Sources and
		  uses
		E - Resourcing party
		  Mad money
			A - Jar
			B - Intuitive
			C - Negotiate
			D - Sources and
			  uses
			  Round table
			  Fireside chats
			E - Resourcing party
			  Mad money
				A - Jar
				B - Cash code
				C - Delegate
				D - Sources and
				  uses
				E - Resourcing party
				  Fun fund

	Protective	**A -** Binder
		B - Fail-Safe
		C - Negotiate or
		  delegate
		D - Written
		  Round table
		E - Fun fund
		  Fixed rewards
			A - Binder
			B - Fail-Safe
			C - Delegate
			D - Round table
			E - Fun fund
			  Fixed rewards
				A - Binder
				B - Fail-Safe
				C - Share
				D - Written
				  Round table
				  Fireside chats
				E - Fun fund
				  Fixed rewards

	Impulsive	**A -** Jar
		B - Intuitive or
		  cash code
		C - Negotiate or
		  delegate
		D - Sources and
		  uses
		  Fireside chats
		E - Fixed rewards
		  Resourcing party
			A - Jar
			B - Cash code
			C - Negotiate
			D - Sources and
			  uses
			E - Fixed rewards
			  Resourcing party
				A - Jar
				B - Cash code
				C - Delegate
				D - Sources and
				  uses
				  Fireside chants
				E - Fixed rewards
				  Resourcing party

Key:
A - Basic *method of accounting* for your system
B - *Recommended options* to that system
C - Basic ways to *implement* that system
D - Basic ways to *communicate* about the system
E - Basic menu of *incentives* for participation

Entry A: The Basic Resourcing System

The first entry in each box of the chart tells you which of the two basic Resourcing systems works better for the personal spending style in that particular household. Detailed descriptions of the Resource Binder system can be found in End Paper No. 1 at the end of this book. The Resource Jar system is described in End Paper No. 2. Here is a brief description of each system:

1. *Resource Binder system.* This system of resource accounting is closest to the traditional budgeting method. However, there is an important difference: it uses a loose-leaf binder and special ledgers you develop yourself as a means for recording and controlling your family's spending.

In the next section we outline the two options available to the basic system depending on the degree of control you require. This method satisfies the careful spender's instinct for order, documentation, and numerical detail.

2. *Resource Jar system.* This method works on the principle of physically separating the money you use for different important purposes. It relies primarily on the checking and savings accounts and statements you already have. It puts minimum demands for paperwork on the more impetuous spenders. Basically, with this method you put money into separate accounts ("jars") that have been set aside for specific spending purposes. You then draw on them as required.

You can never accidentally or impetuously spend yourself into trouble since your important special purpose jars are physically different from your general purpose fund. There are also two different variations for the Jar method that are described in the next section.

Entry B: Variations on the Basic System

Since there is more than one kind of careful or impetuous spender, no one version of either the Resource Binder or Resource Jar system is sufficient. We have developed two variations on *both* methods that give you considerable latitude in customizing the basic system to your needs.

1. For the Resource Binder method: The *Flexible* system allows you to carry over surplus or deficit amounts according to your own needs and tolerance for accuracy. The *Fail-Safe* system automatically prevents you from spending more than you have allotted to any particular purpose.

2. For the Resource Jar method: The *Intuitive* approach gives you maximum freedom in using your Resource Jars. The *Cash Code* approach complements the Intuitive system with a means for identifying tax deductions or other special expenditures you want to keep track of.

Entry C: The Ways to Implement Your System

Too often, great sounding money management systems are never used because the intended user is never told how to make them work! Here are a few ways we have used to adapt our systems to the different household spending types.

1. *Negotiation method.* When the household type is highly competitive, try to begin with a negotiated distribution of Resourcing responsibilities (record keeping, etc.) and spending prerogatives. If partners are too strongly committed to their own spending styles, consider using an outside mediator such as a financial planner, accountant, or other financial or family counseling professional.

2. *Delegation method.* If your household works well by compromising, delegate responsibilities for general spending areas. With this method, partners assume responsibility for certain critical spending without continually having to ask permission or seek the concurrence of the other partners.

3. *Shared-decision method.* If your household collaborates well on financial decisions, encourage full participation of both (or all) partners in all major financial decisions. In practice, implementation of all Resourcing systems eventually gravitates toward the Shared-Decision model.

Entry D: The Ways to Communicate About Your System

Planning for any purpose is useless unless you also control its progress. All control eventually comes down to clear communication, either written or spoken. Here are four basic methods for communicating about your system.

1. *Written summary.* If you select the Resource Binder system, the most obvious way to communicate the progress of your plan is to review your records. The Action Papers that accompany End Paper No. 1 will give you the forms you need to summarize your spending and to detect any variances to your plan.

2. *Round Table format.* All households get together once in awhile to transact domestic business. The way that meeting is held can make a considerable difference in its success or failure. The Round Table family meeting is specifically intended for families that use the Resource Binder.

3. *Sources and Uses Review.* This method is suitable for families who use the Resource Jar system. At selected intervals you and your partner reconstruct the success of your Resource Jar accounts. You decide on the new resources each will need to keep your household moving along in the intended direction. End Paper No. 3, at the end of this book, offers a full description of this method.

4. *Fireside Chats.* In order for these chats to work, the atmosphere must be conducive to free give and take. A nonthreatening, low tension environment is required. The last section of End Paper No. 4 delineates the keys to making Fireside Chats work successfully.

Entry E: The Incentives that Will Make Your System Work

Everyone experiences unexpected rough spots in their financial affairs. If your Resourcing system is going to work, there must be some sort of incentives to keep you and your partner on track. Here are a few ideas we have found successful.

   1. *Create a Fun Fund for your household.* Overly protective, security-minded spenders sometimes overlook the more fun aspects of a healthy financial physique. It is a good idea to set aside some money for no other purpose than to reward the household members for their money management efforts. Set it up as a separate account in your Resource Binder.

   2. *Give your more impetuous spenders their own Mad Money jars.* If your household is not Collaborative and you use the Resource Jar approach, you may find Mad Money jars indispensable for keeping everyone happy and working together for common goals. These special jars allow each spender to have his or her own source of money for the things that matter most to them.

   3. *Give yourself a menu of predictable Fixed Rewards.* It is asking too much of most people to expect change for purely altruistic reasons. But you can tempt even the most anxious and doubtful spenders with a well-designed menu of rewards in exchange for their Resourcing participation. End Paper No. 5, at the back of the book, lists some typical Resourcing rewards.

Coping with Change

Regardless of how carefully you create your Personal Profit Plan and Resourcing System, change will occur. You will have to periodically reassess your wants and needs. There is a good chance that at some point you will want to reorder your priorities. The following procedure should help you at those times.

   1. *Reevaluate your "Sacred" assets.* Your list of marketable assets may have changed along with your changing values. A family home, heirlooms, and other possessions of high emotional value may have become more or less important. Make sure your new financial starting point reflects these new realities.

   2. *Reassess your top priorities.* It is often difficult to convince yourself that a brand new want is really more important than a goal you have been pursuing for years. Also the future sometimes brings with it new partners to a decision—people whose values and needs may differ from your own. When these types of complications occur, it is best to reevaluate your priorities from the "bottom up."

Rather than trying to decide what is most important, approach your list of goals from the opposite direction. Determine which goals are least important first. If you are still torn between two equally critical goals, try to establish their relative value by stating just what you are willing to give up to achieve each of them.

For example, you might rank buying a new car and replacing worn-out furniture about equally. But if you ask, "Which of these would I give up in order to preserve my membership in the local tennis club?", the answer might come quickly.

3. *Redefine your tolerance for risk.* More disposable income usually brings with it a higher tolerance for investment risk. This is simply because any assets lost can be more easily replaced. As your lifetime earnings grow, continually reevaluate how much security you can trade in the quest for bigger, faster payoffs.

4. *Take a value-added approach to career and income planning.* When presented with a new career or investment opportunity, ask, "How much *value* does this new opportunity add to my Personal Profit Plan?" If you really need more liquidity to achieve your goals, a promotion having the major compensation of building wealth (e.g., illiquid or undiversified company shares) may actually undermine your career and life goals.

When in doubt about your plan's relevance or success, it is a good idea to work through the goal-setting and goal-getting process again. We recommend a periodic review of all your needs and wants whenever there is a significant change in your career and life situation. Remember, money is only a tool. Personal Profit Planning is the process by which that tool is used to gain and keep a more rewarding life.

Wrapping Up

In this chapter you have gone from the general to the very specific. You now know whether your initial goals were overly ambitious, given your financial starting point. You also have a good idea of what investment rate of return you will need to achieve the goals you have established.

While it is all well and good to work out a detailed financial plan—learning about yourself, your partner, setting goals and even devising a program for getting those goals—too many people fail to take care of the vital day-to-day financial matters that ultimately determine the success of their more grandiose financial plans. You do not have to be saddled with a static home budget to control your finances.

The problem with most budgets is that they do not allow for the wide variances in spending types and styles that characterize individuals and households. If you take the time to structure a Resourcing system that is compatible with family members, you can get control of the *micro-level* of your financial affairs. Once you have that in hand, you can move on to structuring an investment portfolio.

The Personal Profit Plan you have created as you followed through this book is a flexible, workable program for achieving those things in life which you value the most. While you have incorporated methods for keeping close tabs on your finances, do not confuse control with the constraint that many financial plans and budgeting systems imply.

The key is *your* happiness and fulfillment, not the orderly completion of a predefined task. Success comes from an inner psychological satisfaction for you and your partner. It is not accurately measured by numbers or possessions.

CHAPTER 7

WORKING WITH FINANCIAL PROFESSIONALS

CREATING YOUR PERSONAL PROFIT PLAN

In Chapter 6 you saw how the concept of the time value of money applies to you personally. Understanding and knowing how to work with the future and present value of money enabled you to determine your investment specifications. Up to this point you may have been able to complete all the worksheets and questionnaires without having to consult a financial professional. However, unless you have investment experience, you may now want to consider contacting an expert to zero in on the type of investment vehicles you should use to fulfill your plan. You may want advice about the tax consequences of certain actions. You may want to know the best legal structure for pursuing your dream. Most people require professional advice at some point in varying degrees. In this chapter, we provide you with guidelines on, first, selecting professional help and, second, on making the most of it.

In Chapter 4 you learned about different ways that families make decisions. We detailed a number of effective techniques for breaking down communication barriers. Responsive, effective communication among the members of your household is vital to financial calm.

In this chapter we take a look at the types of outside advice you may require. Depending on your experience, this may range from no more than reading additional independent works, such as the other books in this series, financial periodicals like *The Wall Street Journal, Investor's Daily, Business Week, Forbes, Money, Changing Times,* or others.

Going "solo" with your financial planning has some advantages. Among them is speed. If you devoted full time to the effort, you could probably complete the planning work in only a few days or at the most, a few weeks. If you are single, or you and your spouse agree on financial matters, going solo will present few conflicts. And of course, there is that "psychic profit" that we all savor—personal satisfaction from accomplishing a difficult task.

But most people will need to work personally with a financial professional in some capacity. Even after you have completed the pre-planning (getting to know yourself) and the goal-setting (defining where you want to go) phases, there is still the goal-getting phase. You have the specific numbers in dollars and cents that constitute your financial goals. You still need to identify the investment vehicles that are needed to meet each of those goals.

A Cooperative Effort

At this point, you may begin to encounter some of the disadvantages of "soloing." Unless you have made the decision to pursue a career in financial planning or investments, your goal-getting skills will be limited. Your desire to put your financial affairs in order indicates that you have achieved some professional success. Unfortunately, that success does not necessarily constitute knowledge in the specialized area of investments.

By now, you have discovered your financial physique, your spending habits and motivations, your risk-taking quotient, and your household spending type. You are becoming aware of your strengths and weaknesses as a financial decision maker. And you have some idea of how to improve your financial fitness.

But financial well-being is more than self-awareness. Many people simply lack the day-to-day money management skills, such as knowing how to borrow intelligently, that are crucial to long-term success. Even the financial statements sent by stock brokerage firms may seem like hieroglyphics. But those aren't the only problems facing a budding money manager.

Today's financial markets are undergoing revolutionary changes. New investment vehicles are constantly being developed. These innovations are often hyped as "the greatest thing since sliced bread." Many, if not most of them, prove more notable for the hype surrounding them than for their value to the average investor!

However, some innovations, such as money market funds, allow the average investor to obtain yields on short-term savings that previously were available only to the very wealthy. But how can you separate the sensible from the nonsensical, the useful from the useless, the productive from the destructive? What alternatives do you have?

Your first inclination may be to hire a professional advisor. However, that may put a considerable dent in your investable resources. Before taking that step (and of course it may still be appropriate), check into ways to improve your skills without having to become a full-time professional.

Self-Help for the Personal Profit Planner

There are many things you can and should do to help yourself manage your financial affairs. An important first step is to develop your own career and life goals as you've done in Chapters 2 and 3. Sad to say, most financial advisors are ill-equipped to help you in this regard. Doing it yourself before meeting with your advisor will save you money and grief.

Develop your own record keeping and cash management systems. Remember, *you*, not your advisor, have to deal with them every day. Elaborate commercial systems that are promoted as being necessary and comprehensive may actually be unwieldy for a household budget. Be sure your system suits *your* needs. Don't make the mistake of trying to force fit your style into a prepackaged program. That will only result in your not following through with important tasks.

Above all, learn to shop intelligently for your own financial products—investments, insurance, and tax shelters—before relying on the advice of financial salespeople. Here are some ways you can help yourself in these and other areas.

Consumer Publications
There are many self-help guides on the market for personal financial planning—but beware. Financial "journalists" can only write about other people's methods. Few have the kind of hands-on money management experience they need to coach you through the entire financial planning process. Media gurus and money columnists may be very entertaining to read, but you wouldn't want to trust them with your checkbook.

Magazines that regularly feature articles on financial planning matters include *Money, Changing Times, Sylvia Porter's Personal Finance, Personal Investor*, and *Forbes*. Every issue of *Business Week* includes timely investment tips in its "Personal Business" section. *The Wall Street Journal*, in its "Money Matters" column, and *Investor's Daily*, in its "Investor's Corner" column, feature tutorial pieces on various aspects of the financial scene.

Numerous newsletters are devoted to investing and financial planning. These range from "tip sheets"—which tout their recommendations on the best stocks, options, or futures contracts to buy or sell—to full-fledged research reports on the financial markets. There is even a newsletter that claims to design and monitor individual portfolios for its subscribers.

Newsletter advisory prices range from about $30 per year to over $1,000. Unfortunately, price is not a good guide to performance or value in this industry. Keep the following guidelines in mind:

1. *Make sure the newsletter fits your financial physique.* It doesn't make any sense to spend $1,000 for a newsletter to advise you on a $5,000 portfolio. Since the very best money managers historically add only 3 to 6 percent to the normal market rate of return, you should pay no more than 1 or 2 percent of your portfolio for advice about how to manage it.

2. *Find a newsletter that takes a multi-asset approach.* Most newsletters tend to specialize in only stocks, bonds, futures, real estate, and so on. Since one of the most important uses of their information is to help you determine new allocations among the various asset classes, the ideal letter(s) will address how your portfolio should be divided up.

The authors of this book produce a monthly newsletter that features a multi-asset approach. For a sample copy and subscription information, write us at 2755 Campus Drive, San Mateo, CA 94403.

3. *Review the newsletter before you subscribe to it.* Most newsletters will send you a sample copy or offer a low-priced trial subscription. The Select Information Exchange (2095 Broadway, New York, NY 10023) offers low-priced packages of trial subscriptions to many financial advisories. It is important to find a newsletter that feels right to you. As we have said before, what works for one person may not work for another.

Finding the right combination of general information, technical advice, raw data, and price will take some testing. If you elect the newsletter route, don't become enamored with wild-eyed advertising claims of near infallibility. If sommeone was really 90 percent accurate, they could soon absorb all the financial market's resources. Use the newsletters and other sources of information as inputs to your individualized Personal Profit Plan, not as substitutes for your carefully conceived strategy.

Public Education Programs
Community colleges and university extension schools frequently offer courses in financial planning and personal money management. Many of these programs—we know from our own experience as textbook authors—are very good. However, just as with newsletters and financial journalism, you still need to take a cautious approach to these courses.

None of the personal money management textbooks is really designed to be self-instructional. They are intended for use in the classroom. Naturally, the caliber of the instructor is very important. Be sure the instructor has both counseling skills and technical skills. Both skills are important ingredients if you expect to get much help from these courses.

Private Seminars
Many financial consultants and financial planning practitioners sponsor money management seminars. Often they charge very high fees. As with the price of newsletters, don't be swayed by price alone. High prices do not guarantee high quality or even good value.

In the late 1970s and early 1980s, there was a flood of seminars by self-proclaimed financial gurus on how to build riches with little effort and time. Many claimed to teach attendees how to build their fortunes in real estate with no money. If only it were so easy! By the late 1980s many of these "gurus" had themselves filed bankruptcy. Remember, if it sounds too good to be true, it probably is!

This is not to say that there are no good programs. Seminars can be a convenient way to motivate you to get on the right track. Just be sure you are not paying hard-earned dollars to hear a carefully crafted sales pitch for follow-on financial services. Take a close look at the training material and the sponsor. Before you pay any fees, make sure that the wealth that is increased is your own!

No matter which route you take—publications, seminars, or consultants—look for those which stress skill training over simple information passing. You are familiar with the old adage that it is far better to teach a man to fish than to just give him a fish. This maxim applies equally well to financial matters. If you steadily strengthen your skills, you won't be at a total loss if you lose your advisor for any reason.

Using Professional Advice: When to Seek Help

Even the best newsletter, textbook, instructor, or seminar can't train you to handle every contingency. Many people have to consult a professional advisor at some point during their financial planning program. Problems and questions about taxes, legal snafus, or special investment opportunities often require professional assistance.

In fact, regardless of your planning skills, you will still need to depend on other people occasionally for your ultimate financial well-being. Even professional financial planners use CPAs or tax attorneys for knotty tax problems. In complicated special investment deals, the planner and the investor are often best served by obtaining an independent legal opinion.

These partners to your financial future can be *advisors* or *executors*. Advisors suggest what should be done. Executors do what needs to be done. There are some people who do both—give advice and help carry it out. For example, a lawyer who advises you on financial matters while executing transaction paperwork, or a CPA who counsels you about next year's taxes while preparing this year's return are performing both duties.

Where to Seek Professional Help: Whom Can You Trust?

Once you decide to seek professional advice, you must then locate the proper help. You should be aware of the important difference between *fee-based* and *commissioned* advisors. Each offers a smorgasbord of financial products and services from personal counseling to transaction expertise.

Financial planning is a personal skill based on technical training and expertise. Like a pilot or physician, the planner must master certain technical subjects and apply them to real-life situations. This distinction is important. Theoretical solutions often do not measure up in real-life dilemmas.

And as with professional counselors in every field, the planner's way of dealing with a client is often as important as the advice itself. The best answers will draw on the client's resources and solutions as well as the planner's. Although financial planning is a skill that can be learned and practiced privately or professionally, it can't be vended in a supermarket atmosphere. Each plan and each solution must be tailored to the unique circumstances of each individual client or household. Pre-packaged plans miss the whole point of *Personal* Profit Planning!

Beware of Commissions. Most of the so-called financial planners you will meet work on a commission basis. They provide advice essentially for free or at a nominal cost. They earn their money from the commissions charged on transactions you make with them. These financial product and service agents offering both advice and services are really glorified salespeople. They may work for insurance companies, banks, or other financial institutions.

Because of this method of compensation for their services, they are usually more interested in making a sale than in dispensing objective advice. Sometimes that advice is no more than a subtle promotion for the product or service that nets *them*, not you, the highest return. Although many of these advisors may be well-educated and connected with brand-name institutions, they usually rely on volume rather than excellence for their income.

If your advisor offers products instead of strategies when you talk about your goals, it may be time to run—not walk—to the nearest exit. Be sure the "objective" advice you get is really objective. *Distinguish the products you buy from the intermediaries who bring them to you.*

Low Cost: Is It Really Such a Deal? While we have noted above that a high price doesn't necessarily ensure high-quality advice in newsletters, you should also be aware of the dangers of seeking out low-budget advisors. Unfortunately, here you often do get what you paid for—very little! Many of these advisors have good intentions and recent academic degrees or job training, but few, if any, are qualified to guide you through the entire financial planning and money management maze.

Advisors with advanced academic degrees may be inexperienced. That is why they cannot yet command high fees. Those with more practical experience are often technically unqualified. And most important, none is proficient in *all* the areas (law, taxes, finance, etc.) required of most financial plans.

Even if you do find a low-cost, technically qualified, and experienced manager, he or she will likely be unskilled as a personal counselor. Quality financial planning is still more art than science. *It is a goal-driven, not a product- or method-driven, activity.*

The High Cost of Fee-Based Advisors.   Truly objective advice requires not only education and experience but counseling skills as well. Fee-
based advisors such as physicians and attorneys, render services according
to a schedule of fees, rather than commissions. Fee-based advisors usually
work in multidisciplinary teams of specialists rather than as individual practitioners. These teams typically feature a balance of quantitative experts (the
people who do the computer analysis) and seasoned advisors (people who
know when to look past the numbers and make subjective judgments).

Most important, the planner who heads your team will be adept at personal counseling. This person will talk you through the various approaches
you need to explore, and help you define your true wants and needs. For
these reasons, fee-based financial planners are often as expensive as top-
flight doctors and lawyers. Indeed, these very professionals are often the clients of such advisors.

Most fee-based financial planners have minimum fees. It certainly
doesn't make sense to hire an advisor for fees that run to 10 percent or
more of your portfolio. A good rule of thumb is to pay no more than 1 or 2
percent of your portfolio's value for a professional advisor.

For smaller portfolios there are many different alternatives. Using no-
load (no upfront commission for buying or selling) mutual funds is a low
cost way to secure professional management of the investment end of your
financial plan. Using independent newsletter advisories can be much less expensive. Just remember that it doesn't make sense to pay more in fees to an
advisor than the value that advisor can add to your plan.

If professional planning is cost-effective for your situation (typically
$500,000 or more in investable resources), select your advisor as you
would a physician for medical consultation or a lawyer for important litiga-
tion. Check the company's reputation with local financial institutions. Ask to
see a list of client references. Choose your own candidates from the list—
don't accept the first or only name that is offered. (Of course, firms often
treat their clients confidentially and, therefore, no references can be offered.)

Be sure to check the mix of specialists and generalists available for your
account. You will need both for a quality plan. Evaluate the reasonableness
of fees for the services offered. Shop around. Check with a number of different firms to get a feel for fees, organizational structure, philosophies, and
services.

The most important consideration is that you feel comfortable with
your account manager. This is the person with whom you will be sharing
your innermost thoughts about your financial health. We have repeated that
it is important that the approach you take makes sense to you. Not that it
has a good track record, or that it is recommended by a friend, but that it
works for you. The same final decision process should be applied to your
personal working relationship with your account manager.

Getting the Most from Your Financial Advisor

Once you have decided to hire a financial advisor, your job has just started. In order to make the most effective and cost efficient use of his or her expertise, there are several things you should do. Your financial advisor will have a number of clients. To keep your interests at the top of the priority list, you need to know exactly what services you require in advance of any meeting. Top professionals value their time and don't enjoy wasting it in meandering discussions—even for the high fees!

The following guidelines will help you make the process of being helped less expensive and more rewarding.

Know Your Agenda Beforehand. Prior to meeting with your advisor, do your own homework! Know as much as you can about your near- and long-term goals and their priorities. The bane of any professional advisor is a client who is unwilling or unable to do the personal "spade work" required to dig out these important variables.

Try to know the approximate cost of each goal. You should have a good idea when you will want the money to pay for each financial objective. Taking what you have learned about present value in this book, the whole process will be greatly enhanced if you have a good idea how much you must invest today to achieve your future goals.

Coming to the meeting with unrealistic goals and expectations will serve only to frustrate you. Remember, even the best financial advisor is not a miracle worker. You will wind up paying high fees for your trips down fantasy lane. Be realistic. Take along the worksheets you have completed in this book. This advance preparation will save much time and aggravation, as well as money.

Your advisor will not be able to change the numbers, but can give you insight on how realistic your projections are. He or she can outline the alternative approaches you can take for achieving your goals. There is no perfect investment for every situation. However, your advisor can give you sufficient background information to make an intelligent decision based on the odds for success, the risks, and the costs involved.

Make Your Advisor's Role Clear to Other Financial Partners.
More than once, after accepting discretionary money management accounts (that is, accounts for which we have the client's authorization to make investments without prior consultation), we have run into stockbrokers, bankers, accountants, and even spouses who knew nothing of our involvement in these matters. You can save a lot of grief and misunderstanding by ensuring that all parties to your financial dealings know that an independent advisor is assisting you.

This is especially important when taxes, legal partnerships, or personal dependents are concerned. Financial affairs are complicated enough without having your own team working at cross purposes. If you take the time to clearly define each person's expected role, you will save much time and effort later trying to straighten out misunderstandings.

Put It in Writing. Be sure that your agreements with your professional advisor are formalized on paper. This is particularly important if you envision a long-term relationship. Your advisor won't want to surprise you with unexpected charges. You certainly do not want to pay for unauthorized expenses. Full written disclosure of all fees is an important cornerstone to ensuring a long, trusting relationship.

You should make it a practice to review in writing your discussions with other financial intermediaries who will be working with you. For example, after you have gone through the selection process to find a stockbroker (interviewing different brokers, comparing fees and services, etc.), it is a good idea to spell out in writing your goals, risk tolerance, and the types of investments you are considering. A good broker will have already interviewed you to find out this information. But people's memories about the same events often differ. A written record will serve to protect your interests if a dispute does arise.

In dealing with an independent advisor, stockbroker, banker, accountant, and/or other financial intermediaries, you'll have many good opportunities to exercise the money management skills you have learned here.

What Makes a Good Money Manager?

Whether you elect to use a professional financial advisor in a major role (giving them discretionary authority over your investment portfolio) or a minor one (occasional technical advice), the success of your Personal Profit Plan depends on you. If you practice sound money management skills, you will be able to focus on those things that are most important in fulfilling your plan.

There are three key traits that all successful money managers possess:

1. *They plan for the future.* They are not afraid to stand apart from the crowd and say, "This is what I want. Here is how I intend to get it."

2. *They influence people around them.* They know that attaining their financial goals requires the combined efforts of brokers, lawyers, relatives, and others. They actively coordinate and motivate these people to get them working together for the same goals.

3. *They control their plan's development.* They measure their plan's performance and compare it with the results desired, making corrections when necessary. In turbulent economic times, they command the ship, not a life raft!

FIGURE 7–1
The Money Management Functions

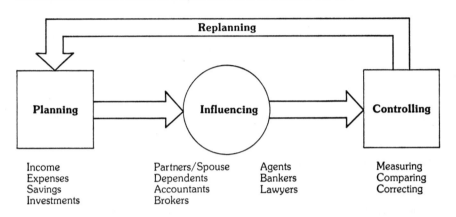

Figure 7–1 shows graphically how these functions relate to each other. The process of money management is very systematic and can be learned by almost everyone. The following guidelines will help you develop your skills as a money manager.

Being an effective Personal Profit Planner means you are able to organize your wealth and income to acquire those things you desire. They may be cash, property, goods, or services. It is more than building net worth. Many people have been unable to pay their current bills, even gone bankrupt, though they were millionaires on paper. Some of the personal assets that characterize a successful personal planner include:

1. *Analytical ability.* The knowledge of goal-setting and goal-getting methods in conjunction with the drive to sort through the mountain of financial facts to find the kernels of relevant information.

2. *Knowledge of the outside world.* The awareness of the overall economic environment with all its dangers and opportunities.

3. *Knowledge of the inner world.* The insight into one's personal needs and wants, strengths and weaknesses.

Controlling Your Personal Profit Plan

The last trait we listed for successful money managers is the ability to control their financial plans. Even the best financial plan will need a few mid-course corrections to keep it on track. Economic conditions can change quickly. Your initial expense, income and investment estimates must be updated with the latest, most accurate information.

Also your goals may very well change as you grow older. Marriage, divorce, birth, death, career changes, or illness can all change your initial assumptions. Of course, even if your goals stay the same, better ways to achieve them may develop. The financial markets are in a state of constant flux. A good money manager is always on the lookout for safer, more productive ways to employ the household's financial assets.

Effective control of your financial future means comparing your plan's progress with some expected level of performance and correcting it if things have strayed off course. This necessity to control your plan is the reason we specify criteria for your goals and objectives. If you don't devise appropriate ways to measure your plan's progress you cannot know if it is staying on track.

Keeping Your Goal-Getting Plan on Track

As you completed your worksheets, you no doubt found that your circumstances differed from that of our Lean and Quick example. Once your goal-getting plan is well on its way, you will encounter unexpected situations. We have found it best to be very conservative about your future prospects. As you progress in your career, your income will most likely increase with cost-of-living adjustments and merit raises. Your spouse will also enjoy further income increases. But we suggest you do not calculate these potential gains into your future at the outset.

Why not? The answer lies not only with an unpredictable economy but also with human nature. Things may go just as you expect. But then Murphy's Law should not be forgotten! And when incomes increase, people tend to spend more as a way of rewarding themselves. Rather than depend too much on income increases, it is better to concentrate on other easy ways to expand your investable resources. Here are a few ideas:

1. *Reduce your variable expenses.* This is the most painless step you can take when you need to get back on track. Variable costs are those over which you have already indicated you have some degree of control.

2. *Reduce your fixed expenses.* If cuts in your variable expenses are not sufficient, look to your fixed expenses. Be careful, however! Your fixed expenses reveal your true money values. Even a small reduction in an important fixed expense can trigger lifestyle changes or inconveniences that may seriously undermine your motivation to achieve your goals.

3. *Reduce your total taxes.* Tax reduction is a strategy that grows in importance as your total income grows. One important way to reduce your tax exposure is to spread your income into areas other than salary. Investigate investments that feature tax-deferred or tax-exempt provisions. Even though the 1986 Tax Reform Act eliminated many so-called tax shelters, annuities and municipal bonds are examples of investments that still offer some tax benefits.

4. *Increase your total income.* Why didn't you think of that?! Actually, there are often-overlooked techniques for increasing the income your assets earn. For example, if you maintain a checking account balance of under $1,000 and a 5 ¼ percent passbook savings account, you can increase the return on these assets by combining them into a single money market account with check writing privileges. In times of high interest rates, the difference can be substantial. Also remember, most banks assess fees for maintaining your checking account. That all comes out of your total return.

Wrapping Up

The business of financial planning is more complex than it may appear at first glance. In addition to your spouse or life partner, your financial affairs inevitably involve many others. Depending on your own desire for active involvement, these others can be mere order takers and executors, legal or tax advisors, or at the other end of the spectrum, financial advisors to whom you give discretionary authority over your own money.

Learning to bring these different financial intermediaries to work together on helping you achieve goals is a key part of your Personal Profit Plan. However, it won't work unless you take the time to determine exactly what it is you need from each party.

You will find that the time and effort it takes to ferret out the advisors who work well with you and others pays off in big dividends down the road. Though you can hire high-priced professional help, only you are responsible and ultimately pay or reap the rewards of your decisions.

We have tried our best to present a comprehensive approach to understanding where you are, what you want, and how to get there. But filling out forms, completing questionnaires, and running computer simulations will do nothing to provide for your future years. You have to act confidently and with discipline. If you do so, you will reap financial and psychological benefits that make all the effort well worthwhile!

APPENDIX A

END PAPERS

End Paper No. 1

Setting the Record Straight

In short, we believe your Resourcing record-keeping system should be, at minimum, *logical* (or you and your spending partner will never use it reliably), *accessible* (or you won't use it when you should), and *compatible* with your household spending type (or you'll never use it, period!).

Here's a system that can do these things for you.

The "Drawers" of Your BB&K 5-Drawer System

In antiquity, people kept their valuable things in a small chest known as an *arca*, or "ark." The top drawer of this chest was used to store the things that were needed most often—costume jewelry, writing implements, etc. The second drawer held records of transactions ("How many *ducats* did you get for that painting, Leonardo?"), letters to answer from friends, and so on. The bottom drawers held more important, seldom used things—heirloom jewelry, wills, land grants and deeds, and other important legal documents. These were usually kept under lock and key to prevent unauthorized tampering or theft. The BB&K 5-Drawer System follows this venerable custom in spirit, if not in fact, as shown in Figure A1–1. Here are the compartments you'll use, in one form or another, for your own "chest of valuables."

Drawer No. 1:
Your Personal Information Sheet

Action Paper No. 3, Your Personal Information Sheet, located at the back of this book, is the key to the rest of your system. Complete this worksheet now and inspect the entries it requires. Now imagine yourself in a crisis—your house has just burned down or been burglarized by a pro. Would you be able to inventory the financial records (including negotiable securities) that might have been lost? Would your irreplaceable documents still be safe—having been placed in another location? If you had been incapacitated by the incident, would your spouse or partner know whom to call for help in reconstructing your household's financial affairs?

Of course, you don't have to be in trouble to use Your Personal Information Sheet. Important but seldom used papers (life insurance policies, birth certificates, diplomas, etc.) have a way of blending into the woodwork over the course of many years. When you need to find an important document, the reason for finding it is usually important, too, and you don't want to have to scour the attic every time you apply for a loan or renew an expired passport.

The "first drawer" of your 5-Drawer system, then, is Your Personal Information Sheet; and you should keep a copy of it in your general file (see Figure A1–2), with a copy in a fireproof container or otherwise physically separated

FIGURE A1–1
Your 5-Drawer Record-Keeping System

Drawer No. 1

Your Personal
Information Sheet
(Action Paper No. 3)

Drawer No. 2

Your Current Activity
(Suspense) File
Desk drawer
Envelope stand
In/out basket
Folder or envelope

Drawer No. 3

Your Current
Year's Records
Tabbed folders
Expanding file
Metal/cardboard box
Filing cabinet

Drawer No. 5
Your Permanent Records
Safe-deposit box
Wall safe
Steel lockbox

Drawer No. 4

Your Long-Term
Records Storage
Packing box
Trunk
Large envelope

from the papers whose location it describes. Wherever you keep it, your information sheet should not be so hard to get hold of that you can't easily update it.

Drawer No. 2:

**Your Current Activity
(Action or "Suspense")
File**

Most people pay their bills once or twice a month, either for convenience or because of the timing of their bills and paychecks. They also receive solicitations in the mail for a variety of products, many of which may be fine values, and notices from various institutions or people requiring eventual response. The documents that occupy this record-keeping "twilight zone" also fill the second drawer of your 5-Drawer system: your Current Activity file. The file itself may actually be a drawer (such as the top drawer on the right of that old roll-top desk in the den); or it could be a desktop envelope stand (the kind you can buy at stationery stores),

FIGURE A1–2
Contents and Checklists for Each File of Financial Records

Heading	Contents	Checklist
General	Personal information sheet (Action Paper No. 3)	Update personal information sheet to reflect any changes.
	List of items in safe-deposit box	
	Letter of last instructions	Update safe-deposit box list as new items are added or old ones eliminated.
	Copy of will (the original should be kept with attorney or in a safe-deposit box)	
Resourcing	List of goals	Review Action Papers.
	Income statement (from *Setting and Achieving Your Financial Goals*)	Revise goals, if necessary.
	Forecasts of income and expenses (binder or jars)	
Housing	Purchase contract and receipt (deed in safe-deposit box)	Keep records of all permanent home improvements so that you can establish accurate cost basis if you ever sell your home.
	Mortgage papers	
	Title insurance policy	
	Home improvement receipts (including landscaping expenses)	
	Property tax receipts	
	Termite inspection and policy	
	Copy of lease or rental agreement	
Property insurance	Details of property insurance coverage (insurance policies or data sheet in a safe-deposit box)	Update property insurance annually to reflect changes in personal property holdings and/or changes in replacement costs of all structures.
	Personal property inventory (from *How to Get the Insurance You Need at the Right Price*; copy in safe-deposit box)	Update personal property inventory once a year: add new items; revalue old items; eliminate items sold or lost; take more pictures, if necessary.
	Pictures of highly valued items (negatives in safe-deposit box)	

FIGURE A1–2 (*continued*)
Contents and Checklists for Each File of Financial Records

Heading	Contents	Checklist
		Shop for rates. Get a minimum of three quotes before each renewal date.
		Save old policies for a year or two after expiration date in case of a delayed claim.
Auto insurance	Details of auto insurance coverage	Update auto insurance annually by adding new cars, amending coverages, and raising drivers' ages.
	Records of traffic violations and accidents	Update traffic violations and accident records. Note which violations or accidents occurred over three years ago and stop including them in insurance applications.
	Auto registration receipts (ownership certificate in safe-deposit box)	
		Shop for rates. Get a minimum of three quotes before each renewal date.
Health insurance	Insurance policies or details of present health coverage, including employee plans	Determine income disability needs
	Current medical history for each family member	Update health insurance to reflect changes in limits, coverage.
	List of drugs to which each family member is allergic	Update medical histories to reflect new ailments, diseases, and immunizations received.
		Shop for rates. Get three quotes before each renewal date.
Life insurance	Details of insurance policies owned, including employee group plans (insurance policies or data sheet in safe-deposit box)	Recompute insurance needs using eight-step procedure every five years—sooner if new financial assets are acquired, or if family income or expenses change significantly.
	Results of eight-step procedure (from *How to Get the Insurance You Need at the Right Price*) for de-	Update life insurance to re-

FIGURE A1–2 (*continued*)
Contents and Checklists for Each File of Financial Records

Heading	Contents	Checklist
	termining life insurance needs	flect changes in benefici- aries and coverage increases in employee policies.
		Shop for at least three rate quotes before each change in policy.
		Review the need for bene- ficiary changes.
Investments— general	Replan goals.	Action Papers from *How to Set and Achieve Your Fi- nancial Goals*
	Plot your progress using an- nual balance sheet.	Annual balance sheets
		List of checking/savings accounts
Investments— Stocks and Bonds	Records of purchase and sale (All stock certifi- cates and bonds should be kept either with broker or in safe-deposit box.)	Update records to reflect purchases and sales evi- denced by transaction slips.
	Records of stock dividends and bond interest	Add new stock numbers and dates of issue to list (if certificates are sent to you).
	List of stock certificate num- bers and dates of issue (if you keep certificates in safe-deposit box rather than with broker)	Place each year's trans- actions and monthly state- ments in an envelope.
	Transaction slips and monthly statements (an- nual envelopes)	
Investments— mutual funds	Records of purchase and sale of mutual funds (Keep mutual fund shares with broker, with the mutual fund transfer agent, or in a safe-deposit box.)	Use transaction slips and statements to update records of purchases, sales.
		Place each year's trans- action slips and monthly statements in an envelope.
Tax	Purchase receipts, interest payment records, charita- ble gift confirmations,	File all receipts required to substantiate deductions.
		After your annual tax form is

FIGURE A1–2 (*concluded*)
Contents and Checklists for Each File of Financial Records

Heading	Contents	Checklist
	medical expense records, and so on	filed, place all receipts and other substantiating records in an envelope and file either here or in extra storage boxes.
	Tax forms, schedules, and supporting data for the past three years	
	Quarterly estimated tax forms	
	W-2 forms, 1099 forms, and so on	
	Canceled checks as appropriate	
Guarantees and warranties	All warranties relating to appliances, tires, carpets, and the like	Add items to file as soon as purchased.
	Receipts	Remove once each year all that have expired.
	Repair instructions	
Employment information	Employment contract, if any	Update file as necessary.
	Employee handbook	
	Fringe benefits information	
Personal résumé	Details of previous education: years, major, degree(s), major professors and advisors (with addresses, phone numbers), transcripts, if any	When you switch jobs, put information from employment file in here.
	Employment record: job titles, dates and responsibilities, accomplishments, supervisors' names and addresses	Before you leave a school, update file with addresses you may need.
	Residence record: dates and addresses	
Credit records	Papers showing resolution of prior debts	Update file as necessary.
	Credit card numbers, names, and addresses	
	Notification forms for lost or stolen cards	

an office-type in/out basket, or a plain folder. The point is, your Current Activity file must be just that—active and current—as well as convenient and orderly.

In using your file each day we recommend the "chessmaster" method of sorting and filing. You see, chess etiquette requires that a player who touches a piece *move* that piece. This rule was devised to prevent idle or distracting fiddling with the chessmen during play, and we think it applies to good record-keeping habits as well. Whenever you bring in the daily mail, sit down next to your system's "second drawer" (wherever and whatever it is—drawer, envelope stand, or folder) and keep your wastepaper basket handy. Once you pick up a piece of mail, you are not allowed to put it back on the stack but must either place it in your action file or throw it away. This strategy keeps letters, solicitations, bills, premium notices, bank statements, receipts, and other financial flotsam (not to mention magazines and other mail) from collecting like moss on the horizontal surfaces of your home. It also keeps you aware, on a daily basis, of your upcoming financial commitments—something you'll need for either the Binder or Resource Jar method of accounting.

The chessmaster method works well, too, when you sit down to pay those bills and file those statements or receipts. Some documents can safely be discarded after you've acted on them (your canceled check will be your receipt), whereas others must be moved to your longer-term files. The point is: *If it's important enough to pick up, it's important enough to do something with—so do it!*

Drawer No. 3:

Your Current Year's Records

Once your suspense file has been depleted after a bill-paying session, you'll need a place to store your working records—your receipts, canceled checks, and other documents that show the current year's evolving financial history. The things you don't throw away—that is, the things you're keeping for a *specific* purpose, like taxes, and for a *specific* length of time, like broker's statements, you will put in the "third drawer" of your 5-Drawer system, your Current Year's Records.

This drawer is really what most people think of when they say "financial records." We recommend storing your current year's records in tabbed folders in an expandable file, cardboard (or metal) box, or filing cabinet, depending on your space and needs. Fireproof steel boxes or multi-drawer cabinets are also recommended, but they can be cumbersome; and lockable files, while useful, mean you have to have a key—another housekeeping task some reluctant record keepers don't appreciate!

Figure A1–2 shows the labels (headings) you should put on the tabs of your folders and the typical contents of each. The checklist in the right-hand column of the table should be written on the front or inside front of the folder to which it pertains to remind you how the file should be maintained.

The next question is: When my file gets full—at the end of the year—where do I put the contents?

Good question—and again, the chess-master method of document transfer applies, as you'll see in the next section.

Drawer No. 4:

Your Long-Term Records Storage

There's something magical about the length of time we call "a year." We report our age in terms of years, the desirability of our automobiles (last year's car is seldom as desirable as this year's, unless it's a classic), the vintages of good wine—as well as the regular intervals at which the IRS comes calling. Because of this cosmic harmony, we think short-term records should become long-term records at the end of the calendar year.

As part of your tax-paying ritual, (usually no earlier than the end of January or February, since you must wait to receive your W-2s and other income accounting forms), you should transfer the contents of each file from your Current Year's Records "drawer" to your Long-Term Records "drawer"—usually a packing box, trunk, large storage envelope, or other receptacle kept in a closet, basement, garage, or other unhandy place. Again, the "you touch it, you move it" rule applies, so be sure your trash container is nearby. If the contents of a file meet the criteria for long-term storage, put the file in the box or envelope, and label it with your name, the word "records," and the appropriate year.

Of course, after you've done this for several years, you'll have a collection of neatly labeled boxes or envelopes. What happens to them after that? Look at the year you've written on the oldest envelope. If it's more than three years old, pull it out of the trunk or packing box or off the shelf and open it up. (Some people even leave notes to themselves for this ceremony, like little time capsules—enclosing the front page of the newspaper for the day the records were sealed, etc.) In any event, your purpose here is to double-check for the misfiling of any truly *permanent* records. If none is found, chuck the folder (envelope and all) into the trash. Next year, you'll do the same thing with what is now the oldest file, and so on, keeping only *the last three years'* worth of records in your Long-Term Records "drawer."

Drawer No. 5:

Your Permanent Records

Anything you keep longer than three years goes in the last "drawer" of your 5-Drawer system. For tax purposes, this is any asset for which the cost basis must be retained for future use when the asset is sold—even if it's part of settling your estate 20 or 30 or more years into the future. Furthermore, the IRS may audit you within six years if you omit an item accounting for more than 25% of your reported income—and the statute of limitations on *fraud* is forever! People with widely fluctuating incomes or income from unusual sources are usually more subject to these examinations than others, so let your CPA or tax attorney be your guide if that description applies to you.

For most of us, permanent records include wills, birth certificates, adoption papers, marriage certificates and divorce decrees, share certificates, deeds, military discharge papers, diplomas (particularly if an academic credential is legally required to hold or obtain professional employment), passports, insurance policies, and title papers to automobiles, artwork, or jewelry. The ideal place for this fifth and final "drawer" is a safe-deposit box at your local bank, since it is just about immune from most natural and man-made disasters and protected by a neutral third party in case of your incapacitation or death. If this is not convenient (or you don't like paying the safe-deposit box fee), a wall safe or portable steel lockbox will also serve.

Options for More Impetuous Record Keepers

Admittedly, even when you realize its importance, establishing, and maintaining your records isn't exactly a barrel of laughs. For households where there's no careful (Assertive or Protective) spender to perform these record-keeping duties, there are some suggestions for making that record-keeping task a bit less onerous.

The "Two-Box" Option

It's been said that the world can be divided into two groups: one group that likes to divide things into two groups, and the other that does not.

For those spenders who belong to the first group, we've devised the "two-box" option to the basic 5-Drawer system. When you're ready to transfer your docu-ments and receipts from your second drawer (action file) to the third (current year files), put them instead into one of two boxes (literally). The first box is for any record that has tax significance—as a basis for future-value computations, for preparing the current year's return, or whatever. The second box is for everything else. After you have filed your tax returns, save the tax box for three more years and throw the other box away. You may come up short of records in some financial contingencies, but an IRS audit probably won't be one of them.

The Coded Check Option

This option works well with either the Binder or Resource Jar system, particularly if you pay most of your bills by check. Simply mark an asterisk (*) on each check you write that has some tax or loan significance. When your checks come back from the bank, keep them in a shoebox, replacing the last year's statement (of the same month) with the current year/current month statement. In other words, throw out last year's January bank statement when you file this year's January statement. This will give you a shoebox that is also a running file of one year's worth of checks. When tax time comes around, pull out only the checks that are marked with an asterisk and throw the rest away. These are your loan and tax records and you'll keep these in Drawer No. 4 (wherever that is) as your long-term records. People who *really* hate records sometimes throw these away, too, and keep only their check registers (also marked with asterisks), since they know their bank keeps a microfilm copy of every check. (You'll still need the check register to know *which* checks to ask for in case of an IRS audit.)

How Long Do I Keep What?

Probably no aspect of financial record keeping is more frustrating or confusing than deciding how long to keep your records. Since no single length of time will suffice for all documents (unless you want to keep *everything* forever—hardly a practical solution), we recommend the following rules as an integral part of your 5-Drawer record-keeping system:

First Option
Keep It Until It's Used, Then Throw It Away

The shortest time you can keep anything is to throw it away as soon as you've finished with it. In accordance with the chessmaster method of filing and sorting, this period is sometimes only as long as it takes to read the outside of an unwanted junk mail envelope. But for envelopes you *do* want to open and for business you do transact, you'll have to decide whether the invoice, statement, or other document makes a better or more necessary record than the canceled check you'll have to show for it once the debt has been paid. One way to reduce the volume of your spending records is to use the memorandum space provided on your checks—to write down not only the number of the account the check is crediting, but what the payment is for. Thus, for many items, you can eliminate the need for an institution's statement and keep only your canceled check as your receipt.

Second Option
Keep It for One Year, Then Throw It Away

Most financial records will fall into the one-year category. Bills that have been paid *and credited* with payment (sometimes it takes several months to accomplish this) should be thrown away, unless the bill has tax significance and/or was used to prepare your current tax return.

Third Option
Keep It for Three Years, Then Throw It Away

The IRS observes a three-year statute of limitations on examining personal income tax returns, so you'll have to keep your IRS Form 1040-related information at least that long. Remember, too, the IRS "tax year" runs from April 15 to April 15; you may receive a notice of examination as long as four months after the end of the third calendar year following your return—so don't be too quick to dump out the "fourth drawer" of your 5-Drawer system.

Fourth Option
Keep It Indefinitely

The specific use for some records, unfortunately, is very unspecific indeed.

For example, anything that documents the cost basis of an asset must be saved until that asset is sold or otherwise disposed of and accounted for on an income tax return. Thus the purchase documentation of a home must be retained until that home is sold so that the magnitude of your capital gain (or loss) can be computed. The same is true for stocks, bonds, and other securities, as well as expensive personal property (such as art and jewelry) that might be sold or stolen.

The Peacock Procedure

If you have an artistic flair, you may prefer the "peacock" approach—so named for the wonderful things it does visually to an otherwise drab metal filing cabinet. Here everything you need is color-coded so you can find it in a flash. We'll tell you the colors and contents we recommend, but you may want to figure out different codes, and different files, on your own.

Green Is the Color of My True Love's Cash

The first file is coded green (for moola) and contains your basic financial records. In it, you'll keep your Sources and Uses worksheets (if you use the Resource Jar method of accounting), your personal balance sheets, your brokerage house statements, money market fund statements, and other investment information (except real and personal property. If a single file folder gets too cramped (in any of your categories), add as many as you need so long as they're all the same color.

Orange You Glad You Have Insurance?

Your next file is coded orange, for insurance—the color used by international agencies for emergency equipment: life rafts, life preservers, and other survival-related sundries. In it you'll put your health, life, disability, automobile, homeowners, and liability insurance data, including policies. If you keep your policy numbers on your Personal Information Sheet, you won't have to worry about a fireproof home for the policies themselves—your insurance company can replace them if yours are lost or destroyed.

Purple Is for People

Your passionate purple file is for "people" or "personal"—whichever you prefer. In it, you store your personal records, a copy of your will, educational records, inheritance records, marriage or divorce documentation, etc.

Tan for Land

Reminding us of the good, weedy earth around our homes, we chose brown (or tan or beige) for home purchase and improvement information—as well as any other personal property records you may have, from automobile title and payment books to the warranties for your major appliances.

Don't Forget: Peacocks Like to Preen

Thin out your files when they become too bulky—although you should still observe the time requirements for IRS examinations. The peacock system isn't as orderly as the filing system shown in Figure A1–2, we admit, but it's a lot more colorful and fun to use—especially for more impetuous spenders.

May We Have the Envelopes, Please?

Finally, we've developed a modification to the basic 5-Drawer system that's especially appealing to those (Assertive or Protective) spenders who *want* to keep better records—particularly for their taxes—but just can't seem to do it.

First, collect enough envelopes (letter size will do, but larger envelopes usually work better) to accommodate your paycheck stubs, evidence of other income (IRS Form 1099s, etc.), receipts from your charitable contributions, medical expenses, and other deductions. Be sure to have an envelope for tax payments too, if you remit your taxes on quarterly vouchers. At the end of the year, go through your canceled checks and put them into the appropriate envelopes and store them along with your copy of your IRS Form 1040. Start the new year with a *new* set of envelopes and repeat the cycle again,

throwing out your fourth drawer (long-term) records when you've held them at least three years.

Getting It All Together

Record keeping may not always be fun—but it sure can be rewarding. There are few "highs" you can experience greater than the one you'll feel after leaving an IRS income tax examination with a "no change" notice on your return. Of course, there are many other reasons to keep complete and timely records—such as never again paying late charges on a misplaced bill or simply feeling *in charge* of your financial paperwork, and not its victim.

Like doing your homework when you were in school, you should pick a regular time to "do" your records (pay bills and file) and stick with it—playing music in the background or rewarding yourself with a nice long walk in the park—or ice cream and a movie!—when you're through. Remember, there's more to the care and feeding of your financial physique than a steady diet of numbers, no matter how big those numbers become!

Notes

_____

_____

_____

_____

_____

_____

_____

_____

_____

| **End Paper No. 2** |

Constructing Your Resource Binder

Many methodical people go wrong when they depend on bookkeeping systems to organize and control their family spending. The most elaborate, carefully designed "budget" (in the traditional sense) is bound to fail if the people who use it don't understand that *people*—not textbooks or worksheets—spend money. Before you create your Resource Binder, then, you should learn a little more about the human factor in all bookkeeping systems.

The Human Side of Resourcing

It's been said that creating a Resourcing System is a little like going on your first date or having a baby. It's an *experience* —one that's unique for each individual yet one that has enough in common with other individuals' experiences for them to empathize with your problems and successes. No amount of analysis or explanation, therefore, can take the place of simply having the experience yourself; so (perhaps a bit like cautious parents who've been through all this ourselves) we'd like to forearm you with some wisdom about what you can expect when theory gets down to practice.

The Key to Controlling Spending Is *Commitment*

As we outlined in Chapter 4, spending is really a *process* that begins with obtaining and allocating funds and ends with actually transferring money from one party to another—in the form of either a bank debiting your checking account or your physically plunking down cash into someone else's hand. Somewhere along the way, the *commitment to spend* is made. It does not occur at the beginning of the process, since "allocation" simply shows the *intention* to spend in some general area. It doesn't occur at the "expense" end either, since by the time your bank debits your account (or you plunk down that handful of cash) the commitment to spend is old history. No, the *commitment to spend* occurs somewhere between the allocation of funds and the actual transfer of cash that backs up a specific spending decision. Why is this distinction important? Because it is here—*in controlling the commitment to spend*—that your Resourcing System will work or fail.

Foreseeing this commitment and making sure it's aimed at the goods and services that will contribute to your financial well-being in the way you'd planned are at the heart of your Resource Binder system. Remember this as we go through this End Paper, and everything else we say will make sense —and work well—when you implement your system.

Overview: Making Your Binder Fit Your Family

Have you ever been to a New Year's Eve party and the next day tried to recall *exactly* what you did and what you said? Other peopel who were there agree they had a good time, but no one remembers clearly what that good time was. Spending money without some forethought—or afterthought—can leave you similarly perplexed, wondering just what it was you wound up with after spending your hard-earned cash.

Creating a bookkeeping system to clarify and control the whats and whys of spending is what your BB&K Binder is all about—but it won't happen without some effort. To help you through this growing and learning process, you'll use the following procedure:

Phase I: Cultivate awareness of your current spending patterns. The first phase in the Resourcing process is to document how your household *actually* spends its cash. Thus your first attempt to create and maintain a Resource Binder will be based on the realities of your own particular household, rather than wishful thinking or a set of abstract principles.

Phase II: Experiment with a trial balloon. No auto maker would dare put a new car on the road without first testing it thoroughly. Why should you be less careful with the Resourcing System that will help you gain and keep financial fitness? The next phase of your Resourcing plan will be to create a trial version of your Binder and test it under "battlefield" conditions—in the trenches of daily spending.

Phase III: Finalize your Binder based on your experience. Once you've seen what works and what doesn't work for you, you'll modify your Binder by reviewing its performance—and your own!—and apply the Flexible or Fail-Safe method for controlling your commitments.

By the time you've finished Phase III, the Resource habit will be almost second nature and the rewards you'll reap—both financial and emotional—will be apparent to every spender in the family.

Phase I: Becoming Aware of Your Spending Habits

Throughout this book and this series, we've said how futile it is to try to manage money in a way that doesn't feel right to you. This is doubly true when it comes to spending the money that you've managed. The first phase of your Resource Binder development, then, is to find out what those spending patterns really are.

Awareness Step 1:

Enlist a Volunteer Spending Coordinator

To map out your true spending patterns, you'll need a financial pathfinder. This person's job will be to set up a "money log" (according to the directions we'll give you in a moment) and circulate it among your household's spenders at a set time every day. We call this person a "coordinator" rather than a monitor or manager because all we need at this point is someone to collect a reasonable *history* of a typical spending cycle in your household—not someone to supervise spending or dictate financial morality. The ideal coordinator, in fact, is an Assertive or Protective spender who backs up his or her methodical ways with compassion and good humor. Since these traits are not the exclusive property of careful spenders, Active and Impulsive spenders can make good coordinators too as long as they're willing to experiment with more formal spending methods. The idea here is to find a person who believes in your Resource System strongly enough to put his or her talents and enthusiasm to work during this very sensitive phase.

Awareness Step 2:

Establish Your Money Logbook

Your coordinator's first task is to procure a three-ring loose-leaf binder and stock it with lined paper. This book is your family's Resource Binder and although you'll add more Action Papers and worksheets to it later, its function now is simply to capture your family's spending habits. Although some coordinators like to pencil in categories for subsequent entries (such as those listed later in Figure A2–1), we discourage this practice. Preestablished expense categories give your binder the "look" of a conventional budget and that can inhibit, rather than encourage, participation by reluctant Resourcers.

Awareness Step 3:

Circulate Your Money Logbook Once a Day

When your binder is ready, the coordinator's next task is to pick a convenient time when the household is assembled (at the dinner table is usually best) and pass the binder around to everyone. Ask them to list any money they spent that day, rounding each amount to the nearest dollar (or nearest ten dollars if that's appropriate) and indicating for what (or how) the money was spent. Entries should include payments made by check for rent, utilities, etc., as well as money placed in savings accounts, time deposits, or other investments. Ask also for any comments about how the day went for the various people. Were they happy about how they spent their money? Did they feel pleasure or guilt or mixed emotions about spending for a particular purpose?

We've found that these little daily ceremonies quickly become a popular feature of family life. Before long your binder will likely become covered not only with comments and numbers but poems, anecdotes, jokes, and cartoons. We even had one family call their logbook "The Peanut Butter Book" because of its lived-in appearance after a few trips around the dinner table. Binders also have a way of sprouting colorful stickers, telephone numbers, and random doodles—and this is all to the good. To do its job, your money log must capture the "feel" of your family's daily life and become a member of the family. If your coordinator gets squeamish about handling a book that, after two or three months, looks like a cross between the creature from the Black Lagoon and a '60s hippie van—don't worry. Tell him or her that your binder's youthful, store-bought appearance was sacrificed for the best of causes—your family's financial fitness!

Awareness Step 4:
Take a Look Inside Your Binder

After two to three months of regular money logging, enough time for your different spending categories to surface on their own, you'll be ready to sit down with your binder and decipher its many secrets.

First, take a large sheet of paper (11 by 17 inches or wider—even a sheet of butcher paper works well, although several notebook pages taped together along their sides will do in a pinch). List down the side the expense classifications shown in Figure A2–1. The idea here is to transfer the money log information onto one big "scratch pad" from which your eventual cost categories will be drawn. If you have additional or different categories from the ones shown in the figure, use the ones that seem right for you. If you've prepared a personal income statement like the one in this book, you'll see that these categories match closely the categories used in the income statement and its supporting schedules. In fact, the income statement was designed as a *cash flow* statement precisely to help you control your spending. In any event, label two broad categories at the top of the sheet, one for fixed expenses (the left half of the worksheet), the other for variable expenses (on the right)—again, to match those shown on the income statement. If you have a lot of categories, you'll probably

want to turn your scratch pad so that the long side is vertical, giving you enough room to list them all.

Now, with the help of your partner (although the coordinator can do this alone if desired), go through the binder page by page and call out items and amounts listed. Locate the category in which the items should fall on your scratch pad sheet and record the amount as either a fixed or variable expense. If you can't decide on its classification or whether the cost is fixed or variable, refer to any comments listed in the binder with it. Don't be afraid to create new categories if you need them. Items that show a lot of emotional attachment or turmoil may be important enough to be considered fixed expenses even if they seem frivolous and wouldn't qualify for this category for objective economic reasons. Keep your entries readable, but don't worry about neatness or lining up your costs in vertical or horizontal rows. This step is simply a "quick and dirty" dump of your logbook information onto a summary scratch pad. Later on, we'll give you formal Action Papers to use as spending records and control sheets.

When you've gone through the money log in your binder, you'll have a scratch pad filled with gobs of numbers for both fixed and variable costs—and sometimes a bit of each for a single category, such as automobile expense for recreational (variable) versus business (fixed) purposes. Using your trusty hand calculator, compute a total for each cost category (for example, "Housing, Fixed," and "Housing, Variable"). Cross out each rough number as you add it so that you won't count it twice. Circle the subtotals so that they stand out from the other numbers on your scratch pad. Now add each circled subtotal (variable plus fixed) for each category

FIGURE A2–1
Suggested Resource Binder Expense Categories and Percentage Guidelines for a Typical Household

Housing (20–35%)
Rent
Mortgage payments
Repairs and improvements
Property insurance
Property taxes

Utilities (4–7%)
Gas and electricity
Waste disposal
Water
Telephone

Food (15–30%)
All food items
Meals taken out
Pet food

Family necessities (2–4%)
Laundry and dry cleaning
Toiletries and cosmetics
Barber and hairdresser
Postage and stationery
Minor home furnishings

Medical (2–8%)
Insurance
Drugs and medicines
Hospital bills
Doctor bills
Dentist bills

Clothing (3–10%)
All clothing purchases
Alterations
Repairs (shoes and so on)

Automobile
and transportation (6–20%)
Purchase or installment payments
Gas and oil
Insurance and license fees
Repairs, parking, and tolls
Rental, taxi, and bus fare

Recreation
and entertainment (2–6%)
Admissions
Games and hobbies
Club dues
Alcoholic beverages
Tobacco
Photographic supplies
Musical supplies
Sporting goods

Personal improvement*
Books
Magazines and newspapers
Tuition and course fees

Short-term goal fund*
Vacations
Other special purchases

Savings and investment (5–9%)
Long-term goals

Outlays for fixed assets (2–8%)
Major purchases or installment
  payments on appliances,
  garden equipment,
  and furniture
Repairs (appliance and television)

Fun fund (1–4%)

Gifts*

Church and charity*

Life insurance*

Taxes*

Contingency*
Legal services
Unspecified debt repayments
Union/professional dues

(Figures in parentheses are suggested spending limits for each category, in percentages of total disposable (after tax) income. Variations are due to income levels, family size, and—primarily—personal choice.)

*These categories have no suggested limits since such expenditures vary greatly from family to family.

How to Tell a Fixed Expense from a Variable Expense

If you have not yet prepared your financial statements as described in this book, here are some guidelines that will help you set up and analyze your expense classifications.

Fixed Costs Take a While to Change

A fixed cost, like a fixed asset, is relatively permanent. Suppose you own a house—a fixed asset—and a lender (a savings and loan company, for example) holds a mortgage on that house. Very likely you make monthly payments on that debt, reducing steadily the principal and interest of your loan. You *could* sell your house and ret rid of the debt, but that would take a long time, probably several months. Similarly, you *could* change the amount of your monthly mortgage payments, but only after selling the house and acquiring a less expensive home, or refinancing the mortgage at a lower rate

of interest. This lack of flexibility in converting an asset to cash or changing the magnitude of an expense is what gives fixed assets and fixed expenses respectively, their names. In terms of monthly income and expenditures, they are "fixed" at their current value.

Variable Costs Can Change from Month to Month

Variable costs, on the other hand, are more flexible. Your food budget, for example, can vary depending on the quantity and type of food you buy. Similarly, entertainment expenses are very flexible and are, in fact, the first things most families cut when economic "belt-tightening" is required.

This distinction between fixed and variable costs is all-important in creating and controlling your Resourcing System. It will pay you many dividends to start thinking in these terms from the moment you create your first trial system.

and write it down in the right margin. For example, total housing cost would be the sum of its fixed and variable components. Next, add the circled variable subtotals and write the variable Grand Total at the bottom of the pad. Do the same for your fixed costs as well. These two sums show you the total costs that you can and can't (respectively) do something about in the short term.

Now push your papers, pencil, and calculator aside and relax! You have just completed the most important part of your Resourcing task: creation of a realistic model of the way your household spends its money. It's something few people even try to measure, but something that's more responsible than anything else for making your Resourcing System work!

Phase II: Send Up Your Trial Balloon

Now that you know something about how your family *actually* spends its money, you're ready to direct that spending behavior into certain positive channels. You'll do this by convening a Round Table family meeting (always a festive event!) and assembling a working version of your Resource binder for a test spin in the real-live world.

> Experimental Step 1:
> **Prepare for Your Resourcing Meeting**

In this section, we'll deal with the *specific* things you'll have to do to prepare for the Binder business you have to transact.

First, ask your household members to submit ahead of time (or come to the meeting with) five goals they'd like to achieve in the coming year, assuming they had the money. These goals should have an estimated cost attached to them and should be realistic enough to be attainable. (Becoming president of the United States won't count, but becoming president of a local service club might.) Most goals, of course, will be related to goods or services, such as buying a stereo or new clothes, starting a college fund, or taking a special vacation.

Next, have the Resource coordinator divide the expense categories shown on your scratch pad by three (if a 90-day money log was used) or two (if a 60-day log was used). This will give you the monthly average of your actual living expenses. The coordinator should trans-

fer these categories and numbers to a clean sheet of paper (8½ by 11 inches so it will fit your binder) for use during the Round Table meeting.

The principal breadwinners in the household (the coordinator may be one of them) should then complete Action Paper No. 10 "Your Forecast Income Worksheet." Locate this worksheet now at the back of this book. Figure A2–2 shows this Action Paper completed for a typical Lean and Quick couple. If you've already completed the income statement in Chapter 3, and it can reasonably apply to the coming year, you may use that value (Item 5, Amount Remaining for Living Expenses, Savings and Investments) divided by 12 as your monthly income. If you don't have this information available, here's the way you'll fill out the worksheet:

1. Estimate your annual after-tax income for each income category other than salary. For our Lean and Quick couple, this was interest on a small passbook savings account, and dividends from a small amount of stock.

2. Enter the amount of both partners' after-tax (net) paycheck in the appropriate month of the coming year. Use gross pay *only* if you have listed income tax and Social Security payments (and other automatic deductions) as expense items on the fixed and variable cost worksheet.

3. Divide the annual total by 12 to get your average monthly income.

4. Add up the monthly amounts to see the total income available from all sources for each month. Enter this figure in the boxes at the bottom of the chart.

5. To check your calculations, the sum of the Total row should equal the

FIGURE A2–2
Sample Income Forecast

Action Paper No. 10

Your Forecast Income Worksheet

Name(s) _Jean and Quick_
Date _December_

Months from Now: Source	1	2	3	4	5	6	7	8	9	10	11	12	Estimated 12-Month Total	Average Per Month	Actual Year's Income
Partner A's take-home wages or salary	1936	1936	1936	1936	1936	1936	1936	1936	1936	1936	1936	1936	23,232	1936	
Partner B's take-home wages or salary	938	938	938	938	938	938	938	938	938	938	938	938	11,256	938	
Bonuses or commissions															
Interest	75			75			75			75			300	25	
Dividends			30			30			30			30	120	10	
Rents															
Annuities, pensions															
Other												1300	1300	108	
TOTAL	2949	2874	2904	2949	2874	2904	2949	2874	2904	2949	2874	4204	36,208	3,017	

sum of the Estimated 12-Month Total column. For our Lean and Quick couple, this total was $36,208.

Experimental Step 2:
Hold Your Resourcing Meeting

On the day you hold your Resourcing meeting, the coordinator will check to see that he or she has (or will accept at that time) all the goals submitted by the family. Without screening them or otherwise making comment, the coordinator will add up their cost and divide the total by 12, entering the total desired goal-related spending as a new variable expense category on the Binder summary sheet. The coordinator will then add up all expenses and compare that total to the total income available for the month. If the expenses are greater than the income, the subject for the Resourcing meeting will become (a) what goals to leave out, or (b) how to generate more income, or (c) how to arrive at new priorities, deferring some goals until the next Resourcing meeting.

To those unfamiliar with Resourcing dynamics, this may seem like the place where your Resourcing meeting begins to fizzle. Actually just the opposite happens. This is where you really begin to experience the payoff from your other Resourcing planning. If your implementation style is collaborative, you'll begin right away to share in those spending decisions. If your decisions are made through compromise and negotiation, you'll find ample grist for your give-and-take mill. If delegation is your means of resolving sticky issues, you'll find that areas of spending responsibility begin to

form. Above all, the goal of the meeting at this point should be to make visible to every spender the trade-offs between limited resources and the use of those resources to benefit the household as a unit. Here are a couple of ways to expedite this process.

Logjam Breaker No. 1:
The 48-Second Speech

If the jockeying for high priority numbers becomes too contentious, or if the household has one or two members who are more vocal than the others, the coordinator can stipulate that each spender has 48 seconds (and *only* 48 seconds!) to explain why his or her goals are most important. At the end of this go-around, the favorites will probably begin to appear. If a priority list is still unattainable, have everyone repeat his or her speech using completely *new* reasons. Not only will this tease out hidden agendas, but people will begin to see how superficial, or how important, the contested goals really are. It's also possible to establish priorities by tackling the *least* important goals first. Have the people amend their speeches to describe their less important goals, and your priority list will begin to take shape in reverse order.

To resolve intractable disputes, the coordinator may announce that the family spender who shows by the speech that he or she is *least* likely to be able to wait (that is, smaller kids, people facing schedule dilemmas, such as going away to school, or highly impetuous adults) may automatically receive a high priority number for his or her most important goal. To some people, this may seem like "giving in" to the most impetuous spenders—fostering indiscipline among the troops and all that—but we've found that this simply is not the case. When those with less self-control are given this obvious favor, they become less anxious, less contentious, and far more willing to cooperate with others later on spending.

Logjam Breaker No. 2:
Go Back to the Money Log

If the priority discussion gets too free and easy with the facts, the coordinator can go back to the foundation of your Resourcing plan, the money log, and review (for everyone's benefit) the annotations each spender made for purchases similar to those under discussion. For example, if Susie's highest priority is a new sofa because she's "ashamed" to have her friends over to the house to hear records, it might be instructive to see the comments she made concerning home improvements in the past. Or, if Warren believes a new video cassette recorder should be part of his family's future, it might help everyone to see just how much the family spent for—and how much they seemed to receive in value from—going out to movies or investing in other forms of home entertainment. However the money log is used, it should *not* be applied as an instrument of punishment or ridicule. On the contrary, if the Binder can be seen as an arbiter of just and equitable spending decisions, then it will have gone a long way toward establishing itself for that purpose in the future.

In the end, you'll have negotiated and revised your basic cost categories to accommodate most of the goals that

will motivate your tribe of spenders to participate in the system.

Experimental Step 3:
Launch Your Prototype Binder

When you've allocated your available income to the fixed and variable categories you've established (including your new short-term goals), the coordinator should transpose the agreed-upon figures to Action Paper No. 11, "Your Forecast Expenses," and place this worksheet in your Resourcing Binder. Be sure to modify or change any category on this worksheet that does not match your scratch pad summary.

You are now ready to implement your basic system, since you have matched your available resources to the fixed and variable costs that will satisfy your household's needs. All that remains now is to put your plan into practice—which means, primarily, controlling your individual spenders' *commitments* to spend. How you do that depends on the degree of freedom you want your spenders to have and how comfortable you are about living with deviations from your plan. Eventually, this will mean choosing either the Fail-Safe or the Flexible method for controlling your expenditures. Before we help you make that choice, however, you'll need to establish the basic bookkeeping procedure you'll use to keep your Binder up to date.

Phase III: Finalizing Your Binder System

Even though your Resourcing efforts so far have been aimed at research and

FIGURE A2–3
Sample Expenses Forecast

Action Paper No. 11
Your Forecast Expenses

Name(s) Lean and Quick Date December

Expense Category	Fixed and Variable Subcategories	1	2	3	4	5	6	7	8	9	10	11	12	12-Month Total	Average by Month
Housing	Rent, mortgage payments, insurance, taxes	750	750	750	750	750	750	750	750	750	750	750	750	9000	750
	Repairs and improvements			115			115			115			115	460	38
Utilities		175	175	175	175	175	175	175	175	175	175	175	175	2100	175
Food		435	435	435	435	435	435	435	435	435	435	435	515	5300	441
Family necessities		40	40	40	40	40	40	40	40	40	40	40	40	480	40
Medical	Insurance					— PAID BY EMPLOYER —									
	Doctor, dentist, drugs, hospital	45	45	45	45	45	45	45	45	45	45	45	45	540	45
Clothing		160	160	160	160	160	160	160	160	160	160	160	240	2000	166
Automobile	Purchase payments, insurance, and license fees	752	368	368	368	368	368	368	368	368	368	368	368	4800	400
	Gas, oil, repairs, parking, tolls, and so on	130	130	130	130	130	130	130	130	130	130	130	130	1560	130
Recreation and entertainment	General	250	250	250	250	250	250	350	350	250	250	250	250	3200	267
Self-Improvement	Magazines and newspapers	15	15	15	15	15	15	15	15	15	15	15	15	180	15
Short-term goals		100	100	100	100	100	100	100	100	100	100	100	100	1200	100
Savings, investments	For long-term goals	150	150	150	150	150	150	150	150	150	150	150	150	1800	150
Outlays for fixed assets	Repairs	20	20	20	20	20	20	20	20	20	20	20	20	240	20
	Purchases and installments	50	50	50	50	50	50	50	50	50	50	50	50	600	50
Fun Fund		50	50	50	50	50	50	50	50	50	50	50	50	600	50
Gifts		30	30	30	30	30	30	30	30	30	30	30	30	360	30
Church and charity		25	25	25	25	25	25	25	25	25	25	25	25	300	25
Life insurance									110					110	9
Taxes															
Contingency	Legal services, debt repayments, union dues	100	100	100	100	100	100	100	100	100	100	100	100	1200	100
Total by Month		3277	2893	3008	2893	2893	3008	2993	3103	3008	2893	2893	3168	36,030	

planning (documenting your spending habits and creating expense and income forecasts), you may have noticed something interesting about your household's spending habits. Because people were *paying attention* now to whys and whats of spending, they probably tended to be more conscientious about how that money was spent—even though no control system was in place yet to enforce it! Does this mean that such bookkeeping and control systems are superfluous? The answer, oddly enough, is yes and no. Yes, because all spending discipline is really *self*-discipline, and cannot be enforced by a piece of paper, no matter how clever or coercive the system is behind it; and no, because without the constant reinforcement of measuring and comparing actual versus planned results, the incentive for self-control seldom lasts. This is the way both the Flexible and Fail-Safe control systems really work to control your household's spending. By conscientiously applying self-discipline when you are *not* spending money, it becomes easier to exercise that discipline when you are.

Implementing Your Basic System

Figure A2–4 shows Action Paper No. 12 "Your Resource Binder Control Sheet," filled out for the Lean and Quick household. Here are the steps they followed (and you will use) to finalize their system:

1. Have your coordinator establish and label one page in your binder for each expense category. Be sure there are plenty of extra (blank) pages available, since you want to encourage all spenders to make entries. Some coordinators make neat, ledger-type pages with vertical columns set up for each item, amount, current balance, and annotations for tax significance. We think this approach is probably too professional for family use, but if this method feels right to you—by all means, go ahead and use it. It's also helpful, too, to put loose-leaf tab dividers (properly labeled, of course) to help your spenders find the right categories easily, although you can accomplish this just as well by using paper clips or bookmarks or other section finders.

2. The coordinator should next instruct the household spenders to make an entry on the logsheets for every type of spending they made during the day. It helps to make these entries all at once and to do it at a regular time each day—before dinner, before retiring (unless thinking about money keeps you awake!), as soon as you get home in the afternoon—these are all acceptable times. Some households make their recording chore a daily family ritual, doing it all at the same time (there's moral support in numbers), which also helps the more forgetful or recalcitrant Resourcers to participate. Probably the best idea is to do it just before dinner, since that's the time you previously set aside to fill in your money log during Phase I, and the habit is already well established. However you decide to do it, make sure it's easy to accomplish and hard to forget this responsibility.

3. At the end of each month, the coordinator should "close the books" and fill out the Resource Binder Control Sheet shown in the figure. The totals from each logsheet should be transferred to this form and the dif-

FIGURE A2–4
Sample Binder Control Sheet

Action Paper No. 12

Your Resource Binder Control Sheet

Name(s) *Lean and Quick*

Date *Jan – April*

Expense Category	Allotted Monthly Average	Month: Jan		Month: Feb			Revised Monthly Average ?	Month: March			Month: April		
		Actual	Plus or Minus	Balance Forward	Actual	Plus or Minus		Balance Forward	Actual	Plus or Minus	Balance Forward	Actual	Plus or Minus
Housing	788	750	+38	826	795	+31		819	750	+69	857		
Utilities	175	125	+50	225	125	+100	✓	275	140	+135	310		
Food	441	466	–25	416	430	–14	✓	427	450	–23	418		
Family necessities	40	45	–5	35	30	+5		45	42	+3	43		
Medical	45	50	–5	40	15	+25		70	60	+10	55		
Clothing	166	246	–80	86	106	–20		146	75	+71	237		
Automobile	530	420	+110	640	650	–10	✓	520	600	–80	450		
Recreation entertainment	267	120	+147	414	280	+134	✓	401	200	+201	468		
Personal improvement	15	22	–7	8	10	–2		13	20	–7	8		
Short-term goal fund	100	100	0	100	100	0		100	100	0	100		
Savings and investment	150	150	0	150	150	0		150	150	0	150		
Outlays for fixed assets	70	0	+70	140	0	+140	✓	210	0	+210	280		
Fun Fund	50	50	0	50	50	0		50	50	0	50		
Gifts	30	15	+15	45	35	+10		40	50	–10	20		
Church and charity	25	25	0	25	25	0		25	20	+5	30		
Life insurance	9	0	+9	18	0	+18		27	0	+27	36		
Taxes	0	0	0	0	0	0		0	0	0	0		
Contingency	100	0	+100	200	75	+125		225	0	+225	325		
Total	3001	2584	417	3418	2876	542		3543	2707	836	3837		

ference computed between the Actual and Planned amounts. This "Plus or Minus" balance is then recorded in the space provided for that month and summed vertically, yielding a plus, minus, or zero balance overall for the month. The deviations are then added to or subtracted from the planned amount for each category and the result entered in the Balance Forward column. Thus an overspending for one category one month will lead to a reduced balance forward the next.

For example, the Lean and Quick couple overspent their $441 monthly food allotment by $25, yielding a "−25" entry in the Plus or Minus column. When this shortfall was used to adjust the next month's allotment amount, only $416 was available for food.

4. During your family Round Table meetings, you should analyze each expense category and decide on next month's spending policy. A typical spending review might go something like this:

He: "Gosh,—we spent $80 more for clothes this month than we'd planned! What happened?"

She: "Oh, don't worry. I had to buy some clothes while they were on sale. I'm all set for the year now."

He: "Okay, but that means we've got a balance of only $86 carried forward for clothes into February. You'll have to cool it in the haberdashery department for at least another month."

And so she tried. In Feburary she spent $106 for the rest of her clothes, leaving a deficit in the category of minus $20. In March, the negative $20 reduced their new $166 allotment to a beginning balance of $146. She spent $75 of this on a pair of shoes, which left a monthly surplus of $71. When this surplus was added to the next month's allotment, they discovered they had $237 in the till.

We could go on with other examples, but you probably see the pattern of measure-compare-and-correct that is the essence of spending control. When they begin the next calendar quarter, our couple may want to revise the allocations, taking from underused categories (such as "Recreation" and "Outlays for Fixed Assets") and adding the recurring surplus to overspent categories (such as "Automobile" and "Food"). To remind them of this, they checked the "Revised Monthly Average?" boxes shown. During the next Round Table meeting, they'll review their spending habits and family needs in these categories and reallocate their resources as required.

The Flexible Method of Controlling Spending Commitments

Now that you've seen how the basic system works, here's the first of two possible ways to control it effectively. Remember, the Flexible system is intended primarily for Assertive or Protective spenders who will be maintaining a Binder system in concert with more impetuous or less methodical spenders. Its aim is to provide all the benefits of numerical control while allowing the widest possible freedom in spending and borrowing (between categories and from the bank) to preserve a desired lifestyle.

Here are the rules that make this option work.

> Rule No. 1
> for the Flexible Binder System:
>
> **Positive variances may be carried over to increase the surplus month after month.**

This means that you have the latitude to increase the value (spending potential) of one cost category by continued underspending, giving you the freedom to make a larger than normal outlay in later months. Under the Fail-Safe system, this surplus would usually be absorbed into a safety reserve and the normal monthly allocation would not be increased by previous underspending.

> Rule No. 2
> for the Flexible Binder System:
>
> **Negative variances may be carried over to allow deficit spending (when desired) month after month.**

This means that you can tailor each month's spending policy to unforeseen needs. As long as the *total* variance is a manageable number, it can be negative (and continue to be negative) in any particular category. If the total for all expenses is negative, it means you're using credit to finance your current lifestyle. There's nothing inherently wrong with this provided you know that's what you're doing. Two warnings go along with the Flexible system, however, and we think you should take them both to heart:

1. Don't get intoxicated with living beyond your means. A little "red ink" in one category won't hurt your system as long as it doesn't become a way of life. Use the checks and balances inherent in different spending styles to put the brakes on excessive spending in a negative category when necessary. If the deficit appears to reflect a new and genuine need, you may have to rethink your basic allocations and pull the resources out of another area to make up the difference.

2. Don't let the red ink spill over into too many categories at once. Flexibility is one thing—no willpower is another. Your Resourcing System should help you *control* your spending pattern, not simply document how and when you went bankrupt! Again, use the communications and incentive methods described elsewhere in this book to help you help yourself keep your plan on track.

The Fail-Safe Way to Control Your Spending

When the spending habits in your household require a tighter grip on the purse strings, there's no more reliable way to do it than to use the Fail-Safe method—a procedure that is virtually guaranteed to prevent you from ever getting over your head in turbulent financial waters. Here's the way it works.

> Rule No. 1
> for the Fail-Safe System:
>
> **Never spend more than the allotted amount in any one category.**

This means that *any* negative numbers in the variance column are flags for immediate action. They may *not* be carried over to the next month, but *must* be made up by transferring cash from an underused cost category. If the total in the Plus or Minus column for any month is negative (that is, if there is no surplus in any one cost category to make up for the deficit in another), then a "sinking fund" (or debt account) is opened as a separate category and cash is drained from the other categories until a zero balance, or surplus, is restored. For example, if our sample couple did *not* have a positive balance in the Total column from month to month, they would have to pare down their spending in selected categories to make up the difference *and* be sure that they incurred no negative numbers in the Plus or Minus column during the process.

Rule No. 2
for the Fail-Safe System:

A surplus in one category cannot be allocated to another category except in an emergency.

This means that you are forced to keep "apples with apples" in your Resourcing plan. If your annual expense forecast assumes a total of $1,200 for clothing, and you spend only $500 in the first six months, you cannot transfer your $100 savings to another cost category (except in an emergency as shown in Rule 1 above). In other words, you must "use it or lose it" once cash has been apportioned to a specific category—although the money you don't spend is really saved and available for next year's allocations. If you re-allocate your resources between categories in response to temporary surpluses and shortfalls, you may be building in a major deficit in one or two particular categories later

down the line when larger lump sum payments are due. This is particularly true for surpluses in insurance, gift, and goal-fund categories.

Living with the Fail-Safe System

As sure-fire as the Fail-Safe method may be for avoiding financial embarrassment, it has a couple of important shortcomings, and you should strive to overcome them if you adopt it as your system.

First, administer the Fail-Safe system with a velvet glove and not an iron fist. The method itself is rigorous enough without a slavish or too literal interpretation of its provisions. It *is* possible to become "penny wise and pound foolish," particularly when you allow a misallocation of resources at the beginning of your plan to rob your family of things it really needs.

Second, don't try to "homogenize" all your expenditures to fit an arbitrary monthly pattern. For example, if your insurance premiums run $1,200 per year, don't incur an unnecessary finance charge just to even out your payments to $100 per month. Instead, pay the premium in full, out of your cash reserve when it's due, and run a negative balance in your "$100 per month" insurance category until time has replenished it completely. In such cases, negative numbers are compatible with both the spirit and the letter of your Fail-Safe Resourcing System.

Conclusion: Making Your Binder Work Better for Everyone

Whether your method of control is Flexible or Fail-Safe, you'll find there are many easy ways to keep your spending team feeling good about their system. Here are a few to get you started.

Participate in Each Other's Joy of Spending

Since Resource planning is a communal affair, there's no reason that spending for individual goals must be a solo event. The first personal goal that is achieved through use of your system should be a cause for household celebration. If teenager Bob's new ten-speed bike is the first goal that's achieved, there's no law that says the entire family can't accompany him while he picks one out. You've participated in the commitments that made your system work—now participate to the greatest extent you can in the rewards that make it all worthwhile.

Create New Categories As You Need Them

Life comes at us from many different angles and we may not have anticipated, in our list in Figure A2–1, all the contingencies you'll have to face. If unexpected costs recur, make separate categories for them; but don't create too many "catchall" accounts or you'll have difficulty allocating to and controlling them. We *do* recommend that you have a petty cash account from which incidental and last-minute money can be drawn without forcing other accounts into the red—for things such as taxicab and bus fare, babysitter expenses, or flowers for a suddenly ill friend. Finally, you may want to have a "fudge factor" account to help you balance your books at the end of the month. It's a rare household that balances its accounts to the penny, and having a handy place to put the difference can reduce frustration and save you hours of wasted effort hunting for missing cash.

Let Everyone Have a Turn at Coordinating

Unless there's a good reason not to do so, it's wise to share the responsibility of closing each month's books. Most junior high school students can handle the math involved, and more people will feel more commitment to the system if they participate in its upkeep. One client even credits her binder with saving her daughter from marrying too young. "Once Anne saw what was *really* involved in raising and feeding a family," Mrs. P. told us one day about her then 17-year-old daughter, "She set her sights on college and a job and never looked back. Well—that's not quite true. She eventually married Don, of course, but that was after a B.S. in chemistry and a few years of work experience under her belt. Now as mother of her own little brood, she's a smarter money manager then *I* ever was!"

Develop a Resourcing "Comfort Zone" that Tells You When to Replan

A lot of living takes place in a single year. Changes in your personal or financial status will obviously suggest changes in your Resourcing System. Chronic variations (either plus or minus) in any category may be telling you something important about your household's true wants and needs, so listen to your system when it speaks to you. Peaks in spending may also be seasonal—new clothes for children beginning school, more medical bills when the flu season hits, and don't forget birthdays, vacations, and gift-giving holidays. And whatever you do, don't try to revise your Binder allocations at tax time—you've got too much on your mind already! Use a pencil and paper—not lightning on stone tablets—to develop and administer your system.

Some Final Words for Extra-Compulsive Money Managers

The Binder (bookkeeping style) Resourcing approach naturally appeals more to Assertive and Protective spending styles than to the others. While a well-kept Binder system can help a family toward financial fitness, it can, if misused or overused, become a disruptive emotional force. Here are some suggestions to help you perhaps too zealous bookkeepers from overdoing a good thing.

1. *Don't let variances become goals in themselves.* If Dad's or Mom's attention is assured (even between each other) by overspending or underspending certain categories in the family binder, chances are that's what will happen. Don't let communications about your Resourcing System take the place of communications about other family matters. Keep money in its place—as the servant, not the master, of a better life.

2. *Making accounts smaller than they have to be is not smart money management.* One of the first mistakes some "smart" money managers make is to purposely underallocate their categories, keeping a bit (or a lot!) of cash hidden from the other household spenders. Fortunately, the BB&K Resourcing approach gives you other means to preserve these discretionary funds if that's your desire. Stacking the financial deck will only cause everyone to distrust the dealer and undermine the purpose—as well as the fun—of playing the game.

3. *Don't use the Binder as a "needler"* for thrift. Another common misconception about good money management is the idea that spenders ought to be harassed to stay within their allotments. This only drives the people needled away from cooperating with others who could help them with their decisions and forces them to find surrogate issues for their money-related problems. Use your Binder as a force for integration—not frustration—in your home.

Notes

End Paper No. 3

Creating Your Resource Jars

If you're an Impetuous (Active or Impulsive) spender, here are a few important questions you should ask yourself:

1. How much did I pay last year in consumer (bank card, credit card, department store, or other) interest charges?

2. How many of my charge card and credit card balances could I pay off *right now* if I had to? What would be the remaining unpaid balances?

3. How many lump-sum "annual surprise" payments (insurance premiums, taxes, *etc.*) do I wind up paying in installments? What are the finance charges or other penalties exacted by these institutions for "lending" me this money?

For many Impetuous spenders, these numbers are startlingly large, particularly when credit is consciously used to achieve and maintain a desired lifestyle. For many more, however, it is the unwanted price tag for living without an adequate Resourcing system. If you equate systematic spending with the drudgery of bookkeeping, keep reading. You're in for a pleasant—and profitable!—surprise.

The Penny Jar Principle Revisited

When you were young, you very likely learned to put your extra pennies away "for a rainy day." For most of us, those pennies usually come back out as fast as they went in—for movies, comic books, hobbies, and other important purposes—whether it was raining outside or not. You may even have been one of those kids who was taught to apply that "penny jar principle" to other areas of life, setting aside a jar or box for buttons, stamps, safety pins and paper clips, and other useful objects. The system worked well because you *knew* that when you needed that particular resource (a stamp to mail a letter or a pin to hold up your pants), it would be there when you wanted it.

The Resource Jar system of spending follows this example closely. By *physically separating* the funds you use for different important purposes, you are assured that they'll be there when you need them. You cannot overspend your reserves inadvertently, because you must consciously do something (writing a check against a specific account, for example) to gain access to the funds, giving yourself time to consider and control your commitments. Here's an example of what we mean.

Richard and Marie, life-partners for several happy and successful years, finally decided to "make it official" and tied the marital knot. While their social affairs worked nicely under this new arrangement, their financial lives did not. Marie, a staff attorney for a nonprofit institution, was a methodical Assertive spender. Richard, on the other hand, was a senior sales rep for a high-tech manufacturer and an Active spender. Since they wanted their marriage to make their partnership more collaborative, they pooled their incomes into one communal account and adopted Marie's bookkeeping budgeting method. Almost at once, however, they ran into trouble. Richard's income, based largely on bonuses and commissions, was high but erratic. He tended to focus on short-term goals and used credit to tide himself over between checks. Marie, more careful about planning and using her income, was frustrated by Richard's apparent financial indiscipline. She believed her lower but more regular salary could and should add stability to their household finances, but was worried about Richard's impulsive spending. For his part, Richard liked "splurging" occasionally—particularly on gifts for Marie—and dreaded the idea of counting each financial bean, even if doing so would give his new spouse more peace of mind. Although they both wanted to reap the emotional and financial benefits of pooling their resources, they saw after the first few weeks that the plunge they had made at the altar just wouldn't work at the bank. What were they to do?

———

Fortunately, Marie had a friend at the office who was familiar with the BB&K Resource Jar system. She learned that by setting up individual "jars," or separate accounts, for each major area of expenses, they could have not only the freedom to spend but the spending discipline necessary to keep even an affectionate spender like Richard in the black. She learned that the system was especially helpful for couples with:

1. *Irregular cash flow.* Fixed budgets and bookkeeping systems (such as the Resource Binder system) work best with regular income. It's hard (and often frustrating) to keep to a set pattern of expenditures when the wherewithal to do so is unpredictable. Resource Jar accounting works well for couples like Richard and Marie who have financial highs and lows—some months with great surpluses and some where they feel lucky to pay the rent without dipping into savings. We'll show you later how your Resource Jar system can dampen these cycles while preserving the spending freedom you need to enjoy the periodic windfalls.

2. *Independent short-term goals.* Although they are a very loving couple, Richard and Marie have individual goals as well as mutual financial desires. Instead of competing for the money they need, the Resource Jar system gives them separate accounts to pursue those goals without constant justification to each other or rationalization over the individual use of joint household funds.

3. *Unpredictable short-term expenses.* Richard travels a great deal, but Marie sticks close to home for most of her legal work. Although his company reimburses him for most of his expenses, Richard must pay for them as they're incurred—including such major (and sometimes last-minute) expenses as airline tickets, hotel rooms, and cus-

tomer entertainment. Without a separate and well-provisioned "business expense" account, Richard's ability to support other spending commitments would seem pretty chancy. The Resource Jar system gives him the latitude to meet these commitments without continually juggling their other resources.

4. *Complex tax payment schedules.* While Marie's income taxes are withheld from each paycheck, Richard pays the IRS via quarterly vouchers based on forecast earnings. During the months when his bonus checks come in, he must guard against spending his surplus for other things. Similarly, when the cash tide is low, he must make sure there's enough for Uncle Sam, who exacts not only his "pound of flesh" but, if the tax is not paid in full and on time, interest and penalty payments as well. The Resource Jar system gives Richard and Marie the funds they need to meet these and other lump-sum expenses.

As you can see, Resource Jar accounting covers the entire menu of life's banquet. It can be used to plan for major purchases as well as daily expenses. It can be a mechanism for freer personal spending and a control device for keeping those spending commitments in line. It can suit the careful spender's desire for plans and records while it gratifies the impetuous partner's need for spontaneous spending. Most important, it provides a means for reconciling partners with different spending styles and keeps partners with similar, impetuous styles out of financial trouble. Here are the two basic ways to make it work: the Intuitive and the Cash Code approaches.

Option 1: The Intuitive Approach

The basic Resource Jar system is the simplest way imaginable for controlling your spending. We put it together specifically for spenders who not only dislike the idea of planning but absolutely refuse to keep traditional budget books.

Step 1: Review Your Short-Term Spending

Using the records you already have—your check register, credit card statements, and other records provided by your financial service institutions (or your own recollections, if necessary)—review the major things you spent money on during the last two or three months. You'll probably find they can be grouped into convenient categories similar to those used for the income statement in this book. If you don't have yours, or if it's too much trouble to locate, simply jot down on a sheet of scratch paper the following categories:

	Partner **A**	Partner **B**
1. Taxes		
2. Insurance		
3. Vacation		
4. Holidays		
5. Goals (Investments)		
6. Personal		

Now enter rough amounts (rounded to the nearest ten or hundred) for each category based on your check register, statements, or memory. Be sure to make a separate tabulation for each partner, depending on who made which commitments to spend. Once you've started, you may want to add categories of your own—such as spousal or child support, savings plan deductions, or whatnot. The idea is to list those major expenditures that somehow seem to intrude—once, twice, or more often each year—on your normal intuitive spending.

Step 2: Create Your Resource Jars

Now find Action Paper No. 13, "Your Resource Jar One Sheet," *at the back of this book.* Because this is the only piece of paper you'll need to set up and monitor your Resource Jar system, we've nicknamed this Action Paper the "One Sheet" and you can use it with either the Intuitive or the Cash Code option.

First, notice that we've numbered your Resource Jars for you, although this does not necessarily imply priority. (Bills have a way of claiming priority when they fall due anyway!) Next, inspect (or just think about) the expense categories you have created. Can any of them be grouped or regrouped according to some more logical scheme? For example, Richard and Marie decided that Richard's quarterly tax payments belonged in a separate jar and that they usually spent their vacation dollars together. Thus Richard made Jar 1 his quarterly tax fund, and they combined both of their vacation amounts into Jar 2. They named Jar 1 "Richard's taxes" and Jar 2 "vacation." The source of Jar 1 would be "Richard's bonus checks" and the use, "state and federal tax voucher payments." Because it was paid out quarterly, Richard decided that the jar should be a passbook savings account, which he indicated in space 5. Since they are not using the Cash Code option, he left space 6 blank and put "Richard" in space 7 as the owner of the jar. Under notes, he wrote a memo to himself that the vouch-

ers the jar represents must be paid quarterly.

Jar 2 was filled out in a similar manner. The source would be "Marie's salary and Richard's commissions" and use would be "skiing trips and summer vacation," although they could have left space 4 blank and let the name of the jar speak for itself. Fill out the uses space only if the purpose of the fund is ambiguous or may conflict with the use of another jar. Space 5 was the number of their joint checking account and space 7 indicated that they would *both* have access to it as desired. Had they wished to do so, they could have used space 8 to indicate a target level—perhaps the amount shown in their review of their previous spending habits, or a larger amount of this total was inadequate.

You can probably see by now how the Resource Jar system works. By setting aside specific, physical places for your money, you begin to match important needs and wants to your resources. By showing where the money for each jar comes from and who controls it, you begin to make your system accountable.

Step 3: Put Your Resource Jar System to Work

When you've completed your One Sheet, you're ready to implement your system. For some couples, it means a trip to their bank or savings and loan office to open the required accounts. For others, it simply means doing what they've always done but now knowing who has the "right" (or obligation) to spend from which jar for what purposes—and when and from what source the jar must be replenished. In this last mode, the Intuitive option is *truly* intuitive, and must be complemented by regular Sources and

Uses Reviews, described in End Paper No. 4.

However once your system is set up, you'll keep it going by allocating cash from your paychecks into each jar account, according to your anticipated spending. Whatever is left in your joint (or personal) account is your general fund, and you'll use that for your ongoing daily spending. In essence, you have skimmed the money you need for your most important spending "off the top" of your paycheck and put it into the appropriate Resource Jars so that you *know* it will be there when you want it.

Notes

_____

_____

_____

_____

_____

_____

_____

_____

_____

_____

_____

_____

Option 2: The Cash Code Approach

The Cash Code approach is essentially the same as the Intuitive option except for the use of spaces 6 and 8 of the One Sheet. This second option was created for spenders who have a slightly higher tolerance for paperwork, and rewards them with a foolproof system for documenting tax returns as well as controlling their expenditures. Here's how it works.

Step 1: Devise a Code for Your Important Expenses

After you've set up and implemented your Intuitive Resource Jar system, prepare a short list of codes for expenditures in the special categories you want to keep track of. For example, the code letter "H" may stand for "home improvements"—which can be summed and deducted from the capital gain on your house when it is sold. If your Resource Jar 1 is "housing expense," you should enter the code letter "H" in space 6 of your One Sheet. Suppose you then decide to give all tax-deductible interest payments the code letter "I." If Resource Jar 4 happens to be "car payments," enter "I" in space 6, showing that any payments made from this jar should be marked with the letter I, for "interest." Simply write the appropriate code letter on the check at the time you draft it. If the expenditure is made in cash, write the code letter on the receipt or bill of sale. If the payment is made by credit card, write the code letter on your copy of the credit card carbon. The idea here is to give yourself a simple way to relate any evidence of payment to its tax-deductible purpose. While the IRS won't care which Resource Jar your payment was drawn against, it *will* care about the tax-related purpose of the expenditure. Your code is the key to tracing that expenditure for preparation and examination of your returns.

Of course, what will work for tax deductions will work for any important spending you want to keep track of. Many people devise codes for contributions to specific investments, entertainment, child support, hobby expenses, or other costs that require some sort of control.

Once you've made your list of codes, jot it down on a wallet-sized card (the back of a library card, supermarket check guarantee card, club membership card, or other nonplastic card makes a good place to do this) and carry it around with you. Refer to it as necessary whenever you write a check or make an expenditure away from home. If you are like most people, you'll have only a few codes to use, so you'll memorize them before you know it.

Step 2: Sort Your Coded Checks and Receipts Each Month

When your checking account statement arrives from the bank (or once a month if you have more than one checking account, sort your checks by code and encter the total in space 8 on your One Sheet. Be sure to add in the total of any receipts or other noncheck documents.

When your totals are complete, bundle your checks and receipts by code and file them in the appropriate "drawer" of your recordkeeping system. (See End Paper No. 1.)

Step 3: Control Your Spending by Comparing Coded Totals to Your Resource Jar Balances

From time to time you'll want to compare your Resource Jar account balances to the spending you have done and intend to do in the future. This is more important for jars from which you'll be making predictable lump-sum payments, such as taxes and insurance; but if you've set intuitive limits on your other spending (such as vacations or personal hobbies), you'll want to keep an eye on those as well. The Sources and Uses Review, described in End Paper No. 4, will help you accomplish this necessary step.

Hints for Making Your Resource Jar System Work Better

No matter which option you choose, there are several things you can do to make your Resource Jar accounting easier for everyone.

Hint No. 1:

Create a "Cash Bowl" Resource Jar

As we said at the beginning of this End Paper, the "penny jar principle" runs deep in our culture. In some homes, we've seen this principle carried to amazing extremes—from a coin-filled brandy snifter to a silver-lined cigar box filled with hundred dollar bills! If you make a lot of cash transactions, however, it's easy to lose sight of your spending commitments, even when you use the Resource Jar system with your checking and savings accounts.

Because of this, we recommend that you make your petty cash fund (cookie jar, cigar box, wall safe, or kitchen drawer) a separate Resource Jar. Establish the size of the jar during your Sources and Uses Review and keep a small pad of paper with it at all times. Whenever anyone makes a withdrawal from the jar, he or she must leave a voucher for the amount of cash taken. This voucher also states the date the cash was withdrawn and its intended use. By the time your next review comes up, you'll have converted your paper cash to paper notes that record the timing and use of all withdrawals. Adjustments to other jars, tax coding, or other "administrative" actions can then be taken based on the notes you find.

Hint No. 2:

Let Your Bank Take the Work Out of Saving

One of the more important tasks in any allocation system is making sure the cash is in the proper jars when it is needed. It may be fun to put money in your vacation fund, but stocking up your tax or insurance account can be sheer labor. If that's the case for you, why not let your bank do the dirty work for you? Most institutions will automatically apportion cash into specific accounts at your request from a single deposit. Since bookkeeping and reporting are the bank's stock and trade, why not let them do the hard part?

Hint No. 3:

Round Off Your Checks to Happiness

Some impetuous spenders are so averse to bookkeeping that they even refuse to balance their checkbooks—taking the bank's word for everything in their monthly statements. While the chances of your bank's making a mathematical mistake are small, there is a much higher possibility that you will overlook a check that you have written, a check will be debited twice from your account or a hold will be put on a check that you needed to fund a big expenditure. For these and other reasons, it's a good idea to keep track of the checks you've written. The trick is doing it with minimum pain and maximum financial safety. With the check-rounding technique, we believe we've satisfied both of these requirements.

First, open a new checking account for the particular Resource Jar against which you'll be making expenditures. Obviously, this should be a fairly large jar and one that you'll be using quite often.

Next, whenever you write a check, round off the total in your check register (*not* on the check itself!) to the next ten. For example, if you wrote a check for $75.80 for clothing, you would enter $80.00 in your check register. When your monthly statement comes, simply compare the number of checks enclosed with the number of checks logged in your register for the period—do not bother with a reconciliation of your balance. If your bank deducts a service charge for your account, round this amount, too, to the next ten.

At the end of the year, open a second checking account and stop using the first one. Make all subsequent deposits to, and withdrawals from, this new account using the check-rounding method. When all checks have cleared from the first account (that is, when you have received in the mail all checks you have previously written), go to the bank and have them tell you your balance. By rounding your checks to the next ten, you will have accrued a handsome nest egg. Write a final check for this amount, closing the account, and treat yourself to something special (or invest the proceeds, if you're so inclined) as compensation for your trouble. At the end of the following year, repeat the process by opening another new account and closing out the second.

This way you will let the bank keep track of all your balances and build a surplus at the same time—ensuring (while you do it) that your account, and Resource Jar, is never overdrawn.

Hint No. 4:

Vary Your Options and Techniques to Make Things Interesting

One of the more fascinating characteristics of impetuous spenders is their love of things new and novel. If variety is the spice of life, it is, for these people, the sauce of successful spending. If you've used the Intuitive option the first year, try the Cash Code option the second—just for the fun of it. If you're tired of coding your checks and receipts A, B, C, and D, switch to colored ink or roman numerals. The point is, make each Resourcing technique *a game* in itself and you'll look forward to using and improving it. For many impetuous spenders, familiarity with any system not only breeds contempt; it fosters *boredom*—something your Resourcing System should never be accused of!

Notes

End Paper No. 4

How to Conduct Your Sources and Uses Review

An alternative to the Binder-type Round Table meeting, the Sources and Uses Review was designed specifically for the Resource Jar system. The assumptions behind it are clear and simple:

1. People have better things to do than talk about how to spend their money.

2. Unless people *take* some time to talk about how they spend their money, that's *all* they'll wind up talking about!

As a technique to facilitate family financial conversation, then, we think the Sources and Uses Review is unsurpassed—particularly when used with Fireside Chats and other informal communication. Here's the way it works.

First: Have Reviews Only When You Need Them

At work, people call meetings whenever they must solve complex problems or capitalize on new opportunities. And since both problems *and* opportunities arise regularly during the course of a given week, many employers call meetings every Monday just to ensure that things never get out of hand. Your Sources and Uses Reviews follow this pattern closely. You'll hold them only when they'll do you some good—when you're facing some problem, some new opportunity, or when it's just been "too long" since you last checked on how you were doing.

Have a Review When Your System Uncovers Financial Problems

We are firm believers in the rule of *management-by-exception*, and the management of money is no exception to this rule. It states, very simply, that if your system is not broken, don't fix it. If your plan is a sound one and it's proceeding on course, you're probably doing things right. Further tinkering will probably do you more harm than good. Of course, this philosophy also supposes that your method of feedback and control is sound and that when problems *are* detected, you will move against them swiftly.

In family finances, problems of this type usually stem from shortfalls of income (loss of a job, a failed investment, extended illness, etc.), or too many expenses (the bills from that illness, a balloon loan payment, high taxes in April, to name only a few). In these cases the brainpower, as well as earning power, of both partners (and other family members) should be applied to solving the problem. It doesn't mean that your Resourcing System has failed you—only that the ground rules on which it was based may have changed. Like participants in any sport, you must change your strategy to keep up with, and take advantage of, the changing rules.

Have a Review When Your System Uncovers Opportunities

Life, of course, sends us many surprises—not all of them bad. Legal awards, insurance benefits, unexpected inheritance, a raise in salary—all these can increase your spendable resources. You may also spot the chance to make a great new investment, to change jobs or careers, or to sell a valuable asset at a higher than expected price. These things may imbalance your previously balanced system and call for a reallocation of resources or new spending patterns. As such, you'll want to make your decisions affecting them with the full knowledge and participation of your partners.

Have a Review When Things Get Too Quiet

Remember the John Wayne movie (*any* John Wayne movie!) where he peeks out of the foxhole (or over the logs at Fort Apache) and says, "I don't like it—it's too quiet?" Real life can get "too quiet" too, and the day-after-day plod of ordinary spending may lull you into a false sense of security. Like an airplane with a sleepy pilot (*never* John Wayne, of course), your Resourcing plan may drift off course and venture over dangerous territory. You must periodically monitor its progress—*especially* when everything seems to be going right.

How to Conduct Your Review

As the name itself suggests, your review is concerned primarily with *where* your money comes from and *how* you intend to use it. Satisfaction with the job that produces that income or things you wished you had done with your money in the past are relevant only to the extent that they influence your future decisions. Here's the sequence of events we think your review should follow:

Agenda Item 1:

Identify your sources of income for the period in question.

First, list your current cash on hand and the balances of your various accounts. If you have a large number of Resource Jars, this "bean counting" is doubly important, since most people tend to forget the resources they *could* apply to other areas if they had to. Remember, the main purpose of the review is to rethink, as necessary, your current balance of resources and the way in which you're using them.

Second, list the cash you expect to receive from various sources. If you have a stable job that provides a steady salary, you may include that in your figuring for several months into the future—but beware. The economy can change quickly (so can office politics!) and even top executives with many years' seniority have been surprised by a pink slip with their paycheck. If you hold your reviews biannually, use six months as your period of forecast. If your reviews are quarterly, make three months the horizon for your plans. The worst that can happen in these cases, then, is that your commitments to spend may be off by a matter of weeks, rather than many months—or, in the case of unwise credit commitments, several years.

We recommend that you have a Sources and Uses Review at least every six months, even if you have no particular problems or opportunities to talk about.

Events in your personal life (and even the national economy that affects your investments) have a way of changing and sneaking up on you. It's a good idea to check them after a while just to see if they are really as you remembered.

Agenda Item 2:

Identify the uses to which these resources will be put.

From the total resources available, subtract the current bills you have accumulated. Usually, this will be any unpaid bills in Drawer No. 2 of your "5-Drawer" recordkeeping system. (See End Paper No. 1.) Some people include any unpaid balances on their credit cards with this amount, although it's probably more practical to use the monthly payments you've been handling.

Next, total all the bills that you know you have coming, even if they aren't shown in your monthly payment file. For example, you know that you have several mortgage or rent payments due in the period covered by your review. It would be foolish, then, to count on this money for other uses. Other costs in this category would be tax payments, insurance premiums, and charges for credit purchases that have not yet appeared on the institution's (bank's or retailer's) statement. Don't forget to include any planned investments if periodic contributions to savings or investment accounts are part of your goal-getting plan.

Finally, list the short-term goals you have earmarked for accomplishment in this period. (Remember, even long-term goals eventually become short-term goals if you pursue them long enough!) If you have any investments to draw down for

goal accomplishment in this period, make a note of them—stating exactly which accounts will be closed (or which assets sold), what the proceeds from this sale will be (including the cost of sales commissions or early withdrawal penalties, etc.), and the cost of the goal itself.

Agenda Item 3:

Compare the balance of resources remaining to the new goals you have in mind.

At this point in your review, your powers as an intuitive money manager come strongly into play. Most people will have either a modest shortfall or a modest surplus in spendable cash after subtracting the cost of their near-term goals. If your balance is positive, you may spend this surplus as a windfall—without guilt—knowing that your foreseeable expenses (including goal accomplishment) have been covered. If your balance is negative, you will have to work backward through your list, postponing certain goals or replacing them with less costly alternatives.

Agenda Item 4:

Set a date for your next review.

Above all, don't forget one of your review's most important pieces of business—the scheduling of your next review. When things are going well, it's tempting to let these meetings slide—to assume that things will go on as they have been. That, as the sailors say, may be only the calm before the storm. Never adjourn your review without setting a date for the next one—with the understanding, of course, that either partner (or any other spending partner in your household) can call for a review whenever new problems or opportunities present themselves.

Hints for Making Your Reviews Go Better

Any review of your records will go better if those records are not in disarray when you need them. Keep up with your 5-Drawer system and your hunt for the required numbers will be short and sweet. Get out Action Paper No. 13 (Your Resource Jar "One Sheet") and use it regularly in your reviews. Make several copies and add to or change your Resource Jars as required.

About Fireside Chats

By nature, most impetuous spenders get antsy when they sit too long. If that impetuous spender is also anxious about money, a formal review (even of the Sources and Uses variety) may provoke more worry instead of confidence. We've known some Impulsive spenders, in fact, to sit up nights stewing about their spending habits, afraid that the review will become a "tribunal" where all their financial faults will be trotted out before the family. This attitude, of course, contradicts the spirit, as well as the letter, of your reviews. If you have an extra-anxious spender in your house, a bit of reassurance—both technical and emotional—may be in order. This is the role of the Fireside Chat.

As many people remember, President Franklin Delano Roosevelt spoke to a worried nation at the height of the Second World War through a series of radio broadcasts that featured a personal, rather than ceremonial, look at the chief executive. He called these broadcasts "fireside chats," and although much information was transmitted to the public in this way, its intent was to reassure rather than inform.

We think this model is appropriate for a wide variety of family financial communications. Simple, earnest conversations about things that matter most are often more effective than long or elaborate meetings. Choose a relaxed setting for your Fireside Chat (as the name implies, a homey, hearthside location works well) and create a positive environment for candid discussion. Here are some dos and don'ts that will help these discussions along:

Do pick a time that's conducive to productive discussion, such as early evening or late in the weekend.

Don't try to tackle your financial problems when people are distracted by other things, such as weekend activities or problems at work (Monday night is probably the worst time of all!), or when they are fatigued.

Do be an active listener. Half of any solution probably lies with your partner. Be receptive to what that person says and encourage him or her to say it.

Don't monopolize the floor or use the chat to gripe about things you cannot fix.

Do make the chat a pleasant occasion.

Don't mix too much alcohol with your money if you expect a cogent conversation. A bit of wine may warm the spirit, but it also dulls the senses and can intensify negative emotions about a very emotional subject.

Do deal with the question at hand in a straightforward, honest way.

Don't try to manipulate the other person or catch him or her off-guard in the mellow moment you've created.

Above all, stay aware of the six basic barriers to family financial communications and know how to overcome them. Keep the substantive part of your Fireside Chat short and to the point. If your partner seems disinclined to pursue the issue, wait until another time.

Notes

End Paper No. 5

How to Plan Rewards for Your Resourcing Effort

Have you ever been asked "What do you want for your birthday?" and been unable to give a reasonable answer? Quite often we think in intangible terms (peace in the world, more personal security, more obedient children, you name it!) or wish for things that are well beyond our power to get—a Rolls Royce, a private jet, or a lifetime supply of bubble gum. Matching meaningful, attainable rewards to the people who'll make your system work is an important part of your Resourcing effort. The idea behind it is to convince your team that if they control their spending now, they'll gain certain rewards in the future. These rewards should be predetermined, predictable, and well matched to the individual's dominant spending motivation. Ideally, your spending partners will tell you what they want—but if they don't (and some reluctant Resourcers try to withdraw from the system by acting as if they were indifferent to its rewards), here are some suggestions that might rekindle their interest and participation.

Rewards for the Pleasure-Seeking Spender

If your partner (or another spender in your family) is mostly motivated to spend for pleasure, that person's earliest Resourcing rewards should gratify that desire. For example, it would be foolish to promise that person a $100 U.S. savings bond if what he or she really wants is a night on the town with friends. Depending on the resources you have for such purposes and the individual's age and personality, pleasure-motivated spenders usually respond well to:

1. Dinner at a favorite restaurant.
2. Being pampered for an evening at home (favorite meal, candlelight, etc.)
3. An unusual outing they can brag about later (helicopter sight-seeing ride, behind-the-scenes tour of some local attraction—use your imagination!)
4. Gift certificate to a favorite store.
5. Membership in a health or athetic club.
6. A costume party.
7. A night at the movies, theater, symphony, or opera.
8. Something funky or outlandish to wear.

The list could go on and on, and you'll want to tailor it to your own pleasure-seeking spender. The point is, these spenders get enjoyment not just from what they buy, but from how they enjoy it. Chances are, if it involves some form of social activity and/or sensory enjoyment, your pleasure-seeking partner will value it as a Resourcing motivator.

Rewards for the Status-Seeking Spender

Spending for prestige has only one hard and fast rule: something will work as a motivator only if *someone else* values it as highly as the recipient does. Status symbols will vary from person to person, but there are some general categories of prestige-related spending that will get you started in the right direction.

1. Designer-label clothing.
2. Recordings or memorabilia of a popular rock star.
3. The latest fad novelty gift (as were Hula Hoops, Pet Rocks, and Cabbage Patch Dolls).
4. Trendy diet, exercise, or other personal improvement books, tapes, or programs.
5. Items with traditional "snob appeal," such as antiques, fine art, old wine, and first-edition books.
6. Any addition to the status seeker's collection of prestigious possessions, depending on their values and interests (rare stamps, autographs, baseball cards, etc.)
7. A chance to meet a famous person—attend a concert or book-signing party, etc.
8. Subscription to a trendy magazine.
9. A weekend at a posh resort.

In general, let your status-seeking spenders be your guide. If you want to find a motivator, go less by what they say (status seekers are sometimes unnecessarily embarrassed by their healthy desires to follow the crowd), and more by what you see them do and admire.

Rewarding Value-Seeking Spenders

Many people become frustrated trying to find motivators for value-driven spenders because they seem to be so picky. However, if you understand the basic equation these people use in their spending (price divided by satisfaction equals value!), you'll see there are a large number of ways to make them happy.

1. A shopping expedition—they may not buy anything, but they'll enjoy the opportunity to compare the prices of the things they see!
2. A gift certificate to a discount store.
3. Subscription to a consumer-affairs or "buyer's guide" magazine.
4. Something practical, such as kitchen appliances or household goods.
5. A product known for its quality, such as shoes that "never wear out" or a jacket that can be worn on many occasions.
6. A novelty gift that performs some function, such as a goose-necked lamp that looks like a goose. (But be careful that the product isn't too frivolous!)
7. Membership in a buyer's club.
8. Something to replace something that's about to wear out.

Again, let your value-seeking spenders guide your choice. You will probably know them well enough to guess which rewards will work and in what areas their value-driven tendencies are strongest. Since making spending decisions is a big part of their motivation, they'll probably be happy simply with the opportunity to analyze your selection!

Rewarding the Security-Minded Spender

People concerned with economic safety tend to be very future oriented, so investments of any kind, even small ones, can please them. When it comes to products or services, they tend to enjoy those things that can be used or experienced closer to home.

1. Open an IRA or make a contribution to an existing account.
2. Buy mature-growth stocks or bonds.
3. Invest in any fixed dollar (liquid) instrument, such as a passbook savings or time deposit account.
4. Purchase home security devices, such as sonic alarms, cash box, bicycle lock, or auto theft device.
5. Make any home improvement, such as having the bedroom painted, new fixtures installed, or buying some much-needed piece of furniture.
6. Buy any collectible with market value, such as stamps or coins.
7. Buy a teddy bear or puppy.
8. Choose any activity that will not cost the household money.

All this is not to say that security-spenders are stodgy, paranoid, or penurious. Many security-minded people we know are very generous and outgoing, forcing their more conservative spending philosophy only on themselves. This, we believe, is the key to finding rewards they will truly enjoy. You may find that by emphasizing nonmaterial rewards you will enhance your family's ability to look beyond the purely monetary side of your Resourcing System.

Rewarding the More Emotional Spenders

While all of the previous spending motives have an emotional component, they tend to depend basically on rational processes. Pleasure spenders *choose* among pleasurable options. Status spenders *compare* their current situation to what the in-crowd seems to be doing. Value-seeking spenders *analyze* their purchases before they make them, and so on. People who spend to gain power or control, however—as well as those who spend to show or obtain affection or to "get even" with a partner—all rely on less rational processes in their spending decisions. How do you find predictable and attainable rewards for people who are currently sensitive to these needs?

First, don't try to beat them at their own emotional games. If your partner seems motivated chiefly by a desire to control the family's spending but is willing to give Resourcing a try, suggest that he or she be the first Resource coordinator. Quite often a need to control is simply a dressed-up *need to know* (or a need to feel more certain) and, once those needs are met, the power-collecting tendencies may begin to go away. If your partner likes to give gifts to show affection, increase the size of his or her gift-giving jar, showing in the meantime appreciation for the many nonfinancial things he or she does. If your partner still seems disposed to spending contests, direct those competitive instincts toward "winning the Resourcing game."

We think you'll find that most of these emotional spending urges are brought about largely by fears and uncertainties. Once your Resourcing System begins to have its effect, other spending motivations will take precedence (the power spender begins spending for pleasure, or the affection-seeking spender begins to share your desire for prestige, and so forth). This development will make your system of rewards more straightforward, enjoyable, and certainly much easier to manage.

And What About Our Fun Fund and Mad Money Jars?

Of course, your system of motivators should include *communal* as well as individual rewards. Resourcing is a family business and the family—as a whole—should share in the benefits it brings.

Making the Most of Your Mad Money Jar

If you use the Resource Jar method (which means you have at least one impetuous spending partner in your midst), you will probably want to set aside a separate Resource Jar for spontaneous communal spending. The only rule that goes along with this allocation is that it *cannot* be spent for anything practical, except in an emergency. Some families use this jar of money for the frills associated with their semiannual Resourcing parties. Others depend on it for impulsive shopping sprees, come-as-you-are parties for friends, or picnics in Tahiti (depending on

the size of their reserves!) Paradoxically, these Mad Money jars keep some sanity in a system that might be, for some impetuous spenders, insanely level-headed.

Financing Fun Where Fun Is Needed Most

What the Mad Money jar is to the Resource Jar approach, so the Fun Fund is to your Resource Binder system. Since the Binder is used by more careful (and often security-motivated) spenders, it's easy for the quality of their daily life to slip while they're preparing for the future. Too often, that future never happens the way it's supposed to, and the most careful spenders wind up building huge estates for no particular reason. To protect these compulsive savers from themselves (and to help lend color to the lives of the more impetuous spenders who love them), we think a Fun Fund should be an important account in every Binder. As with the Mad Money jar, this fund must not become a perpetual "emergency reserve" (of which the careful spender will already have quite a few) but a source of genuine enjoyment for the family. If you're the careful spender in your household, let your more impetuous partners suggest how the money should be spent. We promise you, it will go for the best of causes—the success of your Resourcing System—and you'll have the time of your life to boot!

Notes

_____

_____

_____

_____

_____

_____

_____

APPENDIX B

ACTION PAPERS

| **Action Paper No. 1** |

Your Career and Life Inventory

Name ————————————————————————————————— **Partner A**

Date ——————————————————————————

This inventory was developed to help you (Partner A; and your spouse or life partner, Partner B) assess your career and life circumstances in three important areas:

  I. Your General Financial Condition
  II. Your Personal and Vocational Resources
  III. Your Cultural and Economic Attitudes and Values

Please answer the following questions briefly but completely. A duplicate set of questions is provided for Partner B immediately following Part III of this questionnaire. There are no right or wrong answers to these questions. Self-knowledge and understanding should be your goals for this exercise rather than a tidy worksheet or socially acceptable answers.

When you've finished the inventory, share your answers with your spouse or life partner (who has completed an identical survey) and go on together to complete Action Paper No. 2, "Your Needs/Wants Assessment," following the guidelines in Chapter 2.

Part I: Your General Financial Condition

I-1. Consider your current cash resources (salary, wages, commissions, etc.). Do you usually have adequate cash income to meet your current expenses?

I-2. Do you have some form of cash reserve (money not needed for daily living expenses) that can be applied toward unanticipated emergencies or opportunities?

I-3. Do you loan money privately to others on an informal basis? What has been your success rate in obtaining repayment (in cash or "in kind")?

I-4. Do you have any long-term investments (profit sharing, stocks, bonds, other securities, IRA or Keogh accounts)?

I-5. Are your life and property (home, automobiles, possessions, etc.) adequately insured?

I-6. Do you own your own home?

I-7. Do you have any other real estate investments?

Your Career and Life Inventory   **Partner A**   Continued

I-8. List your major personal property (non-real estate) such as automobiles, jewelry, furs, antiques, or artwork.

I-9. Do you have an ownership interest in any small businesses?

I-10. Do you have any potential inheritances or capital gains income?

I-11. Do you tend to run short on ready cash to pay your short-term expenses?

I-12. Do you have any installment loans (for automobiles, furniture, etc.)?

I-13. Do you have any substantial long-term debt, such as a home mortgage?

I-14. Do you have any current or anticipated legal judgments to consider in your financial planning (such as spousal support, or child support?

I-15. How do you handle your annual income tax, Social Security, property tax, or other tax liabilities?

I-16. Do you have any cash left over each month after paying your current expenses?

I-17. How dependable is your primary income? Is it very predictable (such as a salary from a stable company), or does it fluctuate, as do sales commissions, professional fees, and dividends?

Your Career and Life Inventory   **Partner A**   Continued

Part II: Your Personal and Vocational Resources

II-1. What is your current occupation or profession? Describe your official job title and responsibilities; then devise an "unofficial" job description that more accurately reflects your day-to-day activities.

II-4. (a) In your last three positions (starting with the most recent and working backward), which tasks were the most satisfying to you?
  (b) In these same three positions, which tasks were the *least* satisfying?

II-2. Briefly describe the other significant jobs you have held.

II-5. Which characteristics (behaviors, personality traits, attitudes, etc.) do you currently have that enhance your job performance?

II-3. List the other vocational choices you have seriously considered at one time or another.

II-6. (a) What personal recreational activities do you enjoy the most?
  (b) What personal or technical skills do you show while undertaking these activities?

Your Career and Life Inventory   **Partner A**   Continued

II-7. List your formal educational achievements (degrees, awards, etc.).

II-8. List any courses or special training taken since the completion of your formal education (professional credentials, community college courses, military training, etc.).

II-9. Which extracurricular activities did you enjoy the most during your years of formal education?

II-10. What strengths do you discover when you compare your total educational experience to that of others in your career field? What weaknesses?

II-11. How has your health influenced your vocational and recreational activities?

II-12. What characteristics (behaviors, personality traits, etc.) do you currently have that *detract* from your job performance?

II-13. What worries, if any, do you have about your health, appearance, physical limitations, etc.?

Your Career and Life Inventory   Partner A   Continued

Part III: Your Cultural and Economic Attitudes and Values

III-1. What are your primary personal time activities?

III-2. What social activities do you enjoy most?
Which least?

III-3. What contributions have you made to
community activities? How important are
these activities to you? What would you
like to accomplish in this area in the future?

III-4. (a) What aspects of your childhood do
you remember as being most pleas-
ant? Most unpleasant? Mention the
education, work history, achievements, and the like of both your
mother (or female who raised or influenced you) and your father (or male
who raised or influenced you) and any
brothers, sisters, or other family members who may have influenced you.

Your Career and Life Inventory   **Partner A**   Continued

(b) Describe the attitudes and values you have that resemble those held by these people. How are they different?

III-5. (a) If you are married or sharing a life partnership with someone, write a short description of your partner's personality, achievements, education, work history, social and community life, and personal interests.

(b) Regarding the person described above, write a brief paragraph describing his or her chief attitudes, values, and concerns about the future and how those attitudes, values, and concerns might differ from your own.

Your Career and Life Inventory   **Partner A**   Continued

III-6. (a) If you have any children, list their names and ages and write a brief paragraph about their personalities and the hopes you have for each.

III-7. Write a brief paragraph about your current personal cultural/economic status. Would you describe yourself as lower, middle, upper middle, or upper class? What prerogatives and responsibilities has this classification given you? How has it affected your feelings about your past and your expectations for the future?

(b) Briefly describe how your children have influenced your career and life decisions in the past and how you expect them to influence you in the future.

Your Career and Life Inventory   **Partner A**   Concluded

III-8. If a change in your physical condition (for better or worse) seems likely in your future, how will this affect your earning potential?

III-9. Break down the amount of time you spend each day sleeping, at work, at play, with your family, pursuing community affairs, etc. Record these values as the percentage (fraction) of a 24-hour day.

III-10. What personal characteristics (attitudes, values, behaviors, etc.) do you like most

(a) about yourself?
(b) in others?

III-11. Identify the three personal values you think account best for your current success in life.

III-12. What personal characteristics (attitudes, values, behaviors, etc.) do you like least

(a) about yourself?
(b) about others?

III-13. Identify the three personal values you have had the hardest time living with in your career and life thus far.

III-14. What are the three things in life you are most afraid of losing?

Action Paper No. 1

Your Career and Life Inventory

Name _____   **Partner B**

Date _____

This inventory was developed to help you assess your career and life circumstances in three important areas:

    I. Your General Financial Condition

   II. Your Personal and Vocational Resources

  III. Your Cultural and Economic Attitudes and Values

Please answer the following questions briefly but completely. There are no right or wrong answers to these questions. Self-knowledge and understanding should be your goals for this exercise rather than a tidy worksheet or socially acceptable answers.

When you've finished the inventory, share your answers with your spouse or life partner (who has completed an identical survey) and go on together to complete Action Paper No. 2, "Your Needs/Wants Assessment," following the guidelines in Chapter 2.

Part I: Your General Financial Condition

I-1. Consider your current cash resources (salary, wages, commissions, etc.). Do you usually have adequate cash income to meet your current expenses?

I-2. Do you have some form of cash reserve (money not needed for daily living expenses) that can be applied toward unanticipated emergencies or opportunities?

I-3. Do you loan money privately to others on an informal basis? What has been your success rate in obtaining repayment (in cash or "in kind")?

I-4. Do you have any long-term investments (profit sharing, stocks, bonds, other securities, IRA or Keogh accounts)?

I-5. Are your life and property (home, automobiles, possessions, etc.) adequately insured?

I-6. Do you own your own home?

I-7. Do you have any other real estate investments?

Your Career and Life Inventory   **Partner B**   Continued

I-8. List your major personal property (non-real estate) such as automobiles, jewelry, furs, antiques, or artwork.

I-9. Do you have an ownership interest in any small businesses?

I-10. Do you have any potential inheritances or capital gains income?

I-11. Do you tend to run short on ready cash to pay your short-term expenses?

I-12. Do you have any installment loans (for automobiles, furniture, etc.)?

I-13. Do you have any substantial long-term debt, such as a home mortgage?

I-14. Do you have any current or anticipated legal judgments to consider in your financial planning (such as spousal support, or child support?

I-15. How do you handle your annual income tax, Social Security, property tax, or other tax liabilities?

I-16. Do you have any cash left over each month after paying your current expenses?

I-17. How dependable is your primary income? Is it very predictable (such as a salary from a stable company), or does it fluctuate, as do sales commissions, professional fees, and dividends?

Your Career and Life Inventory **Partner B** Continued	
Part II: Your Personal and Vocational Resources	

II-1. What is your current occupation or profession? Describe your official job title and responsibilities; then devise an "unofficial" job description that more accurately reflects your day-to-day activities.

II-4. (a) In your last three positions (starting with the most recent and working backward), which tasks were the most satisfying to you?
(b) In these same three positions, which tasks were the *least* satisfying?

II-2. Briefly describe the other significant jobs you have held.

II-5. Which characteristics (behaviors, personality traits, attitudes, etc.) do you currently have that enhance your job performance?

II-3. List the other vocational choices you have seriously considered at one time or another.

II-6. (a) What personal recreational activities do you enjoy the most?
(b) What personal or technical skills do you show while undertaking these activities?

Your Career and Life Inventory   **Partner B**   Continued

II-7. List your formal educational achievements (degrees, awards, etc.).

II-8. List any courses or special training taken since the completion of your formal education (professional credentials, community college courses, military training, etc.).

II-9. Which extracurricular activities did you enjoy the most during your years of formal education?

II-10. What strengths do you discover when you compare your total educational experience to that of others in your career field? What weaknesses?

II-11. How has your health influenced your vocational and recreational activities?

II-12. What characteristics (behaviors, personality traits, etc.) do you currently have that *detract* from your job performance?

II-13. What worries, if any, do you have about your health, appearance, physical limitations, etc.?

Your Career and Life Inventory   **Partner B**   Continued

Part III: Your Cultural and Economic Attitudes and Values

III-1. What are your primary personal time activities?

III-2. What social activities do you enjoy most? Which least?

III-3. What contributions have you made to community activities? How important are these activities to you? What would you like to accomplish in this area in the future?

III-4. (a) What aspects of your childhood do you remember as being most pleasant? Most unpleasant? Mention the education, work history, achievements, and the like of both your mother (or female who raised or influenced you) and your father (or male who raised or influenced you) and any brothers, sisters, or other family members who may have influenced you.

Your Career and Life Inventory   **Partner B**   Continued

(b) Describe the attitudes and values you have that resemble those held by these people. How are they different?

III-5. (a) If you are married or sharing a life partnership with someone, write a short description of your partner's personality, achievements, education, work history, social and community life, and personal interests.

(b) Regarding the person described above, write a brief paragraph describing his or her chief attitudes, values, and concerns about the future and how those attitudes, values, and concerns might differ from your own.

Your Career and Life Inventory   **Partner B**   Continued

III-6. **(a)** If you have any children, list their names and ages and write a brief paragraph about their personalities and the hopes you have for each.

III-7. Write a brief paragraph about your current personal cultural/economic status. Would you describe yourself as lower, middle, upper middle, or upper class? What prerogatives and responsibilities has this classification given you? How has it affected your feelings about your past and your expectations for the future?

(b) Briefly describe how your children have influenced your career and life decisions in the past and how you expect them to influence you in the future.

Your Career and Life Inventory   Partner B   Concluded

III-8. If a change in your physical condition (for better or worse) seems likely in your future, how will this affect your earning potential?

III-9. Break down the amount of time you spend each day sleeping, at work, at play, with your family, pursuing community affairs, etc. Record these values as the percentage (fraction) of a 24-hour day.

III-10. What personal characteristics (attitudes, values, behaviors, etc.) do you like most

(a) about yourself?
(b) in others?

III-11. Identify the three personal values you think account best for your current success in life.

III-12. What personal characteristics (attitudes, values, behaviors, etc.) do you like least

(a) about yourself?
(b) about others?

III-13. Identify the three personal values you have had the hardest time living with in your career and life thus far.

III-14. What are the three things in life you are most afraid of losing?

Action Paper No. 2

Your Needs/Wants Assessment

Name

Date

From Action Paper No. 1	Needs	Wants
Part I Your General Financial Condition		
Part II Your Personal and Vocational Resources		
Part III Your Cultural and Economic Attitudes and Values		

Action Paper No. 3

Your Personal Information Sheet

Date _____

Name(s)   Social Security Number(s)

_____   _____

_____   _____

_____   _____

_____   _____

	Account Number	**Institution Name**
Checking accounts	_____	_____
Savings accounts	_____	_____
Safe-deposit box (Location of keys)	_____	_____
Brokerage account	_____	_____

Location of stock certificates _____

Location of deeds _____

Location of other securities _____

Location of will _____

Name of executor(s) _____

Lawyer's name _____ Phone _____

    Address _____

Broker's name _____ Phone _____

    Address _____

Accountant's name _____ Phone _____

    Address _____

Insurance agents, other brokers, etc. _____

_____

This sheet should be kept in your general file and a copy stored with your permanent records.

Action Paper No. 4

Your Supporting Financial Schedules

The following instructional worksheet is your guide for assembling all the information necessary to complete Action Papers 5 and 6, your financial statements. For both the balance sheet and income statement, we'll list each item number and then define the terms associated with that item, describe typical places in your records to find those items, tell how to compute the item amount (where applicable), and give you space to list your answers.

Don't let the length or apparent complexity of the schedules discourage you. You have probably already had experience with such material before when applying for a loan at the bank or assembling information for the IRS 1040 "long" form. Finally, since we're concerned with financial planning rather than accountancy, don't be afraid to round off numbers to the nearest ten or even hundreds of dollars. Comprehensiveness and sound methodology are more important to good financial statements than false "double decimal place" accuracy.

**For Action Paper No. 5, Your
Personal Balance Sheet**

Item 1, Cash and Equivalents:

This includes currency on hand plus a wide variety of "near money" instruments. Cash balances can be counted up quickly by checking your wallet, wall safe (or mattress!), and the last entry of your updated checking account register and savings account passbook. Also include the balances of any NOW accounts or money market funds. Certificates of deposit, corporate or municipal bonds, or any other cash equivalent instrument should be included as well, provided its period of maturity is less than one year.

Item 2, Notes Receivable:

This is any money you have loaned to someone else with the expectation of repayment, regardless of terms. "Loans" that are actually gifts to dependents, friends, or charitable causes are not receivable notes, even if they have value as tax deductions. Finally, even if you expect to earn interest on the loan, list only the principal here. Your profit will be shown later in your income statement.

Your Supporting Financial Schedules Continued

Item 3, Investments:

These are any sums of money employed for the purpose of generating current or future income. Current income is usually realized through periodic receipt of dividends or interest. Future income is usually realized on the sale of the asset after its value has grown in the marketplace. This is true even of investments whose primary purpose is to generate tax "losses" (deductions or credits) for the owner. Investments include U.S. common and preferred stocks, whether traded on the major exchanges or "over the counter"; corporate or government bonds with a maturity date of more than one year; international securities; shares in real estate companies, real estate investment trusts, or real estate partnerships; stock issued to you under company profit-sharing or incentive plans; shares held in mutual funds; assets held in individual retirement or Keogh accounts; the cash value of any life insurance policy (as specified by that policy or as computed by your insurer); and the lump sum value of any annuities to which you are entitled. The value of your profit-sharing plan is reported periodically by your employer or may usually be obtained on request. Compute the market value of your stocks and bonds from the bid-price quotations appearing in most major newspapers. If your holdings are not listed, obtain a current quotation from your broker. The value of Keogh/IRA/mutual funds can be obtained from the institutions maintaining them, although many mutual funds are quoted daily in the business section of most newspapers.

Item 5, Home and Property:

This is the estimated market value of your principal residence (if you are the owner). You may obtain this figure by asking your realtor for a formal appraisal and deducting the probable closing costs. Do not deduct the remaining balance of your home mortgage(s), if any, because this will appear on the liabilities side of the sheet.

Your Supporting Financial Schedules Continued

Item 6, Automobiles/Vehicles

This includes all vehicles you own (regardless of make, model, or age) that you use for personal transportation and recreation. (Cars owned for business use and carried "on the books" of a small business are listed under item 8.) Use the *Kelly Blue Book* value (found at your local library or by consulting an automobile dealer) or by comparing the prices for similar makes and models in the classified advertisements of your local paper.

Item 7, Other Personal Property:

Include here furniture, appliances, clothing, jewelry, art, etc. Your insurance records may be of help here.

Item 9, Other Real Estate

This includes any investment property (such as homes, condominiums, cabins, apartments), residential or commercial, that you personally own. It does not include shares in group real estate investments (such as trusts, limited partnerships, or corporations). Estimate the market value (without mortgage deductions) as you did for item 5 above.

Item 10, Ownership in Small Businesses:

This is your "owner's equity" in a sole proprietorship, shares held by you in a closely held corporation, or limited partnership interest in any business not publicly traded. If you are the proprietor, consult the "owner's equity" portion of your latest company balance sheet. If you are a shareholder, reduce this amount in proportion to your percentage of ownership of stock outstanding. If you are a limited partner, consult the general partner for current share valuation.

Item 14, Unpaid Bills:

This is the money you owe in your "bills payable" file. It includes only those debts for which you have been invoiced or know you have a commitment to pay within the next 12 months. For example, the unpaid balance on a physician's or dentist's statement belongs in this category. Your current month's rent belongs in this category too (if it has not yet been paid by the date of the balance sheet), but not the rent you expect to pay for the remainder of the year, even if you are on a lease. Taxes should be listed only if you have an unpaid balance due or are on a quarterly voucher (self-employed) system. Depending on your circumstances, you may have many more (or fewer) categories than those shown on the sheet. Remember, this is *not* a budgetary listing of what you plan to spend or did spend during the year. It is *only* those bills which you have already received and expect to pay.

Your Supporting Financial Schedules Continued

Item 15, Installment Loans:

This is the balance (including principal and interest) on any loan falling due within the next 12 months. Your book of payment stubs or lender's statement should give you this amount.

Item 17, Non-Mortgage Loans:

These are any loans that mature outside the short-term period, including principal. Examples of this are long-term government loans for college education and personal unsecured loans for longer than one year. Accrued (contingent) capital gains taxes represent an estimate of the taxes and other costs of sale you would have to pay if you were to liquidate all your assets today. To compute this value, follow the steps below:

1. Identify your marketable assets from item 3.

2. Document their purchase price (or the tax basis used as the acquisition cost).

3. Use the current market value of the asset that you have already estimated for the balance sheet.

4. Subtract (2) from (3) above to obtain your unrealized capital gain (or loss) on this asset.

5. When this computation is completed for each marketable asset, add up the individual gains (and subtract the losses) and enter this number as your accrued net capital gains (it may be negative).

6. Multiply any net capital gain (any positive number) by .35 (35%) to reflect federal and state taxes and probably closing costs, such as fees and commissions you would pay should you liquidate all your assets.

Contingency taxes on assets not taxed (such as IRAs) should be computed by taking the market value established for those assets in item 3 and multiplying this value by your current marginal tax rate. (Consult the IRS or your accountant/tax preparer.)

Item 18, Mortgages Loans:

These are loans secured by first, second (and subsequent) trust deeds on your home. Record the balance remaining on these loans (including principal and interest) by checking your payment stubs or by contacting your lender. List any other mortgages against vacation houses or commercial property in a similar manner as may be applicable.

Your Supporting Financial Schedules Continued

**For Action Paper No. 6, Your
Personal Income Statement**

Item 1, Income:

Include all income from any source, including earned income (salary, wages, bonus payments, fees, commissions, or other direct compensation) and unearned income (such as dividends, interest or rent). Include also the annual amounts received from pensions, trusts, or other annuities if not already accounted for as an asset on the balance sheet.

2. *Food.* Include all grocery costs and household consumables (such as cleansers and sponges) but do not include restaurant meals or entertainment.

Item 3, Taxes:

This is the amount shown on your IRS Form 1040 for the year pertaining to the above income. Do not include property or other special taxes since these are listed separately in item 6.

Item 6, Living Expenses:

(See Chapter 3 for a discussion of fixed versus variable costs.)

3. *Clothing.* Include the purchase price of clothing, laundry and dry cleaning expenses, tailoring expenses, and cost of personal accessories.

1. *Housing.* Include all utilities (gas, electric, telephone, etc.) and actual costs of repairs (tradesmen's fees and materials). Include too your homeowner's insurance premiums, but do not double-count the fire insurance that may be included in your mortgage payments. In addition to those mortgage payments (or rent), list property taxes (as applicable), domestic servant or gardener's expense, pool maintenance (as applicable), and any other recurring or nonrecurring costs associated with your residence, such as homeowner's association dues, building maintenance fees (for condos), furnishings, and improvements.

Your Supporting Financial Schedules   Concluded

4. *Transportation.* Include all automobile and commuting expenses, such as gas, oil, lubricants, repairs; car insurance; licenses and parking fees; auto installment loan payments and down payments; and cost of public transportation (bus, train, etc.) as applicable.

5. *Recreation.* Include movies, theater, sports events, pet expenses (if not listed already under household expenses), vacations (including air fare and lodging), and any other entertainment or hobby-related costs.

6. *Medical.* Include the cost of physicians, dentists, prescriptions, over-the-counter remedies and medications, psychotherapy, eyeglasses or contact lenses, health insurance, and of any special medical or therapeutic equipment.

7. *Personal.* Put here any expenses of a personal nature not included in the above categories such as books, jewelry (investment quality rather than clothing accessories), artwork (not included as household furnishings or entertainment), gifts, charitable contributions, and allowances for dependents.

8. *Life Insurance.* Premiums for anyone you insure, regardless of who "owns" the policy.

9. *Outlays for Fixed Assets.* This is the cost to replace a fixed asset (such as a major appliance) whether or not such an expenditure actually took place during the year. In other words, it is a reserve fund to make post-warranty repairs or replacements of washing machines, dryers, TV sets, etc. To compute this amount, figure the *cost to replace* your major appliances and take 10% of this total. Once this fund is in place, it need not be duplicated on subsequent income statements unless depleted by use or outdated by the addition of new appliances. Remember — this represents the cost to replace failed items, not upgrade to better models or add new equipment. If you anticipate outlays for newer or more expensive appliances, make this desire a need or want on Action Paper No. 2.

10. *Other Expenses.* This may include such things as attorney's fees, CPA's fees, and broker's fees and any other expenses unique to your situation and not reflected in the above categories.

Action Paper No. 5

Your Personal Balance Sheet

Name

Date

ASSETS	LIABILITIES

ASSETS

Monetary Assets

1. Cash and Equivalents

    Cash/checking/savings   _____
    Money market funds   _____
    Certificates of Deposit   _____
    Bonds (< 1 yr. maturity)   _____

    Total Cash and Equivalents   _____

2. Notes Receivable   _____

3. Investments

    Stocks   _____
    Bonds (>1 yr. maturity)   _____
    Real estate (REITs,
    partnerships)   _____
    Cash value of life
    insurance   _____
    Cash value of annuities   _____
    Retirement plans   _____

    Total Investments   _____

4. Total Monetary Assets
    (1 + 2 + 3)   _____

Fixed Assets

5. Home and property   _____
6. Automobiles/vehicles   _____
7. Other personal property   _____

8. Total Personal Assets
    (5 + 6 + 7)   _____

9. Other real estate   _____
10. Ownership in small business _____

11. Total Fixed Investment
    Assets (9 + 10)   _____

12. Total Fixed Assets (8 + 11)   _____

13. Total Assets (4 + 12)   _____

LIABILITIES

Short-Term Liabilities

14. Unpaid Bills

    Taxes   _____
    Insurance premiums   _____
    Rent   _____
    Utilities   _____
    Charge accounts   _____
    Credit cards   _____
    Other_____   _____

    Total Unpaid Bills   _____

15. Installment Loans
    (balance due)

    Automobile   _____
    Other_____   _____

    Total Installment Loans   _____

16. Total Short-Term Liabilities   _____
    (14 + 15)

Long-Term Liabilities

17. Non-mortgage Loans
    (balance due)
    Bank   _____
    Educational   _____
    Other_____   _____
    Accrued capital gains
    tax liability   _____

    Total Non-mortgage Loans   _____

18. Mortgage Loans (bal. due)
    Home   _____
    Other_____   _____

    Total Mortgage Loans   _____

19. Total Long-Term Liabilities   _____
    (17 + 18)

20. Total Liabilities (16 + 19)   _____

21. Net Worth (13 minus 20)   _____

22. Balance (21 + 20)   _____

Action Paper No. 6

Your Personal Income Statement

Name

For the Year Beginning January 1, 19_____ and ending December 31, 19_____

---

1. **Income**
   - Spouse or Partner A   _____
   - Spouse or Partner B   _____
   - Total wages or salaries   _____
   - Dividends and interest   _____
   - Rents   _____
   - Other _____   _____

2. **Total Income**   _____
3. **Taxes**
   - Personal income taxes   _____
   - Social Security and disability taxes   _____
4. **Total Taxes**   _____
5. **Amount Remaining for Living Expenses, Savings and Investments**   _____

6. **Living Expenses**

	Fixed	Variable
Housing		
Utilities	_____	_____
Repairs	_____	_____
Insurance	_____	_____
Taxes	_____	_____
Rent or mortgage payments	_____	_____
Other _____	_____	_____
Food	_____	_____
Clothing (including laundry, dry cleaning, repairs, and personal effects)	_____	_____
Transportation		
Gas, tolls, parking	_____	_____
Repairs	_____	_____
Licenses	_____	_____
Insurance	_____	_____
Auto payments or purchase	_____	_____
Fares	_____	_____
Recreation, entertainment, and vacations	_____	_____
Medical		
Doctor	_____	_____
Dentist	_____	_____
Medicines	_____	_____
Insurance	_____	_____
Personal	_____	_____
Life insurance (term)	_____	_____
Outlays for fixed assets	_____	_____
Other expenses _____	_____	_____
Subtotal	_____	_____

7. **Total Annual Living Expenses**   _____

8. **Amount Remaining for Savings and Investment**   _____

Action Paper No. 7

Your Goals Priority Worksheet

Name

Date

Priority	Goal	Price

Your Goals Achievement Schedule

Name _____

Date _____

From Action Paper No. 7				
1 Goals (in Priority)	**2 Goal Price, Current Value**	**3 When Desired** (Years From Now)	**4 Future Value Factor From Figure 6-1** (or Figure 6-3) if using annual contributions at _____ %	**5 Future Value** (at _____ %) (2) x (4)

(6a) Total Goals Current Value

(7) Total Investable Assets (Balance Sheet items 4 + 11)

(8) Total Annualized Surplus Income (Income Statement item 8 times factor from Figure 6-5)

(9) Total Investable Resources, (7) + (8):

(10) Current Goal Achievement Surplus (or shortfall), (9)-(6a)

(6b) Total Goals Future Value:

(9b) Record item (9), from left, here:

(10b) Future Goal Achievement Surplus (or short fall), (9b)-(6b)

Your Investment Specifications

Name _____

Date _____

From Action Paper No. 8

Item (1), Goals (in Priority)	Item (5), Future Value (at ___ %)	Year Needed

Present Value of Goals for Various After-Tax Rates of Return
(Factor from Figure 5-1 or 6-5/Present Value Tables)

High Priority, Near Term

High Priority, Long Term

6%	8%	10%	12%	14%

Low Priority, Near Term

Low Priority, Long Term

Final Investment Objectives (Selected from left)

Present Value Sum	% Return

(A) Total Present Value of Goals: _____

(B) Total Investable Resources (From Action Paper No. 8, Item 9): _____

(C) Final Goals Achievement Surplus (or Shortfall) (B) — (A) above: _____

Action Paper No. 10

Your Forecast Income Worksheet

Name(s) _____

Date _____

Source / Months from Now:	1	2	3	4	5	6	7	8	9	10	11	12	Estimated 12-Month Total	Average Per Month	Actual Year's Income
Partner A's take-home wages or salary															
Partner B's take-home wages or salary															
Bonuses or commissions															
Interest															
Dividends															
Rents															
Annuities, pensions															
Other															
TOTAL															

Action Paper No. 11

Your Forecast Expenses

Name(s) _____

Date _____

Expense Category	Fixed and Variable Subcategories	Months from Now: 1	2	3	4	5	6	7	8	9	10	11	12	12-Month Total	Average by Month
Housing	Rent, mortgage payments, insurance, taxes														
	Repairs and improvements														
Utilities															
Food															
Family necessities															
Medical	Insurance														
	Doctor, dentist, drugs, hospital														
Clothing															
Automobile	Purchase payments, insurance, and license fees														
	Gas, oil, repairs, parking, tolls, and so on														
Recreation and entertainment	General														
Self-Improvement	Magazines and newspapers														
Short-term goals															
Savings, investments	For long-term goals														
Outlays for fixed assets	Repairs														
	Purchases and installments														
Fun Fund															
Gifts															
Church and charity															
Life insurance															
Taxes															
Contingency	Legal services, debt repayments, union dues														
Total by Month															

Action Paper No. 12

Your Resource Binder Control Sheet

Name(s) _____

Date   _____

Expense Category	Allotted Monthly Average	Month:			Month:			Revised Monthly Average ?	Month:				Month:			
		Actual	Plus or Minus	Balance Forward	Actual	Plus or Minus		Balance Forward	Actual	Plus or Minus	Balance Forward	Actual	Plus or Minus			
Housing																
Utilities																
Food																
Family necessities																
Medical																
Clothing																
Automobile																
Recreation entertainment																
Personal improvement																
Short-term goal fund																
Savings and investment																
Outlays for fixed assets																
Fun Fund																
Gifts																
Church and charity																
Life insurance																
Taxes																
Contingency																
Total																

Action Paper No. 13

Your Resource Jar "One Sheet"

Name(s) _____

Date _____

(1) Jar No.	(2) Label of Jar	(3) Source	(4) Use	(5) Account No. and Location	(6) Check Code*	(7) Responsible Partner	(8) Scratch Pad
1							
2							
3							
4							
5							
6							

*Used only with Cash Code option.

INDEX